OSSIAN, according to Highland and Irish oral tradition, was a third-century bard. He told stories about his youth, especially his father, Fingal, and his son, Oscar. His stories tell of a life full of battles and excitement. However, by the time he is telling the stories compiled by Macpherson, he is alone – both Fingal and Oscar have died – and blind, the last of his race looking back to a heroic past.

JAMES MACPHERSON was born in the Highlands in 1736, in an area that was greatly affected by the Jacobite uprising of 1745. He later went to study at King's College in Aberdeen, and possibly also at Edinburgh University. He published the Ossianic poems, including *Fragments of Ancient Poetry* and the epic *Fingal*, in the 1760s, and they were an instant success across Europe, but he soon came under pressure to prove their authenticity. After spending a few years in America, he became an MP in 1780. Macpherson died in 1796 and is buried in Westminster Abbey.

ALLAN BURNETT was born and brought up in Uist in the Western Isles. He was educated at the University of Edinburgh, gaining a distinction for his postgraduate thesis on constitutional history. Allan worked as a ghost-tour guide in his student days and today gives costumed interpretative performances at heritage sites. Allan works regularly with schools across the country on history and literacy projects. As a journalist he contributes to a number of newspapers and magazines at home and abroad, with a special interest in history and heritage issues. Among Allan's previously published books are *William Wallace And All That* and *Invented In Scotland: Scottish Ingenuity And Invention Throughout The Ages*.

LINDA ANDERSSON BURNETT was born and brought up in Sweden. She is currently completing an AHRC-funded PhD at the University of Edinburgh on 18th-century travel in the Scottish Highlands and northern Scandinavia. She was awarded an MSc with distinction by the same university for her thesis on the Ossianic poems. She has published a number of articles on Scottish and Scandinavian history and is a winner of the Scottish Society for Northern Studies' Magnus Magnusson Essay Prize.

# Blind Ossian's Fingal

*Fragments and Controversy*

Compiled and Translated by
JAMES MACPHERSON

Edited and Introduced by
ALLAN BURNETT and LINDA ANDERSSON BURNETT

**Luath** Press Limited

EDINBURGH

www.luath.co.uk

For Hannah Carin

First edition of *Fragments of Ancient Poetry* 1760
First edition of *Fingal: An Ancient Epic Poem in Six Books* 1762
Luath edition 2011

ISBN: 978-1906817-55-8

The publisher acknowledges subsidy from

ALBA | CHRUTHACHAIL

towards the publication of this book.

The paper used in this book is sourced from renewable forestry
and is FSC credited material.

Printed and bound by
MPG Books Ltd., Cornwall

Typeset in 11pt Quadraat by
3btype.com

Front cover image: *Ossian receiving the Ghosts of the French Heroes* by
Anne-Louis Girodet de Roussy-Trioson
Back flap image: *James Macpherson* after Sir Joshua Reynolds, reproduced
courtesy of the National Portrait Gallery

# CONTENTS

Acknowledgements     6

PART I – THE STORY OF THE POEMS OF OSSIAN
    *Allan Burnett and Linda Andersson Burnett*

Ossianic Timeline     7

'Poetry of the Heart': An introduction to the setting,
themes and characters of Ossian     11

The Poems of Ossian – A Controversial Legacy     25

The Life of James Macpherson     53

PART II – A SELECTION OF THE POEMS

Preface to *Fragments of Ancient Poetry*     67

*Fragments of Ancient Poetry*     70

Preface to *Fingal*     99

Dissertation Concerning the Antiquity of the
Poems of Ossian, Son of Fingal     107

*Fingal, An Ancient Epic Poem in Six Books*     120

PART III – CONTEMPORARY OPINIONS

Hugh Blair     187

Samuel Johnson and James Boswell     206

Malcolm Laing     211

Report of the Committee of the Highland Society
of Scotland     213

Bibliography     221

# ACKNOWLEDGEMENTS

This book is an introduction for the general reader to the Ossianic poems and the controversy surrounding them. It builds on the work of several established Ossian scholars. We would like to pay particular acknowledgment to the essential and extensive work on the subject carried out by Derick S Thomson, Fiona Stafford and Howard Gaskill. All of us who are interested in Ossianic literature and the issues surrounding it owe a debt of gratitude to these and other scholars, not least in their rescuing of the literary Ossian from obscurity and academic neglect in later modern times, and in beginning the process of putting the reputation of Macpherson on a balanced footing.

During the course of our research we made extensive use of library collections at the University of Edinburgh, the National Library of Scotland and the Mitchell Library in Glasgow.

Allan would like to thank Professor Cairns Craig of the Centre for Irish and Scottish Studies at the University of Aberdeen, formerly the Head of English Literature and Director of the Centre for the History of Ideas in Scotland at the University of Edinburgh, for having been an outstanding teacher and supervisor whose approach to such topics as Ossian and on the relationship between literature, history and politics generally is truly enlightening.

Linda is grateful for the feedback from Dr Tom Furniss and his students at the 'The Discovery of Scotland' course at Strathclyde University to her seminar on Ossian and the Scottish Landscape. Linda would also like to thank Dr Andrew Newby at the University of Helsinki for his support and shared interests in 'northern' history and literature. Lastly, she would like to thank her University of Edinburgh PhD supervisors Professor Susan Manning, who also supervised her MSc dissertation on the Ossianic poems, and Dr Thomas Ahnert for their patience, inspiration and great knowledge on 18th-century Scottish history and literature.

# TIMELINE

| 3rd century AD | The time when the Bard Ossian is said to have lived. |
| --- | --- |
| 1370s | John Barbour's *The Bruce*, which mentions Fingal, written. |
| c. 1500 | The Book of the Dean of Lismore written, which contains references to Ossian. |
| 1707 | The Union of Scotland and England. |
| 1710s | John Addison's series of essays spark off public interest in sublime landscapes. |
| 1736 | Macpherson born at Invertromie in Badenoch. |
| 1746 | Bonnie Prince Charlie's Jacobite rebels burn down government army barracks at Ruthven, near Macpherson's home. The Jacobites are defeated at the Battle of Culloden. |
| 1752 | Macpherson commences his degree at King's College, Aberdeen. |
| 1755–56 | Macpherson believed to have studied Divinity at Edinburgh University. |
| 1757 | The Militia Act prohibits the Scots from raising their own militia, prompting much anger and resentment at the British government in London. Edmund Burke's seminal work, *A Philosophical Enquiry into the Origin of our Ideas of the Sublime and the Beautiful* is published. |
| 1758 | Macpherson publishes the *The Highlander* and 'On the Death of Marshal Keith'. |
| 1759 | Macpherson meets playwright John Home who introduces Macpherson's translation of the Ossianic poem 'The Death of Oscur' to his influential friends. |
| 1760 | Macpherson publishes *Fragments of Ancient Poetry, Collected in the Highlands of Scotland, and translated from the Galic or Erse Language*. Macpherson makes trips to the Highlands to collect more poetry. |

1761    Ongoing Highland research trips. In December Macpherson publishes *Fingal, An Ancient Epic Poem in Six Books: together with Several Other Poems composed by Ossian, the Son of Fingal.*

1762    Lord Bute, Macpherson's patron, becomes the first Scottish Prime Minister of Great Britain. *The Briton* and *The North Briton* are launched.

1763    *Temora, An Ancient Poem in Eight Books: together with Several Other Poems composed by Ossian, the Son of Fingal.* The work is dedicated to Bute. The unpopular Bute resigns as Prime Minister. Hugh Blair publishes *A Critical Dissertation on the Poems of Ossian, Son of Fingal.*

1764    Macpherson appointed secretary to the governor of the Western Provinces. Macpherson spends two years in America.

1765    *The Works of Ossian, The Son of Fingal. Translated from the Galic Language by James Macpherson* is published in two volumes.

1771    *An Introduction to the History of Great Britain and Ireland.*

1773    *The Iliad of Homer, Translated by James Macpherson.* He also publishes a new edition of the *Works of Ossian.*

1774    Goethe publishes *The Sorrows of Young Werther.* It features a key scene in which Werther reads Ossianic poetry.

1775    Samuel Johnson's *Journey to the Western Islands of Scotland*, which criticises the works of Ossian, is published. Macpherson publishes *Original Papers, Containing the Secret History of Great Britain from the Restoration to the Accession of the House of Hanover, with Memoirs of James II*, 2 vols and *The History of Great Britain from the Restoration to the Accession of the House of Hanover*, 2 vols.

1776    Macpherson publishes *The Rights of Great Britain Asserted Against the Claims of America.*

1779    Macpherson publishes *The History and Management of the East India Company, from its Origin in 1600 to the*

*Present Times*, following a stint as a colonial agent in London. He also publishes *A Short History of the Opposition during the last Session*. Reverend Donald MacNicol defends Ossian and Highland culture in *Remarks on Dr Samuel Johnson's Journey to the Hebrides*.

1780     A seat in the House of Commons is bought by Macpherson for £4,000. He becomes an MP for Camelford in Cornwall.

1784     Highland Society of Scotland set up in Edinburgh.

1796     Macpherson dies at his estate in Belleville ('Balavil'), Scotland. Buried in Westminster Abbey.

1805     Highland Society of Scotland publishes *Report of the Committee of the Highland Society of Scotland: appointed to enquire into the nature and authenticity of the poems of Ossian*. It concludes that Macpherson used genuine sources, which he embellished.

         Malcolm Laing publishes *The Poems of Ossian, &c, containing the Poetical Works of James Macpherson, Esq. in prose and rhyme: with notes and illustrations*.

1829     Jakob Felix Mendelssohn visits Staffa, making sketches and notes for his *Hebrides Overture* (known as 'Fingal's Cave') and other works.

2002     Calum Colvin exhibits 'Ossian: Fragments of Ancient Poetry' at the Scottish National Portrait Gallery.

2006     BBC documentary re-examining the 'Ossian Hoax'

2010     Exhibition at Paisley Museum by Sandy Stoddart, Her Majesty's Sculptor in Ordinary in Scotland, including a preview of his most ambitious project yet, 'a national Ossianic monument' on the west coast of Scotland – a huge sculpture of Oscar son of Ossian hewn out of an Argyll hillside, on a similar scale to the American presidents cut out of rock in the American west.

# 'POETRY OF THE HEART': AN INTRODUCTION TO THE SETTING, THEMES AND CHARACTERS OF OSSIAN

ALLAN BURNETT and LINDA ANDERSSON BURNETT

It was a dark and stormy night. Or, as the Ossianic narrator put it to their audience in 1760's *Fragments of Ancient Poetry*: 'It is night; and I am alone, forlorn on the hills of storms.' Such is the depth of irony surrounding the infamous cliché of the after-dark scene with its inclement weather and intense atmosphere of foreboding, it can be difficult to imagine a time when the sentiments it conveys were accepted as refreshing and original. Yet that is precisely how this imagery was received by the reading public when *Fragments of Ancient Poetry* was first published. It is testament to the enormous popularity of the work that its central poetical ideas went on to be widely copied, mimicked and ultimately parodied in the centuries that followed. As with the red, red roses of Robert Burns, the poems of Ossian have a lot to answer for in the realm of romantic writing – good and bad.

The opening sentence above comes, of course, from the popular 1830 novel *Paul Clifford* by Edward Bulwer-Lytton – the key difference being that in Bulwer-Lytton's book the loneliness of the Celtic heath is supplanted by the streets of London, where nature gives a thundering reminder of its authority over man's modern, metropolitan dominion. Similar imagery is found in a host of earlier works of what is loosely termed 'Gothic fiction', where other notable themes from the poems of Ossian crop up; such as its ethereal, ghostly atmosphere, its general emotional fervour, and an attitude that awe, terror and doom are emotional states to be especially savoured and enjoyed. The legacy of Ossianic poetry and its wider influence on literature, art and music is discussed in greater detail elsewhere in this volume. In seeking to offer an interpretative guide to the poems themselves, this introduction deals with the genesis of 'Ossianic' imagery – which has proved so potent, durable and adaptable – and how it came to be deployed to resounding effect in *Fragments of Ancient Poetry* and other Ossianic works through the aesthetic choreography of language, rhythm, landscape, sentiment, character and narrative theme. We hope this background will prove illuminating whether the reader is in the mood for reading Ossian's words with straight solemnity, or with an affectionate giggle.

This volume reproduces the original edition of *Fragments of Ancient Poetry* and an abridgement of its follow-up *Fingal: An Ancient Epic Poem in Six Books* as they were presented by James Macpherson, the editor who translated the works – purportedly composed by Ossian, a third-century Highland bard – from the original Gaelic. Of all Macpherson's Ossianic works, *Fragments*, published in 1760, is the closest in form and content to its original Gaelic sources. Its publication kicked off an Ossianic craze and prompted Macpherson to take his work a stage further. The result was *Fingal*, published in 1761, which is a complete epic poem whose existence was suggested by the preface to *Fragments*. The content of *Fingal*, which relates the adventures of its eponymous hero Fingal, comprises translations of original Gaelic sources with embellishment and editorialising by Macpherson.

The anonymously published *Fragments* comes with a short preface written by Hugh Blair, later Professor of Rhetoric and *Belles Lettres* at the University of Edinburgh. According to Blair, the ideas expressed in the poems, their style, and the manners of the characters, all point to their antiquity. The poems are said to have been composed before the establishment of both Christianity and clanship in Scotland, and passed down through the generations by bards who were employed since very early times by prominent families to record important events.

Of the 15 pieces that comprise *Fragments*, many are untitled. The setting of the poems relates to the landscape of Scotland and

Ireland. They are narrated by anonymous bards and the female partners of absent warriors. The verses tell of fallen heroes, their ghosts, their lovers, and of invaders from Denmark. They are presented as the remains of greater works. The readers are encouraged by the preface to expect to an epic poem, whose content is the following:

> The subject is, an invasion of Ireland by Swarthan [Swaran] King of Lochlyn; which is the name of Denmark in the Erse language. Cuchulaid, the general or chief of the Irish tribes, upon intelligence of the invasion, assembles his forces. Councils are held, and battles fought. But after several unsuccessful engagements, the Irish are forced to submit. At length, Fingal King of Scotland, called in this poem 'The deserts of the hills', arrives with his ships to assist Cuchulaid. He expels the Danes from the country; and returns home victorious.[1]

The last three poems in the collection are said to be part of this epic. Thus *Fingal* duly follows, with the same core story as Blair outlines in the preface to *Fragments*.

*Fingal* opens with the arrival of Swaran's ships in Ireland and the action takes place during six days and nights, sometime in the autumn, until the defeated Swaran returns to Scandinavia. Unlike the melancholic tone of the rest of the epic, it has, as was expected from an epic, a happy ending: 'Spread the sail, said the king of Morven, and catch the winds that pour from Lena. —We rose on the wave with songs, and rushed, with joy, through the foam of the ocean.'[2]

Macpherson, who is named in *Fingal* as the translator, is also the author of both a preface and a dissertation on the work. He discusses the ancient Celts and their society – a society whose existence and heroes he believed needed wider recognition. In

---

[1] Hugh Blair, 'Preface' in James Macpherson, *Fragments of Ancient Poetry, Collected in the Highlands of Scotland and Translated from the Galic or Erse Language*, This Edition, pp.68–69.

[2] James Macpherson, *Fingal, An Ancient Epic Poem*, This Edition, p.188.

raising the curtain on the epic that follows, Macpherson puts the narrator Ossian at centre stage. This is in contrast with *Fragments*, which has a number of narrators. In so doing, Macpherson emphasises the importance of the bard – in this case, Ossian – in ancient society. The bard's job was to inspire the people, and to articulate their moral character.

Although parts of the pieces in *Fragments* are incorporated into *Fingal*, they are often amended. King Garve becomes King Swaran, for example. Descriptions of nature change, becoming more embellished and more romantic. The poems are also given an epic structure. In the interests of maintaining this volume as an accessible introduction to the general reader, the supplementary poems originally presented with Fingal in 1761 are not included here. *Fragments* and the epic *Fingal* can be read as two sides of the Ossianic coin. The former are short, discrete pieces of Ossianic poetry known to be close to the original Gaelic sources. The latter is the first complete Ossianic epic, which sparked off the authenticity controversy.

*Temora: An Epic Poem in Eight Books* is not included in this volume. Macpherson produced this follow-up to *Fingal* in 1763, to satisfy the reading public's hunger for more Ossianic poetry. *Temora* details the supposed further adventures of Fingal, who goes to Ireland to remove a usurper of the throne in the name of the rightful heir. The writing in *Temora* is generally accepted as being markedly inferior to that found in Macpherson's earlier Ossianic works. It is likely this relates to the fact that, save for extensive use of a genuine Gaelic ballad in book one, the vast bulk of *Temora* is not in any real sense a translation of original material; rather, it is a new piece of work created by Macpherson using the general pool of Ossianic material as a source.

As to the texts presented herein, Macpherson's original footnotes have been reproduced since we believe these will aid the reader's understanding. These footnotes provide useful explanations of character and plot, as well as giving an insight into Macpherson's literary agenda.

There are a large number of footnotes. As well as explaining characters and content, these tell the readers about different practices in ancient Ireland and Scotland. Macpherson also uses them to make references to classical authors whose works he compares to *Fingal*. Here was Scotland's epic and he wanted to strengthen its case in every way possible.

## A SUBLIME SETTING

The main narrative of *Fingal* is set in Ireland, Ulster in particular. Readers also get to know the Highland and island landscapes of the Scots. Ossian is, for example, known as the Voice of Cona, or Glencoe. In *Fragments* there are no specific locations, save for the Scottish island of Jura. However, it could be said that the specificity of locations is of less importance than the features and nature of the landscape. The Ossianic world is one of rocks, moors, towering oaks, deer, dogs, mists, winds, clouds, stars, meteors, thunder storms, raging torrents and wild seas. It is a world that both reflected and popularised an emerging literary fashion describing nature and landscapes in terms that were sublime – beautiful, terrifying and disorderly.

Public interest in sublime landscapes can be traced back to the 1710s, when Joseph Addison penned a series of important essays for *The Spectator* under the title 'On the Pleasures of the Imagination'. It foretold a new appreciation for wild and rugged landscapes:

> Such are the prospects of an open champion country, a vast uncultivated desert, of huge heaps of mountains, high rocks and precipices, or a wide expanse of waters, where we are not struck with the novelty or beauty of the sight, but with that rude kind of magnificence which appears in many of these stupendous works of nature.[3]

---

3 Addison, 'From the Spectator' in A. Ashfield and P. de Bolla (Eds) *The Sublime: A Reader in British Eighteenth-Century Aesthetic Theory* (Cambridge: Cambridge University Press, 1996), p.62.

This interest was 'foretold' in the sense that during the early part of the 18th century, far-reaching interest in the sublime was yet to take hold. Neo-classical aesthetics were then the order of the day – celebrating order, symmetry and harmony.[4]

It was not until 1757 that attitudes began a marked shift, with the publication of a seminal work on the sublime by Edmund Burke – *A Philosophical Enquiry into the Origin of our Ideas of the Sublime and Beautiful*. Burke promoted sentiment, or sensibility, as a response to the natural world. The sublime was the strongest emotion that nature could evoke. The concept of the sublime, Burke explained, was linked to human feelings of terror, pain and fear:

> Whatever is fitted in any sort to excite the ideas of pain and danger, that is to say, whatever is any sort terrible, or is conversant about terrible objects, or operates in a manner analogous to terror, is a source of the *sublime*, that is, it is productive of the strongest emotion which the mind is capable of feeling.[5]

Burke advocated the idea of 'agreeable horror'; experiences that threatened man's self preservation and whose enjoyment came from the very fear and terror of the experience.[6] Whereas a pretty meadow is beautiful and lends itself to feelings of joy and pleasure, a thunderstorm is sublime since it has a terrifying and awe-inspiring beauty that mankind cannot control. Burke compares the two concepts thus:

> ... for sublime objects are vast in their dimensions, beautiful ones comparatively small: beauty should be smooth and polished, the great, rugged and negligent [...] beauty should not be obscure: the great ought to be dark and gloomy: beauty should be light

---

[4] For a good discussion on the changing taste in landscapes see for example Malcolm Andrews, *In Search of the Picturesque: Landscape Aesthetics and Tourism in Britain, 1760–1800* (Aldershot: Scolar Press, 1989)

[5] E. Burke, *A Philosophical Enquiry into the Origin of our Ideas of the Sublime and Beautiful* (London, 1757), p.38.

[6] Andrews, *In Search of the Picturesque*, p.42.

and delicate: the great ought to be solid, and even massive. They are, indeed, ideas of a very different nature, one being founded on pain, the other on pleasure.[7]

The sublime ideal put forward by Addison and Burke provided a British cultural vocabulary to compliment the native northern landscape. A Mediterranean classical education was not required in order to interpret and adopt this new aesthetic, and as a result it had a widespread appeal in Britain among the growing middle strata of society.

Macpherson thus used sublime notions to challenge and overturn some deep-rooted, negative perceptions of the Highland landscape. Northern and western Scotland had been condemned for having a barren and unproductive landscape by such early 18th-century travellers as Daniel Defoe and Edward Burt. Burt, travelling in 1730, wrote about the unpleasant Highland mountains:

> Those ridges of the mountains that appear next to the ether – by their rugged irregular lines, the heath and black rock – are rendered extremely harsh to the eye, by appearing close to that diaphanous body, without any medium to soften the opposition; and the clearer the day, the more rude and offensive they are to the sight.[8]

Now, thanks to Ossian and Macpherson, the Highlands would be celebrated for that same stark and irregular landscape. Hugh Blair proudly proclaimed the sublime qualities of the Ossianic Scottish landscape in his *Critical Dissertation on the Poems of Ossian*: 'We meet with no Grecian or Italian scenery; but with the mists, and clouds, and storms of a northern mountainous country'.[9]

---

7 Burke, *A Philosophical Enquiry*, p.151.

8 E. Burt, *Burt's Letters from the North of Scotland as related by Edmund Burt*, Ed. A. Simmons (Edinburgh: Birlinn, 1998), p.157.

9 Hugh Blair, *A Critical Dissertation on the Poems of Ossian*, *The Son of Fingal* (London: T. Becket and P. A Hondt, 1763), p.53.

## PRIMITIVE PASSIONS

The bleak and tumultuous landscape is reflected in the thoughts and deeds of the characters inhabiting the world of Ossian, as this line from the 10th piece in *Fragments* illustrates: 'it is night; and I am alone, forlorn on the hill of storms. The wind is heard in the mountain. The torrent shrieks down the rock. No hut receives me from the rain; forlorn on the hill of winds.'[10]

The Ossianic world is one of primitive passions and impulsive actions, not yet curtailed or controlled by civilization and modernity. Hugh Blair in his *Critical Dissertation on the Poems of Ossian* claims the early society depicted in the poems offers the reader an early history of emotions.[11] The heroes express very strong feelings, in very bold terms. Men and women are found weeping, raging with anger, or desperately in love.

These emotional states are expressed in plot devices that are correspondingly dramatic: bloody pitched battles, family feuds resulting in murder, mistaken identities, doomed love, crimes of passion, the death of major characters, elegies over loved ones, and so on. There is a strong association between love and death, with no happy ending for most of the couples, who often are united only in death. Another common motif is of parents grieving the death of their children. A sense of loss permeates the poems: a lost (bygone) age, lost lovers, lost (dead) children, lost greatness. Spiritually, these are dark times, with no God or religion and no hope in salvation. Although Christian missionaries and druids are mentioned in the poems, the Ossianic heroes do not adhere to either belief system. There is relief only in being commemorated by the bards. In this sense the Ossianic poems prefigure the spiritual concerns of modern nationalism, where national heroes live on not so much in Heaven but are instead immortalised in the history books and statues of their earthly realm.

---

[10]  Macpherson, *Fragments*, This Edition, p.86.
[11]  Blair, *A Critical Dissertation*, p.1

All of this sadness, darkness and doom is intended to provide great pleasure for the readers. Ossian himself refers to 'The Joy of Grief'. This is something he shares with his 18th-century readers; indeed, the late 1700s is often characterised culturally as 'the age of melancholy'. John Aitkin, for instance, noted in the 1790s the importance of melancholy in Britain: 'Melancholy itself is a source of pleasure to a cultivated mind.'[12] The isolation and melancholy permeating the northern Ossianic landscape reflected the vogue for morbid emotionalism. Or, as it is put in *Fragments*: 'SAD! I am sad indeed: nor small my cause of woe!'[13]

The dominant mood is one of gloom and melancholy, even at moments of high drama or action-packed battle. Yet, the red-blooded heroes of Ossian's world often exhibit great warmth and tenderness. The poems are entwined by close friendships, passionate love affairs and strong family ties. The heroes are generous and gentle, or 'noble'. Their honour and gentility holds true during warfare. Fingal, for example, remembers that his foe Swaran is the brother of Agandecca, a woman who had saved his life and was his first love. In light of this, Fingal resolves not kill his arch enemy. Instead they reconcile and feast together before Swaran returns home to Lochlin (Denmark).

Thus at the conclusion to Book Six of *Fingal* we read of the former enemies reconciling, and Fingal recalling happier times with shared toasts from a drinking shell: 'King of Lochlin said Fingal, thy blood flows in the veins of thy foe. Our families met in battle, because they loved the strife of spears. But often did they feast in the hall; and send round the joy of the shell.'[14] The response is equally gracious: 'BLEST be thy soul, thou king of shells, said Swaran of the dark-brown shield. In peace thou art the gale of spring. In war the mountain-storm. Take now my hand in friendship, thou noble king of Morven.'[15] The bards Ossian,

---

[12] Aitkin qtd. in Andrews, *In Search of the Picturesque*, pp.42–44.

[13] Macpherson, *Fragments*, This Edition, p.88.

[14] Macpherson, *Fingal*, This Edition, p.180.

[15] Ibid., p.181

Carril and Ullin, then sing songs of the past with harps accompanying them, and the two mighty heroes listen together.

## THE GOOD OLD DAYS

Fingal and Swaran are, of course, long gone by the time Ossian sits down to recite their epic life stories. Ossian, the poems' principal narrator, is the last of his people. He is old, blind and lonely. With his beard waving in the wind, he laments the dead. He is left on his own, without his family and friends. 'Such, Fingal! Were thy words; but thy words I hear no more.'[16] He can hear only the sounds of the landscape and the ghosts of his ancestors.

The aged bard is happy only when reminiscing, since the present provides no joy. This is illustrated by a passage from the poem 'In The War of Inis-thona':

> When shall Ossian's youth return, or his ear delight in the sound of arms? When shall I, like Oscar, travel in the light of my steel?
> —Come, with your streams, ye hills of Cona, and listen to voice of Ossian! The song rises, like the sun, in my soul; and my heart feels the joys of other times.[17]

Retelling the past also gives Ossian a sense of purpose, since his duty and function is to tell of warriors' heroic deeds. Again there is melancholy as Ossian worries what will happen to the memories of the fallen when he, too, passes away. 'But memory fails on my mind; I hear the call of years. They say, as they pass along, why does Ossian sing? Soon shall he lie in the narrow house, and no bard shall raise his fame.'[18] This sensation of doom is acute, since Ossian's much-loved son Oscar is dead. There is no hope for the future.

The sense of hopelessness is braced against the recurring idea of a lost golden age. In the former times recalled by Ossian, Fingal and his cohorts enjoy a simple but noble lifestyle. Apart from warfare they also enjoy hunting, listening to the bards, sharing the

---

[16] Macpherson, *Fragments*, This Edition, p.83.

[17] James Macpherson, *Fingal, an ancient epic poem, in six books: together with several other poems, composed by Ossian the son of Fingal* (London, 1762) p.104.

[18] Ibid., p.218.

drinking shells and being in love. In the fifth piece of *Fragments*, the bard remarks of Connal: 'Thy family grew like an oak on the mountain, which meeteth the wind with its lofty head. But now it is torn from the earth. Who shall supply the place of Connal.'[19] In the piece that follows, Ossian states that his thoughts are of Fingal and former times.

The poems' emphasis on the ideal of a lost golden age was undoubtedly a feature of traditional Gaelic verse. Yet it also relates to Macpherson's interest in the new aesthetic of 'primitivism', which was put forward by Macpherson's old tutor Thomas Blackwell, among others. Primitivism offered a critique of contemporary, early-modern 18th-century society by comparing it unfavourably with more primitive times. Adherents to the 'primitivist' notion of society argued that the earliest conditions of mankind and society represented the best conditions. Since then, a progressive decline had set in, enfeebling man and nature. Modern commerce and civilization brought only degeneration, selfishness and corruption. Primitivism was in its prime at the time of *Fragments* and *Fingal*'s publication and represented a reaction against Britain's rapid commercial expansion and urbanisation with a corresponding desire to return to a simpler and less sophisticated lifestyle. The sense that something good and pure has been lost, and that the future looks bleak, is an ideal amply articulated by Ossian.[20]

## STORIES WITHIN STORIES

The poems contained in *Fragments* and *Fingal* have a curious texture. They lack a specific form and are instead a mixture of prose and poetry. However, as Ossian scholar Fiona Stafford has pointed out, Macpherson did use vocal patterns to create consistency and there are internal rhymes.[21] Macpherson often repeated sentiments and

---

[19] Macpherson, *Fragments*, This Edition, p.76.

[20] For a discussion on primitivism see for example: L. Whitney, *Primitivism and the Idea of Progress*, 2nd. Ed. (New York, 1973).

[21] Fiona Stafford, *The Sublime Savage: James Macpherson and the Poems of Ossian* (Edinburgh: Edinburgh University Press, 1988), p.108.

words, like a chant that draws the reader into the world of the poems, which are intended to come alive when read aloud.

Similarly, the wider narrative structure of the poems is not straightforward, even in the epic *Fingal*. Sub-plots and mini-narratives create frequent digressions that can easily confuse the readers. Ossian's tendency to relate stories within stories is discussed by Stafford, who argues that since Ossian is 'unable to receive fresh impressions of the external world, his poetry depended on the repetition of the 'tales of the times of old', so the general monotony and lack of definition in his poems seemed appropriate to the ramblings of a blind old man.'[22]

The digressive and fragmentary structure of the poems, even in their continuous epic form, speaks of the nature of human memory with all its complexities and contradictions. Holding it all together is not so much an orderly narrative structure, but the lynchpin figure of Ossian himself. This lack of narrative discipline is in contrast with the emphasis on order and classification that we often associate with the 18th-century Enlightenment era. As such it is indicative of the sublime and the romantic, where free rein is given to the passions and eccentricities of primitive society. Instead of demanding of Ossian a strict narrative discipline, it is perhaps better to go with the flow, reading the poems aloud and savouring the beauty of the language.

## SELECT CAST OF CHARACTERS

The poems of Ossian feature a large cast of characters. There are numerous warriors, kings, bards, love interests, parents, children and animals. Below is a selection of some of the key characters in *Fragments* and *Fingal*.

OSSIAN: Also called the 'Voice of Cona' (Glencoe). The main Ossianic bard and narrator. We also encounter him as a young warrior in his recollections of the past. Also known as 'Oscian'.

---

[22] Ibid p.144.

FINGAL: Ossian's father and King of Morven. Fingal is depicted by his son as a great warrior and leader of his people. Fingal is known for his nobility and kindness of spirit, even among his foes, which is reflected in his nickname 'Fingal of the Mildest look'.

SWARAN (Known as Garve in *Fragments*): A Scandinavian king. The son of King Starno. Swaran instigates the action in *Fingal* by invading Ireland. He is referred to as a 'Man of great size'.

AGANDECCA: Swaran's sister. In love with Fingal, and saved his life. Killed by her brother for betraying him.

CUCHULLIN: Son of Semo. Cuchullin is Lord of the 'Isle of the Mist' (Skye). Acts as general for the Irish tribe during King Cormac's minority. A daring hero. Referred to as Cuculaid in *Fragments*.

OSCAR: Son of Ossian and Evirallin. A young warrior hungry for fame but with great warmth. He is in love with Malvina. Praised and exalted by his proud father. Also known as 'Oscur'.

MALVINA: The lover of Oscar. She is the audience for many of Ossian's tales.

SEMO: Cuchullin's father and Chief of Skye, the 'Isle of Mist'.

CORMAC: A name borne by kings of Ireland. Cormac I is the grand-father of Cormac II. They are assisted by Fingal and Cuchullin.

FILLAN and FERGUS: Two of Fingal's sons. They take part in the wars against Swaran.

ULLIN: Fingal's principal bard.

GAUL: A commander in Fingal's army.

RYNO: The son of Fingal, celebrated for his swiftness. Dies in the battle against Swaran's armies.

BRAN and LUATH: Two dogs. The first is a 'hairy-footed' greyhound belonging to Fingal. The second is Cuchullin's hunting dog.

## SOME KEY LOCATIONS

What follows is a selection of some of the most significant places featured in the poems, and a brief explanation where applicable of how they relate to present-day terrain.

MORVEN: The Kingdom of Fingal and his ancestors. On the west coast of Scotland. Almost certainly related to the region known today as Morvern, although the Ossianic Morven is larger.

LOCHLYN: Gaelic for Denmark, or Scandinavia. Also appears as 'Lochlin'.

TEMORA: Royal palace of the first Irish kings.

SELMA: Fingal's palace in Morven.

TURA: A castle in Ulster.

LENA: 'The heath of Lena', on the coast of Ulster.

CROMLA: A mountain in Ulster.

CONA: A river and mountain region in Morven, related to present-day Glencoe.

INNISFAIL: Ireland, also known as Erin.

INNISCON: Shetland.

INISTORE: Orkney.

# THE POEMS OF OSSIAN –
# A CONTROVERSIAL LEGACY

LINDA ANDERSSON BURNETT and ALLAN BURNETT

The instant success of James Macpherson's first collection of
Ossianic translations, *Fragments of Ancient Poetry*, in 1760, prompted him to swiftly extend the scope of his ambition. His next step
was to produce what he claimed were literal translations of full
and complete epic poems from the third century, beginning with
*Fingal* in December 1761. According to Macpherson these complete epics demonstrated that Ossian, their original narrator, was
an ancient Celtic bard whose talents were equal to, if not greater
than, those of Homer. Soon after the publication of the second of
these complete epics, *Temora*, in 1763, doubts were raised in
public about the authenticity of the poems. Had Macpherson
faithfully translated the poems from ancient Gaelic originals, the
critics asked, or had he in fact fabricated the material himself?
Were Ossian's poems, in reality, a work of fiction?

In the 18th century, the question of authenticity resulted in a
bitter row that was eventually to overshadow the poems themselves, at least in Britain. Present-day authorities have sought to
establish the extent to which Macpherson's translations are
faithful to the original Ossianic ballads of Gaelic tradition. Gaelic
scholar Derick S. Thomson has shown that Macpherson did
embellish his original sources to varying degrees, for example adding
Romantic episodes and descriptions of nature.[1] Ultimately, however, Macpherson's Ossianic poems were closely derived from the
themes, plots and names in authentic Gaelic ballads.

Thomson identifies around 16 authentic Ossianic ballads
within the original Gaelic tradition, several of which were

---

[1]   Derick S. Thomson, 'Macpherson, James (1736–1796)', *Oxford Dictionary of
National Biography*, Oxford University Press, 2004; online edn, May 2006 [http://www.
oxforddnb.com/view/article/17728, accessed 25 Jan 2011]

faithfully utilised in *Fragments of Ancient Poetry*. While *Temora* features a large amount of embellishment by Macpherson, *Fingal* is much closer to the original sources. 'The [original authentic] ballads are used in a range of different ways,' writes Thomson, 'sometimes to provide a basic plot, or an adapted plot, sometimes having a sequence of lines or stanzas loosely translated, with interjections, and often taking names or specific incidents from ballads and using these, or more normally variants of these.'[2]

To source the tales, Macpherson and his assistants went out into homes, halls and meeting places and wrote them down as they were recited by the keepers of the oral tradition. Specialist 'keepers' of oral information had been used for centuries within the *Gàidhealtachd* to accurately record everything from poetry to land records. In addition, Macpherson's team also collected written manuscripts, and consulted mediaeval written records held in archives and institutions, which corroborated to some extent the supposed vintage of the original ballads. These records included John Barbour's *The Bruce* from the 1370s, which contains a reference to Fingal. Another source is *The Book of the Dean of Lismore*, a manuscript compiled in the late 15th and early 16th centuries, which contains significant Ossianic references.

Macpherson was the best-known collector of Ossianic ballads, but he was not the first. In the 1750s, for example, Archibald Fletcher wrote down his own collection; as did the Reverend Donald MacNicol. The minister of Dunkeld, Jerome Stone, likewise translated a heroic Gaelic poem in the Ossianic mould for *The Scots Magazine* in 1756.[3] As to why Ossianic poems had not met with greater interest before, Macpherson offered his own explanation. The poems contained 'ideas so confined to the most early state of society that it was thought they had not enough variety to please a polished age.'[4] With all things primitive being

---

[2] Ibid.

[3] *The Scots Magazine*, January 1756.

[4] James Macpherson, 'A Dissertation Concerning the Antiquity, & co, of the Poems of Ossian' in James Macpherson, *Fingal: An Ancient Poem in Six Books, This Edition*, p.117.

fashionable in the mid-18th century, Macpherson and his supporters realised that the reading public was now ready to receive
the Ossianic poems.[5] However, while Macpherson's translations
were to prove vastly more popular than earlier examples, they were
also destined for a correspondingly greater degree of scrutiny.

Macpherson's Ossianic epics were held up to be the great
literary work of the Scottish nation at precisely the moment when
the very idea of Scotland, Scottish culture and Scottishness were
being critiqued and questioned as never before by educated men
north and south – particularly south – of the Border. The poems
were seized upon instantly as a Scottish totem, assaulted by some
and defended by others. Amid the din of warring cultural
agendas, any unbiased response to the question of authenticity
struggled to be heard.

### THE CELTIC HOMER

On the face of things, following the Union of 1707, Scotland and
England were peacefully incorporated into a fully United Kingdom. The centuries of bloody cross-border war were now behind
them. Yet by 1760 people from north of the Border generally felt
that the English still looked down on them as rebellious and
uncivilised. Many educated middle and upper class Scots were
therefore exceedingly keen to champion Macpherson, because
they saw the Ossianic poems as an opportunity to strengthen
Scotland's cultural prestige within the Union. The Scottish literati
believed that England, as the larger nation of the two, and on
whose constitution the new British state was modelled, did not
respect Scotland as an equal partner.

They were right. 'Scotland', 'Scotch' and 'Scottish' were
common words of abuse in England, and the entire Scottish nation
tended to be depicted in English letters as backward, untrust-
worthy, despotic, insolent and money-grabbing. The height of
this English hostility occurred in the early 1760s when Lord Bute

---

5  Ibid.

became the first Scottish Prime Minister of Britain. Bute had an unusually close relationship with the royal family. This led to accusations of corruption, sexual misdemeanours and excessive favouritism towards Scots at court and in government in London.

In Edinburgh, however, there was little sense that Scotland had been treated favourably of late. Quite the opposite. The Scots felt that they were still being treated as traitors because of the last Jacobite rebellion, in which a mainly Scottish army, under Prince Charles Edward Stuart and backed by the French and other foreign governments, had tried and failed to seize the British throne and overturn the Hanoverian regime. In the immediate aftermath of the Jacobites' final defeat at the Battle of Culloden in 1746, the bearing of arms and the wearing of Highland dress was banned.

English suspicion of Scottish treachery lingered in the following decade, finding renewed expression in the Militia Act of 1757, which specifically prohibited the Scots from raising their own militia for civil defence. When rumours of a French invasion spread in Scotland in 1759, during the Seven Years' War, the Militia Act left the Scots feeling that they were in no position to defend themselves.[6] This Act was taken as a violation of the Scots' traditional right to bear arms, and was seen as especially insulting since the raising of militias was permitted in Wales and England.[7]

Anger was felt widely among the literati of Scotland's Lowland cities, who felt they had worked hard to distance themselves from the 'Jacobite' Highlands and demonstrate their loyalty to Britain. One anonymous writer, styling himself 'ScotoBritanicus', wrote to the popular newspaper *The Caledonian Mercury* in March 1760, suggesting that the Union would not, and should not, have

---

[6] Richard B. Sher, *Church and University in the Scottish Enlightenment: The Moderate Literati of Edinburgh* (Edinburgh: Edinburgh University Press, 1985), p.215.

[7] Alexander Broadie, *The Scottish Enlightenment: The Historical Age of the Historical Nation* (Edinburgh: Birlinn, 2001), p.91.

happened had the Scots known what they were in for.[8] This sense of injustice was to be well catered for by the initial appearance that year of Macpherson's *Fragments of Ancient Poetry, Collected in the Highlands* – since the poems both celebrated Scotland's martial virtues and demonstrated that Scottish culture contained treasures equal to those of the classical world, marking it out as superior to English culture.

It was hoped that the Ossianic poems and their eponymous author – presented by Macpherson as a third-century Scottish poetical genius superior even to Homer – would improve the image of Scotland's independent, pre-Union past. Mediaeval Scotland, the Highlands particularly, was often perceived by the English, and even many Lowland Scots, as having been an unenlightened and savage place, riddled with conflict and plagued by feudal oppression. Faced with a grander Scottish pedigree, it would be harder for the English to discredit the Scottish nation. Moreover, while much of Scotland's pre-Union identity appeared to be defined by the many conflicts with England,[9] this was not what the Ossianic poems were about. Instead it held out the liberating prospect of a more elevated national mythology through which to express Scotland's distinctiveness within the Union.

In order to promote the published Ossianic translations as an ancient Scottish national mythology, Macpherson and his supporters emphasised the historical importance of the poems. In the preface to *Fingal: An Ancient Poem*, published December 1761, Macpherson states that the poems narrate genuine history alongside their mythological and fantastical elements, making them more 'valuable for the light they throw on the ancient state of Scotland and Ireland than they are for their poetical merit'.[10] He also contends that the poems reveal Scotland's antiquity to be

[8] *The Caledonian Mercury* 31 March, 1760.
[9] Colin Kidd, *Subverting Scotland's Past: Scottish Whig Historians and the Creation of an Anglo-British Identity, 1689–c.1830* (Cambridge: Cambridge University Press, 1993).
[10] Macpherson, *Fragments*, This Edition, p.105.

superior to any other European nation.[11] Although there are no gods in the Ossianic world, its heroes appear as god-like. Fingal is described by Macpherson's mentor Hugh Blair in his A Critical Dissertation on Ossian, The Son of Fingal, published in 1763, as the greatest hero of all:

> Wherever he appears, we behold the hero. The objects which he pursues, are always truly great; to bend the proud; to protect the injured; to defend his friends; to overcome his enemies by generosity more than by force. A portion of the same spirit actuates all the other heroes.[12]

Such heroes represented the idea of national genius, or national character, that was becoming popular in the later 18th century. The national character of the Scots depicted in the poems was a martial one of courage, patriotism, unselfishness and friendship. The Ossianic heroes represented the quintessential values behind the ongoing claim of Scottish political and cultural leaders, such as the respected philosopher Adam Ferguson, for a militia.[13] Although the militia supporters did not want to see the break-up of the Union, they wanted to see a change in English attitudes to Scotland. They hoped that the mythical heroes in the Ossianic poems, which they believed had existed in some form, would help bring about this change.

In order for the Ossianic warriors to be effectively mobilised in defence of Scottish culture, they had to be presented as embodying Enlightenment axioms of what constituted proper behaviour. Macpherson boldly claimed that the emerging mid-18th century fashion for politeness, gentility and sentiment was prefigured by Ossian and the Scottish Gaelic past. Of course, the content of the poems spoke for itself. The Ossianic poems are

---

[11] James Macpherson, Works of Ossian, The Son of Fingal, 3rd ed, Vol.II (London: T. Becket and P. A. Hondt, 1765), p.xxiii.

[12] Hugh Blair, A Critical Dissertation on Ossian, The Son of Fingal (London: T. Becket and P. A. Hondt, 1763), p.70.

[13] Fiona Stafford, The Sublime Savage: James Macpherson and the Poems of Ossian (Edinburgh: Edinburgh University Press, 1988), pp.157–158.

permeated by a tenderness and sensibility that appealed directly
to 18th-century readers looking for literature that was instructive
but also touched their hearts.[14]

Fingal and his friends represent both polite manners and
martial heroism. Fingal, for example, never injures or kills the
weak. In the poem 'The Battle of Lora' Fingal states:

> I was born in the midst of battles, and my steps must move in
> blood to my tomb. But my hands did not injure the weak, my
> steel did not touch the feeble in arms.[15]

It is however Ossian, rather than his father Fingal, who exempli-
fies the 18th-century man of feeling, since he is renowned for his
sensitivity rather than his martial prowess.[16] The capacity of the
poems to excite emotions, in Scotland especially, can be seen in
the author Tobias Smollett's review of Fingal in the Critical Review
in December 1761:

> We will defy any person of sensibility to read three succeeding
> pages of it, without feeling strong motions of tenderness and
> admiration.[17]

Ossian was elevated by Scottish readers to the status of the
northern Homer. Blair wrote in his dissertation on Ossian:

> As Homer is of all the great poets, the one whose manner, and
> whose times comes the nearest to Ossian's, we are naturally led
> to run a parallel in some instances between the Greek and the
> Celtic bard. For though Homer lived more than a thousand years
> before Ossian, it is not from the age of the world, but from the
> state of society, that we are to judge of resembling times.[18]

---

[14] Hugh Honour, Neo-Classicism, 2nd ed. (London: Penguin, 1991), p.66.

[15] James Macpherson, Works of Ossian, The Son of Fingal, 3rd ed, Vol.1. (London:
T. Becket and P. A. Hondt, 1765), p.162.

[16] John Dwyer, 'The Melancholy Savage: Text and Context in the Poems of
Ossian' in Howard Gaskill (Ed.), Ossian Revisited (Edinburgh: Edinburgh University
Press, 1991), p.187.

[17] Smollet Qtd. in The Scots Magazine, December, 1761.

[18] Blair, Dissertation, p.22.

Ossian was even claimed to be superior to his Mediterranean classical cousins in many respects. Smollett, for example, argued that
the Ossianic characters were more agreeable than those of Homer
and Virgil, which he saw as vindictive and puerile.[19] David Erskine-
Baker's *The Muse of Ossian*, an 18th-century play that is based on
Ossianic poems, proclaimed the Scottish bard's superiority in its
prologue:

> Methinks I hear the *Greciani* Bards exclaiming,
> (The *Grecian* Bards, no longer worth the naming),
> In song the Northern tribes so far surpass us,
> One of their *Highland-hills* they'll call PARNASSUS
> And from the sacred Mount *decrees* shall follow,
> That OSSIAN was *himself* the TRUE APOLLO.[20]

According to Macpherson, the living representatives of these
remarkable Ossianic warriors – warlike yet noble – were found in
the Scottish Highlands. Scottish Highlanders were portrayed as an
exclusive race that had survived uncorrupted by outside influence
since the third century and had therefore avoided the negative
influences of modernity.[21] Contemporary Highlanders were not
ill-mannered brutes, but had instead retained the virtues of their
heroic ancestors.

This noble portrait of the Scottish Highlands soon found
favour. Adam Ferguson stated that it took: 'genius, learning and
courage' to promote a culture and language whose 'greatest
elegancies were to be learned from herdsmen' and which was
'connected with disaffection and proscribed by government'.[22]
Howard Gaskill has pointed out that the term 'Highlanders' was
a synonym for savages in the 1760s and that the term gradually

---

[19]  *The Scots Magazine*, 22 December 1761.

[20]  David Erskine Baker, *The Muse of Ossian: A Dramatic Poem of Three Acts*, (Edinburgh, 1763), Prologue.

[21]  Stafford, *The Sublime Savage*, p.153.

[22]  Qtd in Dafydd Moore, *Enlightenment and Romance in James Macpherson's The
Poems of Ossian: Myth, Genre and Cultural Change* (Aldershot: Ashgate, 2003), p.25.

lost its pejorative association partly due to Macpherson's positive portrayal of them.[23]

Macpherson also drew parallels between the decline of the heroic ancient Scottish society depicted in the Ossianic world and the decline of Highland culture in the 18th century. Common to both epochs was, in Macpherson's view, the negative influence of the English and the corruption that accompanied the process of 'civilisation'. The decline of Ossianic society, Macpherson argues in the dissertation to *Temora*, started at the time of the departure of the Romans, which he pinpoints to the year 426AD, and when the influence of the Saxons began to be felt in the Lowlands of Scotland.[24] The Caledonians, as a result, settled in the mountain areas, where they formed clans. They were self-sufficient and autonomous, while the Lowland population declined into a modern commercial society. Macpherson's insistence that corruption was external – English – is brought forward to the 18th century at the end of the dissertation of *Fingal*. It does not end with a discussion of ancient Celts, but of the situation of 18th-century Highlanders:

> The genius of the highlanders has suffered a great change within these few years. The communication with the rest of the island is open, and the introduction of trade and manufacture has destroyed that leisure which was formerly dedicated to hearing and repeating the poems of ancient times. Many have now learned to leave their mountains, and seek their fortunes in a milder climate; and though a certain *amor patriae* may sometimes bring them back, they have, during their absence, imbibed enough of foreign manners to despise the customs of their ancestors. Bards have been long been disused, and the spirit of genealogy has greatly subsided.[25]

---

[23] Howard Gaskill, 'Introduction' in Howard Gaskill (Ed.) *Ossian Revisited*, p.5.

[24] Macpherson, *Works of Ossian*, Vol.II, pp.xv–xvi.

[25] Macpherson, *Fingal*, This Edition, p.118.

Fiona Stafford, a scholar of the Ossianic poems, argues that Macpherson's attitude towards the Saxons, as being a negative influence on Scottish society, is significant since it explains Macpherson's own ambiguity and anxiety about the Anglication of the Scottish Highlands in the century after the Union of 1707.[26] In a sense, Macpherson is the last of his people – just as Ossian was in the third century – whose task it is to preserve the spirit of a doomed group. The Ossianic poems are therefore partly an elegy to a past age and a past Scottish nation, and partly an assertion of a new era and a new identity.

A more critical view, on the other hand, is that far from setting Scotland above and beyond the thrall of England, Macpherson's works are merely a capitulation to English power. Macpherson may have depicted a glorious Scottish past, but that past is of little value since it is now gone. Ossian, old and blind, laments the fate of being the last of his race. He is left in a barren landscape, a landscape he can only bring back to life through the recollection of the past, in which his father Fingal and himself were successful and renowned warriors:

> Such, Fingal! were thy words; but thy words I hear no more. Sightless I sit by thy tomb. I hear the wind in the wood; but no more I hear my friends. The cry of the hunter is over. The voice of war is ceased.[27]

Critics have drawn attention to the last sentence of the above section. It has been interpreted as a powerful image of Scotland no longer presenting a military or cultural threat to England. Although there is an emphasis on military valour in Fingal, by the end the two enemies, Fingal and Swaran, reconcile. This has been interpreted as representing the hostility between England and Scotland.[28] Scotland might once have had a distinct society, but

---

[26] Stafford, The Sublime Savage, pp.159–160.

[27] James Macpherson, Fragments, This Edition, p.83.

[28] Mícheál MacCraith, 'Fingal: Text, Context, Subtext' in Fiona Stafford and Howard Gaskill (Eds) From Gaelic to Romantic (Amsterdam: Rodopi, 1998), p.67.

that society is now gone and the nation can therefore be accom-
modated within the Union, since it has been made to appear
acceptable and unthreatening to an English audience. Some
critics, such as Peter Womack, have gone further, arguing that
'the Poems of Ossian idealise Highland culture by reading its extinction back into its very origins'.[29]

The restrictive measures that had followed Culloden struck a
severe blow to Highland society. It was therefore deemed essential to collect the nation's Highland heritage before it vanished
forever. An investigation commissioned by the Highland Society
of Scotland found that there were few people after 1745 who could
recite Ossianic poetry.[30] Some critics have argued that Macpherson and those like him were not really concerned with reversing
this trend, and that they were focused on finding emotional ties
to the Highland past rather than searching for ways to rebuild
Gaelic culture, and wider Scottish culture, for the future.[31]

Yet it was precisely by repairing Scotland's link with its past,
deemed to have been broken by the Union of 1707, and the dis-
aster of Culloden in 1746 in particular, that Macpherson sought to
assert the distinctiveness and value of the contemporary Scottish
nation. The publication of the poems was prompted by a desire
for the Scottish nation to be treated as an equal to England rather
than as a subservient junior sibling. Macpherson made the Scottish
past relevant to its present at a time when it was still controversial to
do so. His Scottish Highlanders were not barbarians but humane,
noble and refined. Extracts from Ossian were published in Scotland's national newspapers. Poems and plays were dedicated to the
third-century bard and leading literary lights, such as the novelist
Tobias Smollett, wrote rave reviews of Fingal and Temora.

---

[29] Peter Womack, Improvement and Romance: Constructing the Myth of the Highlands
(Basingstoke: Macmillan, 1989), p.109.

[30] Highland Society of Scotland, Reports of the Committee of the Highland Society of
Scotland: appointed to enquire into the nature and authenticity of the poems of Ossian (Edinburgh: Constable, 1805), p.78.

[31] See for example Murray Pittock, Inventing and Resisting Britain: Cultural Identities in Britain and Ireland 1685–1789 (London: Palgrave Macmillan, 1997), pp.156–7.

## AN ELABORATE HOAX?

South of the Border, many took a different view. That Scotland was a great and noble nation with an illustrious cultural tradition stretching far back into antiquity might have seemed self-evident to Macpherson and the legions of Ossianic admirers that quickly emerged at home and on the continent. Among many of the English literati, on the other hand, the idea that Scotland could be anything more than wholly inferior to England was considered absurd – even insulting. From the outset, Macpherson and his Ossianic translations were viewed with ridicule, suspicion and outright hostility. In the years that followed the poems' first pub-lication, Macpherson came to be discredited as a forger and his translations failed to become part of the canon of British litera-ture. He is still widely dismissed as a conman, who concocted the poems entirely out of thin air.

The negative English attitude to Macpherson's poems origi-nated not with the poems as such, but rather was prefigured by the fierce Scottophobia that prevailed south of the Border around 1760. Scots were participating in the post-Union state as never before, in government and in commerce, but this had not created a greater sense of unity between the two nations. Instead, it prompted a renewed emphasis on national differences. Ossian was presented as a Scottish-British hero by Macpherson and a Scottish literati who wanted mutual respect and equal status within the Union. Yet this was interpreted as a cultural threat by the English, who were not open to anything that challenged their assumption that Britain was merely a more territorially extensive version of England.

Again, this national difference of opinion over the poems took place in a wider context of antagonism between Scotland and England in the later 18th century. Macpherson's crime was to drop his Ossianic work, with all its provocative Scottish cul-tural ambitions, onto the British reading public at precisely the moment when the Scots were being seen as a renewed political and economic threat to England; a threat in some ways more insidious than anything hitherto presented by Jacobitism or even the Scottish nation's independence.

English fear of a Scottish 'enemy within' was widespread. It was prompted by the sudden increased participation of Scots within the political hierarchy of the Union state and the markets of the Empire. The first half-century following the Union – which had been sold to the Scottish people as an economic boon – brought slow growth and little opportunity to Scotland, contributing to strong anti-Union sentiment and decades of rebelliousness north of the Border. By the 1750s, however, the Scottish economy had finally become properly engaged with the colonial markets. This 'take-off point', the significance of which has been identified by economic historians, brought Scottish industrial capitalism whirring into life.

More significantly, this take-off also prompted many politically minded Scots to cross the Border. Scots were, to a greater degree, finding employment and housing in England, especially London, which was the governmental and administrative core of the Union and the Empire. There was a sense that England was being overrun by Scots, even though the weight of numbers did not bear this out.[32] The exaggerated English reaction to an increased public Scottish participation in the Union was commented upon in *The Caledonian Mercury* on 24 August 1763:

> ... how few in proportion the Scots in place are to the English, – The Privy Council list consists of above eighty; of whom there is scarce a dozen Scotsmen: – Of all the numerous great offices of the Household of all the train of attendants on the Queen, the Princess of Wales, and Royal Family, there is scarce one of ten a Scotsman. – Amidst the band of new-made nobility we don't observe one Scotsman. [...] in the places of the administration and revenue, there is scarce almost a Scotsman to twenty Englishmen.[33]

---

[32] See for example: Pittock, *Inventing and Resisting*, pp.129–30.
[33] *The Caledonian Mercury*, 24 August 1763.

Discontent with the English perception of a Scottish invasion was pointed, since many Scots were fighting and dying abroad for the British Empire. A letter to *The Scots Magazine* in September 1764, with the headline 'On the Insults offered to the Scots', expressed anger at the Scots being labelled traitors when they were: 'bleeding, conquering, dying, for the liberty of Great Britain'.[34] The letter added that if the Scots were to be treated as aliens and enemies, yet defending country that mistreated them: 'Then we are slaves indeed'.[35] Nevertheless, what came to predominate south of the Border was the perception that the country was being overrun by avaricious and scheming Scots, living and working in England and in *her* Empire

This resentment reached fever pitch in 1762, shortly after the publication of *Fingal*, when Bute became Prime Minister. Bute, who took over from William Pitt, proved so unpopular in England that he was said to have hired a group of butchers and prize-fighters to protect him from physical attacks.

There were a number of things that worked against this rather hapless Scottish Prime Minister. Bute was a favourite of the king, which aroused jealousy and suspicion; he wanted peace rather than war against France and Spain, which was deeply unpopular; and last but certainly not least, he was a Scotsman, and therefore an imposter. The English paper *The Monitor*, which had attacked Bute even before he became Prime Minister, portrayed the Bute government as being run by aliens and favourites of the king who ignored the public good of the English nation.[36]

To counter this criticism and whip up support for Bute's policies, *The Briton*, which was edited by Smollett, was launched on 29 May 1762. In its first edition, the paper stated its intention was: 'not to alarm, but appease; not to puzzle, but explain; not to

---

[34] *The Scots Magazine*, no.26. September 1764.

[35] Ibid.

[36] Byron Gassman, 'Note' in Tobias Smollett, *Poems, Plays and 'The Briton'* (Athens, University of Georgia Press, 1993), p.224.

inflame, but to allay'.[37] Only one week later, a satirical anti-Bute and anti-Scottish newssheet The North Briton was published by the English politician and journalist John Wilkes. This paper, which proved much more popular than The Briton, ridiculed the Scottish nation and its inhabitants on a weekly basis until the resignation of Bute on 8 April 1763 following riots against a new cider tax.[38]

Macpherson could not have picked a worse time to publish his works. Nor could he have chosen a worse patron for his endeavours – Bute himself. Macpherson all but invited English critics to heap invective upon him by dedicating his Ossianic poems to Bute. Although Bute is not named in the first edition of Fingal in 1761, and instead is referred to as a 'noble person', Macpherson dedicated Temora to him in 1763. Macpherson received valuable financial support from Bute, yet the public acknowledgement certainly did not help the sales or reputation of his works in England.

While some English criticism appeared measured, with The Monthly Review arguing that the poems did not measure up to the standards of Homer or Virgil, there was no such pretence of objectivity elsewhere.[39] The North Briton mercilessly mocked the Scots, criticising their growing presence in London and their Ossianic hubris. This satirical remark, published in June 1762, is attributed to a Scot scheming to take over England:

> We are certainly growing into fashion. The most rude of our bards are admired; and I know some choice wits here, who have thrown aside Shakespeare, and taken up Fingal, charmed with the variety of character, and richness of imagery.[40]

The editors of The North Briton also sought to undermine Macpher-

---

[37] The Briton, no.1, 29 May 1762.

[38] Leith Davis, Acts of Union: Scotland and the Literary Imagination of the British Nation, 1707–1830 (Stanford: Stanford University Press, 1998), p.76.

[39] The review by The Monthly Review was printed in The Scots Magazine, April, 1762.

[40] The North Briton, 12 June 1762.

son's work by arguing that the poems belonged to an Irish rather than Scottish tradition. In this they latched on to the fact that, from within the common Scottish-Irish Gaelic realm, Macpherson was facing another battle. Macpherson's introduction to *Temora* stressed that the Irish Ossianic ballads were borrowed from Scotland. As far as the Irish were concerned, however, the borrowing was the other way around. Whereas the reaction to Macpherson in England had been cries of forgery, in Ireland people were outraged that he tried to claim what they perceived as their poetry.[41]

Though English critics gleefully added Irish allegations of theft to their arsenal, this was not their ultimate weapon against Macpherson. In the wake of *Fingal* in 1761–2, the English attack quickly began to focus on the assertion that this could not be the translation of a complete Gaelic epic in the classical mould, for given the lowliness of Scottish culture surely no such thing could have existed. The whole thing must instead be an elaborate hoax manufactured by Macpherson – a typical example of Scottish effrontery. Charles Churchill, friend of Wilkes and contributor to *The North Briton*, penned an anti-Scottish poem in 1763 called 'The Prophecy of Famine'. It undermined the authenticity of the poems and castigated the infiltration of Scots into England. 'Into our places, states, and beds they creep,' Churchill wrote, and linked Ossian with Bute:

> From themes too lofty for a bard so mean
> *Discretion* beckons yo an humbler scene,
> The restless fever of ambition laid,
> Calm I retire, and seek the sylvan shade.
> Now be the *Muse* disrob'd of all her pride,
> Be all the glare of the verse by *Truth* supplied,
> And if plain nature pours a simple strain,

---

[41] Michael Mac Craith 'We know all these poems': The Irish Response to Ossian' in Howard Gaskill (Ed), *The Reception of Ossian in Europe* (London: Thoemmes Continuum, 2004), pp.91–108.

Which BUTE may praise, and OSSIAN not disdain,
OSSIAN, *sublimest, simplest* Bard of all,
Whom *English Infidels* Macpherson call,
Then round my head shall honour's ensigns wave,
and pensions mark me for a willing slave.[42]

English antipathy to the Scots' political, economic and cultural ambitions could not have been clearer. Correspondingly, Scots tended towards a haughty dismissal of English criticism of the poems' literary merit and authenticity as being nothing more than mean-minded national envy at the achievements of both Macpherson and Bute. This is seen in a letter written on 14 October 1763 from John Macpherson, Minister of Sleat, to Blair:

> I am not at all surprised that, at a time when the spirit of party, and national quarrels, are risen to such a height, the authenticity of Ossian's poems should be called in question. The glory arising to our country and ancestors, from these noble monuments of genius, cannot miss to give pain to the malevolent in the southern division of the Isle; and, as a great person who has patronized Fingal, must not only be depressed, but made as little as possible in every respect, Mr Macpherson must be involved in the same cruel persecution.[43]

Macpherson himself initially responded to English hostility by appearing to up the ante of the debate. In 1765, in *The Works of Ossian*, he tendentiously compared Bute to Ossian:

> ... there is a great debt of fame owning to the EARL OF BUTE, which hereafter will be amply paid: there is also some share of reputation with-held from Ossian, which less prejudiced times may bestow. This similarity between the Statesman and the Poet, gives propriety to this dedication.[44]

---

42 Charles Churchill, *The Poetical Works of Charles Churchill*, Ed. Douglas Grant. (Oxford: Clarendon, 1956), pp.260–272.

43 The Highland Society, *Report*, Appendix p.6.

44 Macpherson, *The Works of Ossian*, Vol.I, Dedication.

Behind the bluster and provocation, the jibes and the insults, national insecurities were pricked on both sides. Macpherson's Ossianic works were deemed significant enough a threat to force the English to attempt to re-establish their sense of cultural superiority within the Union. This was the impetus behind Dr Samuel Johnson's famous tour of the Scottish Highlands and Islands in 1773 alongside his Scottish companion James Boswell.

Johnson and Boswell went to places where Macpherson had collected the Ossianic poems. Johnson's aim was to debunk Macpherson's heroic vision of Scotland. He therefore placed particular emphasis on the primitiveness of Gaelic culture, which Macpherson had elevated. This was done to undermine Scotland's claim to a distinctive and heroic literary past, which in turn was used to reinforce Johnson's own discourse that the English had civilised the Scots and introduced them to literature. Johnson could not accept that 'culture' could be indigenous to Scotland rather than being adopted from England.[45] Scotland, Johnson argued, began the process of civilisation only after the Union with England in 1707:

> Till the Union made them acquainted with English manners, the culture of their lands was unskilful, and their domestick life unformed; their tables were coarse as the feasts of Eskimeaux, and their houses filthy as the cottages of Hottentots.[46]

Johnson portrayed the whole Scottish population as being prone to fabrication, and contended that Macpherson's publications were a prime example of this. It was only due to 'Caledonian Bigotry' that the poems had become a success story, he wrote.[47] He also claimed, incorrectly, that there were no Gaelic Ossianic manuscripts more than 100 years old.[48] In any case, he demanded to

---

45  See for example Davis, *Acts of Union*, pp.93–94.

46  Samuel Johnson, *A Journey to the Western Islands of Scotland* (London: W. Strahan and T. Cadell, 1775), p.57.

47  Ibid., p.274.

48  Ibid., p.267.

see whatever original written Gaelic manuscripts Macpherson had in corroboration of his translations. In a letter to James Boswell on Saturday 25 February 1775 Johnson wrote: 'There are, I believe, no Erse manuscripts... If there are manuscripts, let them be shewn.'[49]

Personally affronted by what he saw as the condescending attitude of Johnson and other critics, Macpherson angrily announced that he had in fact placed the 'originals' of *Fingal* – perhaps as many as 19 Gaelic manuscripts – with his publisher, Thomas Becket, for these to be inspected by the public at Becket's shop in London back in 1762. The publisher subsequently confirmed this in an advertisement published on 19 January 1775, the day after Johnson's attack in his *Journey to the Western Islands of Scotland* appeared.[50] Given that the original manuscripts had only been put on display for a limited time, and that apparently little attempt had been made to publicise the display, this did little to assuage English suspicions. Johnson, for his part, refused to let the issue lie, culminating with Macpherson rather facetiously challenging the ageing and infirm bibliophile to a duel.

Unsurprisingly, Johnson and others who dismissed the oral sources of the poems also aroused anger among the wider Gaelic community. The Gaelic scholar Reverend Donald MacNicol published a rebuttal in 1779 called *Remarks on Dr Samuel Johnson's Journey to the Hebrides*. Meanwhile the novelist Sir Walter Scott, whose own romantic fiction was to be heavily influenced by the Ossianic poems, commented that Scottish Highlanders would rather 'disavow the Scripture than abandon a line of the contested tales'.[51] Yet, even in circles where there was a greater acceptance and understanding of oral culture, suspicions that the poems contained elements of fabrication refused to die down. These doubts

---

49 Samuel Johnson Qtd. in James Boswell, *The Life of Samuel Johnson*, Vol.1 (London: 1791), p.456.

50 Gaskill, *Ossian Revisited*, p.11; Saunders, *Life and Letters*, pp.197 and 249.

51 Qtd in Susan Manning, 'Ossian, Scott and Nineteenth-Century Scottish Literary Nationalism' *Studies in Scottish Literature* 17 (1982), p.47.

were reinforced by Macpherson's unwillingness or inability to adequately demonstrate that the keepers of the Gaelic oral tradition, for this was said to be the chief repository of the work, could recite the original epics – or at least those sections not otherwise obtained from manuscripts – word for word as they appeared in translation in his text.

As early as 1763, the philosopher David Hume had written to Blair pressing upon him the importance of obtaining from Macpherson such specific and detailed evidence – whether in manuscript or oral form. Blair responded to such requests but only superficially, and failed to present specific materials or individuals that testified in detail and with precision about their contribution to Macpherson's Ossianic translations. For his own part, Macpherson's response was a somewhat dismissive summary of his research fieldwork. 'A detail of this journey would be both tedious and unentertaining;' he wrote in a dissertation in the collected Poems Of Ossian in 1765, 'let it suffice therefore that, after a peregrination of six months, the translator collected from tradition, and some manuscripts, all the poems in the following collection, and some more still in his hands, though rendered less complete by the ravages of time.'[52]

While Macpherson's evasive tone here might warrant suspicion, it perhaps tells us less about the poems and more about Macpherson's character – which during the course of the debate revealed its vanity, arrogance and obstinacy. He intensely disliked having his integrity called into question, and though he conducted some verbose rhetorical defences of the poems' authenticity, his unwillingness to go into detail about his research likely had as much to do with a vindictive desire to confound his anglophone critics as anything else.

The boggy question of where fact ends and fiction begins in

---

[52]  Hugh Blair, A Critical Dissertation on the Poems of Ossian, The Son of Fingal, 2nd ed. (London, T. Becket and P. A De Hondt, 1765); James Macpherson, 'A Dissertation' in James Macpherson, The Works of Ossian, Vol.I., p.xxii ; See also Michael MacCraith 'We know all these poems', pp.91–2.

his Ossianic publications and the circumstances of their creation was clearly as fascinating to some contemporary observers as the poems themselves. Smollett was inspired to reflect on the issue in his popular 1771 novel The Expedition of Humphry Clinker. The poems' authenticity is apparently certified in an episode that sees the main character enjoying a heightened sense of adventure on a Highland estate, as he views it through Ossianic spectacles:

> We have had princely sport in hunting the stag on these moun-tains – These are the lonely hills of Morvern, where Fingal and his heroes enjoyed the same pastime: I feel an enthusiastic pleas-ure when I survey the brown heath that Ossian wont to tread; and hear the wind whistle through the bending grass – When I enter our landlord's hall, I look for the suspended harp of that divine bard, and listen in hopes of hearing the aerial sound of his respected spirit – The poems of Ossian are in every mouth – A famous antiquarian of this country, the laird of Macfarlane, at whose house we dined a few days ago, can repeat them all in the original Gaelick.[53]

It was one thing for the original Ossianic epics to be recited in Smollett's fictional world, but quite another for these originals to be heard in reality. In an attempt to settle once and for all the long-running authenticity debate, the Highland Society of Scotland, a respected cultural and agricultural improving organisation set up in Edinburgh in 1784, commissioned an investigation following Macpherson's death in 1796. While many Scots believed Macpherson had tweaked and edited the poems to appeal to a modern audience, few perceived them to be pure fabrication since they were deemed to be based on a real oral Gaelic tradition. Andrew Gillie, who was the minister of Kincardine in Ross-shire, wrote to Charles MacIntosh, a member of the investigating committee, in 1799:

> Before Mr Macpherson could know his right hand from his left,

---

53 Tobias Smollett, The Expedition of Humphry Clinker, Vol.II, (London: J. Wren and W. Hodges, 1795), p.86.

I have heard fragments of them repeated, and many of those fragments I recognised in Mr Macpherson's translations.[54]

Macpherson's influential friends and supporters justified his alterations by again comparing him to Homer, who also had collected and tied together fragmented stories from the past. The Highland Society's report, published in 1805, concluded that there had been no outright falsification. It was at least a partial vindication of what Macpherson himself had always maintained. Contrary to the supposition of such critics as Johnson, Macpherson never claimed to have sourced all of his material from complete epic manuscripts; he never pretended to have discovered a third-century Gaelic manuscript containing a complete *Fingal* or *Temora*. Rather, as the Highland Society investigation confirmed, Macpherson and his associates had collected a litter of oral and written fragments, which Macpherson then saw himself as restoring and refurbishing to their 'original' epic state.

Whether or not Macpherson had made a grave error in setting himself that task, perhaps misguided by his and Blair's assumptions about what they believed the poems *ought to* have looked like, remains a valid subject for debate – especially since Macpherson failed to be completely open about his methodology in polishing and embellishing the original material in order to turn fragments into whole epics. Whatever the verdict on Macpherson's methods, the claim that he was an out-and-out fraud or hoaxer who completely fabricated the Ossianic poems now seems far fetched. As the Highland Society report put it, if Macpherson was guilty of having committed a literary crime, it was in making excessive editorial amendments to material that was considered 'too simple or too rude for the modern ear'.

The Highland Society's Report was and remains an important bulwark for the defence, at least in part, of the poems and Macpherson's reputation. It should be noted, however, that Scotland was not wholly united in its desire to get behind the poems in the

---

[54] The Highland Society, *Reports*, p.39.

face of criticism from south of the Border. In his last years, Hume grew roundly fed up of Macpherson, whom he described as a 'hot-head', and commented in a letter to the historian Edward Gibbon in 1776 that:

> I see you entertain a great Doubt with regard to the Authenticity of the Poems of *Ossian*. You are certainly right in so doing. It is, indeed, strange, that any men of Sense coud [sic] have imagin'd it possible, that above twenty thousand Verses, along with numberless historical Facts, could have been preservd by oral Tradition during fifty Generations, by the rudest, perhaps, of all European Nations...[55]

Foreshadowing some of the internal cultural squabbles and schisms of the 19th and 20th centuries about the 'true' nature of Scottish identity, further dissenting voices were heard from within, both in the Lowlands and in the north. The Edinburgh-born historian John Pinkerton (1758–1826) initially celebrated the Ossianic publications but turned against it after he decided that its elevation of ancient Gaelic Scotland was an unwelcome subversion of the dominant culture of Lowland Scotland. Pinkerton argued that the Picts who inhabited ancient Scotland were a Gothic people related to the Scandinavians, and that the Gaels were racially inferior imposters from Ireland who had settled in the south-western province of Dal Riata, latterly known as Argyll, and then corrupted the Picts.[56] A contemptuous attitude towards Macpherson's work was also expressed in a heavily annotated edition of the Ossianic poems by the lawyer and historian Malcolm Laing (1762–1818), a native of the Orkney Isles.[57]

The intensity of the debate over the Ossianic poems saw the work attacked with ferocity and on a number of fronts. It is testa-

---

55   Hume to Edward Gibbon, Edinburgh 18 March 1776, cited in the *Electronic Enlightenment* online database http://www.e-enlightenment.com.

56   William Ferguson, *The Identity of the Scottish Nation: An Historic Quest* (Edinburgh, 1998) p.250.

57   T. F. Henderson 'Laing, Malcolm (1762–1818)' in *The Oxford Dictionary of National Biography* (Oxford University Press, 2004).

ment to the intrinsic merit of the poetry that despite its many detractors and the seriousness of their criticisms, it continued to attract admirers. The poems' popularity and influence in the century following its publication was immense. It was as though the heroes in its pages, whether ancient or novel, refused to be beaten.

### BEYOND DISPUTE

For many readers, especially outside of the British Isles and Ireland, the question of provenance was of far less importance than the intrinsic merit of the work itself. The poems became a huge international success and were translated into several European languages including French, German, Italian, Magyar and Swedish.[58] The Ossianic works and their aesthetic proved a key inspiration for the dominant 19th-century tradition in European literature, art and music: Romanticism. The poems offered an alternative to Classicism with a freer attitude to poetry, an emphasis on feeling and a greater sensitivity towards nature. In the world of Ossian, the ancient, the primitive, the remote, the wild, the sublime and the supernatural are venerated.

An appreciation of these qualities was what united personalities as disparate as Johann von Goethe, Napoleon Bonaparte, Oscar Wilde, and the king of Sweden. Each bears the imprint of *Ossian*'s international popularity. The first, Goethe, was inspired to write his greatest works after reading about Ossian. The second, Napoleon, preferred the Ossianic poems to the *Odyssey* and always carried Macpherson's work with him on his campaigns. 'They contain the purest and most animating principles and examples of true honour, courage and discipline,' Napoleon wrote, 'and all the heroic virtues that can possibly exist'.[59] He awarded the Italian translator of the poems, Cesarotti, with a lifetime pension.[60] As

---

[58] See for example, Howard Gaskill (Ed), *The Reception of Ossian in Europe*.

[59] Napoleon Qtd. in Fiona Stafford, 'Introduction: The Ossianic Poems of James Macpherson' in Howard Gaskill (Ed.), *The Poems of Ossian and Related Works* (Edinburgh, Edinburgh University Press, 1996), p.vi.

[60] Stafford, *The Sublime Savage*, p.177.

to Wilde, both he and the Swedish monarch Oscar I (1799–1859), bore the name of one of the works' principal characters. The young Prince Oscar noted in a letter to John Sinclair, the Scottish improver and compiler of the *The Statistical Accounts of Scotland*, the special relationship between Scandinavian and Celtic heroes:

> The Celtic heroes were brothers and friends of the Scandinavian heroes, and their glory interests me doubly, since I happen to bear the name of one of their most famous warriors.[61]

That the Ossianic works were highly regarded by many of the brightest lights of the Enlightenment age is beyond dispute. Although Macpherson opposed the American Revolution, this did not prevent his work from being admired by Thomas Jefferson.[62] The poems were a key influence on the German *Sturm und Drang* movement – which celebrated emotions, individualism and nature – with the philosopher-poet Johann Herder being one of the leading enthusiasts. In England, too, among writers of the stature of Blake and Coleridge, the appeal of Ossian was considered too great to be entirely submerged in national prejudice.[63]

The Ossianic poems impacted on other art forms besides literature. It inspired Scottish painters such as Alexander Runciman and the English impressionist JMW Turner. It also inspired prominent foreign painters such as François Pascal Simon Gérard (*Ossian Conjuring up the Spirits on the Banks of the River Lora with the Sound of his Harp*); Anne-Louis Girodet de Roussy-Trioson (*Ossian Receiving the Ghosts of the French Heroes*) and Jean Auguste Dominique Ingres (*The Dream of Ossian*).

---

[61] Letter from Prince Oscar to Sir John Sinclair. Dated Stockholm 26th of July 1817. In J. Sinclair, *The Correspondence of the Right Honourable Sir John Sinclair*, Vol.1, (London: H. Colburn & R. Bentley, 1831), pp.59–60.

[62] Susan Manning, 'Why Does It Matter that Ossian Was Thomas Jefferson's Favourite Poet?' *Symbiosis* I (Oct. 1997), pp.219–36.

[63] Coleridge wrote the poem 'Imitated from Ossian' in 1793. On the influence of Ossian on Blake see: David Punter, 'Ossian, Blake, and the Questionable Source', in Valeria Tinkler-Villani et al (Ed.), *Exhibited by Candlelight: Sources and Developments in the Gothic Tradition* (Amsterdam: Rodopi, 1995), pp.25–42.

Beethoven, Brahms, Haydn and Schubert all wrote music to accompany the tales of Ossian. The personal interest of Jakob Felix Mendelssohn provides the most vivid illustration of the poems' capacity to inspire in this regard. The German composer went on a pilgrimage to Scotland after reading about Ossian, and toured the Highlands and Hebrides in 1829 in search of romantic scenery. He found the landscape suitably melancholic. On an excursion to the island of Staffa, he was infamously prevented from enjoying the view of Fingal's Cave by a bout of sea-sickness. Nevertheless, during the trip Mendelssohn made notes and even drew sketches that became raw materials for the resulting orchestral compositions – The Hebrides Overture, or 'Fingal's Cave', and Symphony No. 3 (Scotch) in A Minor.[64]

The misty and desolate Highland landscapes described in the poems attracted tourists to Scotland during Georgian and Victorian times. These visitors eagerly roamed the locations suggested by the poems, and continue to do so now. Indeed the work changed forever how people viewed the Scottish landscape. Some enterprising Scottish landlords were quick to harness the appeal of Ossian to attract visitors. At the Duke of Atholl's estate near Dunkeld, for example, there was a summer house that came to be referred to as 'Ossian's Hall' in which travellers could view a portrait of Ossian which was hoisted away to reveal a large window overlooking a waterfall. The site remains open to visitors today, although the portrait is long gone. The 'discovery' of Fingal's Cave on Staffa, visited by Mendelssohn, was attributed to Joseph Banks. A 1772 tour of Scotland by the travel writer Thomas Pennant included Banks's account of Staffa and Fingal's Cave, and this turned Staffa into a major tourist destination.[65]

The impact of the poems on people's understanding of their landscape was felt in nations beyond the British Isles. Translations of the poems influenced the political nationalism of the 19th century and the accompanying trend for supporting nationalist claims by uncovering 'lost' ancient cultural artefacts, such as the *Kalevala* which was championed by Finnish nationalists in their quest to gain cultural and political independence from Sweden and Russia.

It is hard to overestimate the breadth and depth of the poems' cultural impact, even where it is not explicitly stated. An Ossianic influence can be detected in the epic nationalist opera of Wagner in the 19th century; in both the melancholic mood and the poetic evocation of landscape, ancestry, war and fellowship in the Celtic-Gothic fantasy world of Tolkien's Middle Earth in the 20th century; and in the misty Highland mountain imagery and mournful musical accompaniment extensively utilised whenever Scotland is depicted on screen today, a notable recent example being the BBC's *A History of Scotland* television series broadcast in 2008 and 2009.

In recent decades, a more overt appreciation of the Ossianic poems has been sustained by the publication of far-reaching academic re-appraisals of Macpherson's work by Thomson, Stafford, Gaskill, Moore and others. This in turn has been echoed by some renewed popular interest, as evidenced by a BBC television documentary entitled *The Great Ossian Hoax* presented by the author Alexander McCall Smith and first broadcast in 2006. The visual artist Calum Colvin meanwhile has challenged audiences to re-evaulate the work with his exhibition *Ossian: Fragments of Ancient Poetry*, shown at the Scottish National Portrait Gallery in Edinburgh in 2002 and the headquarters of UNESCO in Paris in 2005.

The publisher of this volume, Luath Press, founded in 1981, also does its bit to maintain Macpherson's legacy in Scotland in the 21st century. Luath is the name of Cuchullin's hunting dog in *Fingal* and was given to a collie owned by Robert Burns. The poet's pet is referred to in a poem entitled 'The Twa Dogs', first published in 1786, in which Burns pokes fun at the debate over exactly when the poems were created:

And in freak had Luath ca'd him,
After some dog in Highland Sang,
Was made lang syne,
Lord knows how lang.

While the question mark over the provenance and authenticity of Macpherson's Ossianic translations still casts a long shadow, it is not why the poems endure. As Scottish writer George Chalmers put it in 1805, 'Except the Bible and Shakespeare, there is not any book that sells better than Ossian. This sale seems to arise from the intrinsic merit of the book, and not from the talk about it.'[66] With this in mind, both the work and some of the most influential talk about it is presented here so that you may judge for yourself.

---

[66] George Chalmers Qtd. in Stafford, *The Sublime Savage*, p.171.

# THE LIFE OF JAMES MACPHERSON

ALLAN BURNETT and LINDA ANDERSSON BURNETT

James Macpherson was born on 27 October 1736, at a farm at Invertromie in Badenoch – a land of wooded hills, green shrubbery and teeming marshes in the Highland valley of the River Spey. Macpherson was the only child of his parents, Andrew and Helen. Macpherson's father was a first cousin of Ewan Macpherson of Cluny, a leading Jacobite rebel. Both of Macpherson's parents were related to the clan chief. Macpherson therefore grew up in a comparatively well-heeled, respectable Highland family.[1]

While growing up on the family farm, however, Macpherson saw the society of his parents crumbling around him. He was eight years old when the Jacobite rebellion, led by the dynamic Charles Edward Stuart, aka Bonnie Prince Charlie, took off in the summer of 1745. The aim of the rebellion was to restore the Stuarts to the British throne, from which they had been ejected in the late 1680s. The Prince's supporters, consisting of Lowlanders and Highlanders but mainly the latter, hoped the Stuarts could restore lost stability and security to Scottish society.

The Jacobites felt that the traditions and certainties of Scottish life had been broken by the Union of 1707 with England, which robbed Scotland of its independence. After 1707 Scots were required to anglicise their speech and manners in order to fit in to the new British society. Worse, the ancient, tribal role of the chief as the 'father' of the clan was being replaced by the idea of a commercial landlord with no paternal duty of care to his tenants. These were all complaints that Macpherson heard being made by the grown-ups around him.

To begin with, the Jacobite rebellion seemed to be a success.

---

[1] The biographical information in this essay is drawn extensively from Bailey Saunders's *Life and Letters of James Macpherson* (London: MacMillan, 1894), Fiona Stafford's *The Sublime Savage: James Macpherson and the Poems of Ossian* (Edinburgh: Edinburgh University Press, 1988) and Derick S Thomson's 'Macpherson, James (1736–1796)', *Oxford Dictionary of National Biography*, (Oxford, Oxford University Press, 2004).

The young, impressionable Macpherson almost certainly looked on as around 300 Highlanders massed nearby and laid siege to the government barracks at Ruthven. The Highland warriors then spectacularly set the barracks on fire. That was in February 1746, only months after the uprising had commenced. But even then, the Jacobite army was on the retreat, lacking supplies and denied reinforcements that had been promised by the French royal court.

Before Macpherson had celebrated his tenth birthday, the rebellion was defeated in battle on a bitterly cold April day on Culloden Moor, near Inverness. The Prince was forced to hide out in the Highland hills and then the Western Isles, before escaping to France. He had been greatly assisted in his escape by Macpherson of Cluny, the clan chief, who had for a while hidden the Prince in a cave in Badenoch at grave personal risk. Cluny remained a fugitive for nine years.

For those left behind, the consequences were severe. Clans such as the Macphersons, who had staunchly supported Charlie, were humiliated and their traditional rights violated. Their houses and farms were ransacked. Their weapons were banned. Their traditional Highland dress, meaning the old great kilt, was banned. And, in some cases, their land and homes were confiscated. Captain John Macpherson of Strathmashie, a Jacobite officer, later recalled the aftermath of Culloden:

> Oh heavens! In what characters will what follows be writ! Murders, burnings, ravishings, plunderings! Ane army of fiends let loose from Hell, with Lucifer himself at their head! Barbarities unheard of – no distinction of sex or age – cruelties never as much named among any people who made profession of or pretended to Christianity, and all not only with impunity, but by command.[2]

As Macpherson witnessed this mayhem unfold, with his peers throwing stones at the government troops who harassed the residents of his village, he grew aware of the long-term consequences.

---

[2] John Macpherson Qtd. in Stafford, *The Sublime Savage*, p.18.

The Gaelic language, which had been under attack anyway for being too 'alien' from English, was increasingly seen as something to be rooted out entirely. As a result, a strong sense of loss and melancholy pervaded life in Badenoch into the 1750s, and Macpherson felt it deeply, as he later made clear. There can be little doubt this early experience shaped his aesthetic approach, as a poet and translator, to the Highlands.

Besides imbibing these historic events, Macpherson had an education which, at home, consisted of readings from the Bible and Highland folklore. Gaelic was his first language, and he would later use a colloquial form of Gaelic in his letters to other Gaelic speakers. Macpherson was inculcated with the view that Gaelic was a 'pure', ancient language not derived from any other tongue, whereas English was a mongrel language. The Gaels generally saw themselves as a pure 'race', who had – until now – successfully combated the corrupting influences of foreigners.

Despite the upheavals after Culloden, Highland villages continued to feature Gaelic poets and reciters that kept local history alive. Macpherson learned much from them, in particular tales of ancient heroic characters such as Ossian, Oscar, Fingal and Dermid and the Fiana, an elite warrior band charged with protecting the Highlands from foreign invasion, which formed a storytelling tradition that Gaelic Scotland shared with Ireland. Like other clans, the Macphersons saw the Ossianic heroes as being their own heroic ancestors, which reinforced their strong attachment to the traditional role of the clan chief. Tales of the Ossianic era were told for entertainment, to strengthen Gaelic identity and to encourage people to follow the morals of the heroes.

Macpherson's formal education was at Badenoch Parochial School, possibly followed by a stint at a grammar school in Inverness. It was at school that Macpherson's sense of a divide between the Highlands and the rest of Britain, including Lowland Scotland, was likely reinforced. After all, modern formal education was itself an innovation brought from the Lowlands. The Society in Scotland for the Propagation of Christian Knowledge (SSPCK), which established many schools in the Highlands, took a dim view of the 'traditional' Highland way of life, in particular its adherence to Catholic religious sentiments over the new Presbyterian doctrine. The Highlands was dismissed by the SSPCK as being an unholy place of ignorance, laziness and criminality. There is little doubt Macpherson had similar attitudes impressed upon him, whether by teachers or in school books, when he was a boy.

On the other hand, even in the homes of Highland schoolmasters and Presbyterian ministers, a kind of inverted snobbery towards the 'superior' south was also making itself felt. Lowlanders tended to be characterised as cold and soulless, corrupted by luxury and convenience; whereas Highlanders saw themselves as warm and soulful, honest and down to earth.

Macpherson therefore grew up with a starkly contradictory view of the Highlands and the Lowlands, of Scotland and of England, and of tradition and progress. As an intelligent and inquisitive young man, he could plainly see the benefits that modernisation from the south had brought to the Highlands. In the 1720s and '30s, the government had commissioned General Wade to build a huge network of modern roads and bridges that would allow troops to easily march through the Highlands and quell disorder. Before that road-building programme there had been only dirt tracks, mountain paths and a lot of wet feet.

Now, as a young scholar about to embark on the next stage of his education, Macpherson was able to travel swiftly upon those pristine highways to the universities of Aberdeen and Edinburgh. Shortly after Macpherson left the clan heartlands to make his way in the world, Cluny, his outlawed chief, finally made his own escape to France in 1755. It was the end of one era, and the beginning of another.

There can scarcely have been a more stimulating time in which to attend a Scottish university. Macpherson enrolled at King's College, Aberdeen, in 1752, and then moved to Marischal College. His student life coincided exactly with the age of Enlightenment. Students at this time were being taught to view culture in scientific terms. At Aberdeen, Macpherson also studied classical literature and was introduced to the ancient works of Homer. One of his teachers at Marischal College, Thomas Blackwell, was the author of *An Enquiry into the Life and Writings of Homer* (1735). Blackwell had a great interest in ancient, epic poetry which he shared with Macpherson. Blackwell's work on Homer also illustrates how he favoured the 'natural' and 'simple' manners of so-called primitive people:

> ... they best show human wants and feelings; they give us back the emotions of an artless mind, and the plain methods we fall upon to indulge them: goodness and honesty have their share in the delight; for we begin to like the men, and would rather have to do with them, than with more refined but double characters. [...] We live within doors, covered, as it were, from nature's face; and passing our days supinely ignorant of her beauties, we are apt to think the similies taken from her *low*, and the ancient manners *mean*, or absurd. [...] State and form disguise man; and wealth and luxury disguise nature.[3]

This elevation of supposedly primitive people likely had a great impact on Macpherson. Having been brought up in the aftermath of Culloden when the Highlanders were depicted as brute savages, Macpherson must have been aware that the time was now ripe to rehabilitate them as noble savages, whose minds and bodies were not yet corrupted by wealth and luxury.

In addition to his strong intellect, Macpherson was a good-looking young man and he knew it. Student hi-jinx and romancing the lassies were high on his list of priorities during these years, if his later satirical writings about student life and his string of illegitimate children are anything to go by. He also made some serious first attempts at writing his own poetry. After Aberdeen, Macpherson is believed to have attended the University of Edinburgh as a

---

[3]  T. Blackwell, 'From An Enquiry into the Life and Writings of Homer' in A. Ashfield and P. de Bolla (Eds.), *The Sublime: A Reader in British Eighteenth-Century Aesthetic Theory* (Cambridge: Cambridge University Press 1996), p.164.

divinity student in 1755–6. His father was keen for him to become a minister, but Macpherson had other ideas and did not complete his divinity degree.

Returning to his homeland in 1756, Macpherson started to collect Gaelic poetry. He also ran a charity school in Ruthven while he bided his time and considered his next move. It was not long before an opportunity presented itself. He took up employment as a family tutor for the aristocratic Grahams of Balgowan and, by taking full advantage of the networking opportunities, by 1758 had found himself work as a proof corrector for Balfour publishers in Edinburgh. Among the work Macpherson got published at this time was a long poem called *The Highlander* – a tale about the invading Scandinavians and the Highlanders who defended their land. Below is an extract from the poem:

> The Mountain-chiefs, in burning arms incass'd
> And carrying all their country in their breast,
> Undaunted rear their useful arms on high;
> Now fought for food, and now for liberty:
> Now meet the sport of hills, now of the main,
> Here pierc'd a stag, and there transfix'd a DANE.
> Tho' nature's walls their homely huts inclose,
> To guard their homely huts tho' mountains rose;
> Yet feeling ALBION in their breast, they dare
> From rocks to rush and meet the distant war.[4]

Heavy with Gaelic imagery and heroic and noble Highland warriors who valiantly fight the Scandinavian invaders, this piece was indicative of the direction in which Macpherson was moving.

In 1760, Macpherson's first Ossianic work, *Fragments of Ancient Poetry, Collected in the Highlands of Scotland, and translated from the Galic or Erse Language* was published, followed by translations of full Ossianic epics. The task of bringing the Ossianic poetry to print was a joint effort between Macpherson, who collected and

---

4 James Macpherson, *The Highlander: A Poem: In Six Cantos* (Edinburgh: Wal. Ruddiman jun. and Company, 1758), p.17.

translated the poems from their original Gaelic sources, and leading figures of the Scottish Enlightenment. These figures included
the philosophers David Hume and Adam Ferguson, the historian
William Robertson and Hugh Blair who would soon become the
first Regius Professor of Rhetoric and Belles Lettres at the University
of Edinburgh.

Macpherson's introduction to this powerful circle of men was
through Ferguson.[5] Macpherson probably first met Ferguson
when the former accompanied one of his well-born students to
Ferguson's father's manse in Logierait. Ferguson was impressed
by Macpherson's classical knowledge and enthusiasm for Gaelic
poetry, and wrote him a letter of introduction to the popular playwright John Home.

Macpherson met Home at the spa resort of Moffat in 1759.
Home shared Macpherson's passion for heroic virtue and patriotism, which were the themes of Home's early plays and Macpherson's poem 'The Highlander'. When Macpherson showed Home
a translated fragment of Ossianic poetry – 'The Death of Oscur' –
Home was impressed. The playwright circulated the work among
his famous friends. Among them was Blair, who was to become
Macpherson's strongest supporter. Blair told Macpherson that he
would arrange for publication of the translated poems, provided
Macpherson could produce enough to fill a small book.[6]

That small book duly appeared as Fragments of Ancient Poetry. It
contained 15 short poems and an anonymous preface by Blair
detailing their importance to the readers. The work was an instant
success. The public was soon hungry for more of these supposedly
ancient poems, which Blair suggested were part of a greater epic:

> Though the poems now published appear as detached pieces in
> this collection, there is ground to believe that most of them were

---

[5] Macpherson's introduction to this powerful circle of men has been well docu-
mented. See for example Thomas Bailey Saunders, Life and Letters of James Macpherson
(London: MacMillan, 1894), p.64.

[6] Richard B. Sher, Church and University in the Scottish Enlightenment: The Moderate
Literati of Edinburgh (Edinburgh: Edinburgh University Press, 1985), pp.242–5.

originally episodes of a greater work which related to the wars of Fingal.[7]

Blair's preface also reckoned that more could be found in the Highlands:

> It is believed that, by a careful inquiry, many more remains of ancient genius, no less valuable than those now given to the world, might be found in the same county where these have been collected.[8]

Spurred on by the success of *Fragments*, Blair quickly arranged a fundraising exercise among Edinburgh's literati and lawyers, which would pay for Macpherson to go north and collect more poems.

Macpherson made two trips to the Highlands between August 1760 and January 1761, visiting friends and relatives. Armed with introductory letters from the literati, he also visited Highland and Island clergymen and clan chiefs. Travelling through Perthshire, Argyll, Inverness-shire, Mull, Skye and the Uists, Macpherson's mission was to collect Gaelic manuscripts and write down oral recitations of the poems. Among those who assisted Macpherson were his cousin, the Gaelic poet Lachlan Macpherson of Strathmashie, and the Rev James McLagan. McLagan was himself collecting Gaelic poetry and supplied Macpherson with some Ossianic ballads.[9]

When Macpherson returned to Edinburgh in mid-January 1761, he stayed directly beneath Blair in Blackfriar's Wynd, where he translated and polished his material. Blair later recalled that during dinners together, Macpherson would either read or repeat to him what he had translated.[10] While Macpherson set about

---

[7] Blair, 'Preface' in James Macpherson, *Fragments of Ancient Poetry*, This Edition, p.67.

[8] Ibid., p.68.

[9] Derick S. Thomson, 'Macpherson, James (1736–1796)', *Oxford Dictionary of National Biography*, Oxford University Press, 2004; online edn, May 2006 [http://www.oxforddnb.com/view/article/17728, accessed 25 Jan 2011.

[10] Saunders, *Life and Letters of James Macpherson*, p.149.

marshalling what he had uncovered into a single, complete epic poem, it is likely that Blair, the language specialist, helped him. The help from the literati continued when Macpherson had to find a publisher for *Fingal* in London. It was David Hume who wrote the letter of introduction to William Strathan, who became Macpherson's publisher.[11]

The resulting full Ossianic epic, *Fingal, An Ancient Epic Poem in Six Books* was published at the end of 1761. Although Macpherson was credited as the collector and translator, *Fingal* was essentially a group effort. Much of the incentive had come from the Edinburgh literati, as the historian Richard B. Sher has convincingly argued.[12] They had provided Macpherson with money, letters of introduction, editorial assistance and publishing connections. In return, Macpherson probably moulded his translations into what they expected his 'ancient' poems to look like.

The success of *Fingal* led to the publication of another epic, *Temora, An Ancient Epic Poem in Eight Books*, in 1763. This was followed by a two-volume collected edition entitled *Works of Ossian, the Son of Fingal* in 1765, which included Blair's *Critical Dissertation*, and *The Poems of Ossian* of 1773. Later editions include the Patrick Geddes edition of 1896, published on the centenary of Macpherson's death, followed in recent times by Howard Gaskill's entire edited works entitled *The Poems of Ossian and Related Works* in 1996.

To create his English translations, Macpherson used Gaelic ballads and tales as his original sources. These ballads were infused with material from the shared Gaelic traditions of Scotland and Ireland. They also spoke of the Scandinavian dimension to the Gaelic world, opened up by a long history of contact, conflict and trade across the North Sea that long predated the earliest surviving records of Viking raids on Scottish and Irish monasteries. The publication of Ossian brought Macpherson fame but also infamy revolving around hugely damaging accusations of literary fraud

---

[11] See for example Saunders, *Life and Letters of James Macpherson*, pp.117 and 149.

[12] Sher, *Church and University*, p.254.

that were brought by such high-profile English critics as Samuel Johnson. This furore is discussed in detail in the essay 'Ossian: A Controversial Legacy' in this volume.

While *Ossian* gave Macpherson notoriety in Britain, and a list of enemies as long as a parish register, he found refuge through his contacts in high places – the patron of *Ossian* having been the former Prime Minister, Lord Bute. In 1764, Macpherson was appointed secretary to the governor of the Western Provinces. He duly left for America and spent two years there, also touring the West Indies. On his return in 1766, whereupon he settled in London, Macpherson was allowed to retain his salary. The money was converted into a secret retainer for his ongoing services as a writer of government propaganda.

Next came a spell of history writing. Perhaps in a conscious effort to undo the damage to Macpherson's reputation wrought by the *Ossian* affair, this output was both scholarly as well as patriotically British. It was also intended to please Macpherson's government paymasters. In 1771 he published *An Introduction to the History of Great Britain and Ireland*, a work with a marked Celtic dimension. Four years later there followed *Papers Containing the Secret History of Great Britain*, along with his *History of Great Britain from the Restoration to the Accession of the House of Hanover*. In the intervening time, he also rekindled his interest in classical literature and published a translation of the *Iliad* in 1773.

There can be little doubt that Macpherson, like many ambitious and well-connected Scots of his era, was on the make. In the late 1770s he renewed his association with John Macpherson, a minister's son from Skye whom he had visited while collecting Ossianic poetry in the early 1760s. John Macpherson had gone on to work for the Nabob of Arcot in India and risen to become India's Governor-General. He now needed an agent in London and James Macpherson, for a suitable fee, duly obliged.

By this time Macpherson had grown very wealthy. He used some of his fortune in a manner that was typical of the institutionally corrupt political practices of the time. In 1780 he paid

£4,000 for a seat in the House of Commons, becoming MP for one of the Cornish boroughs – at the opposite end of Britain from those he liked to call 'my people' in the Highlands. He held this seat for the rest of his life.

Dipping into his pockets again, Macpherson bought a tract of land north of Kingussie. He had a mansion built there in characteristically imposing neoclassical style by Robert Adam. The estate was originally known in English as Balavil, but Macpherson anglicised it more thoroughly to Belleville. During his holidays at the house, which still stands, Macpherson was known for his hospitality to the locals. He often threw parties at which he would recite Gaelic poetry.

Macpherson never married. Instead he lived as something of a libertine, notching up love affairs with many women. Of his attitude to England he once quipped that 'I hate John Bull but I love his daughters.'[13] He fathered three sons and two daughters, and treated them generously. Upon his death at the age of 59 on 17 February 1796, Belleville passed to his eldest son, also James. Macpherson was buried in London, in the Poets' Corner at the Abbey of Westminster. In his will he stated that a stone monument of himself was to be erected, and this was duly put up outside Kingussie. Over time the monument's face has been worn away and, along with it, Macpherson's fame. The possibility remains that a renewed appreciation of the poems of Ossian will lead to their restoration.

---

[13]  Saunders, *Life and Letters*, p.238.

# FRAGMENTS

## OF

## ANCIENT POETRY

Collected in the Highlands of Scotland

AND

Translated from the Galic or Erse Language

*Vos quoque qui fortes animas, belloque peremtas Laudibus in longum vates dimittitis ævum, Plurima securi fudistis carmina* **Bardi.**

LUCAN

EDINBURGH
Printed for G. Hamilton and J. Balfour

MDCCLX

# PREFACE

THE public may depend on the following fragments as genuine remains of ancient Scottish poetry. The date of their composition cannot be exactly ascertained. Tradition, in the country where they were written, refers them to an æra of the most remote antiquity: and this tradition is supported by the spirit and strain of the poems themselves; which abound with those ideas, and paint those manners, that belong to the most early state of society. The diction too, in the original, is very obsolete; and differs widely from the style of such poems as have been written in the same language two or three centuries ago. They were certainly composed before the establishment of clanship in the northern part of Scotland, which is itself very ancient; for had clans been then formed and known, they must have made a considerable figure in the work of a Highland Bard; whereas there is not the least mention of them in these poems. It is remarkable that there are found in them no allusions to the Christian religion or worship; indeed, few traces of religion of any kind. One circumstance seems to prove them to be coeval with the very infancy of Christianity in Scotland. In a fragment of the same poems, which the translator has seen, a Culdee or Monk is represented as desirous to take down in writing from the mouth of Oscian, who is the principal personage in several of the following fragments, his warlike atchievements and those of his family. But Oscian treats the monk and his religion with disdain, telling him, that the deeds of such great men were subjects too high to be recorded by him, or by any of his religion: A full proof that Christianity was not as yet established in the country.

Though the poems now published appear as detached pieces in this collection, there is ground to believe that most of them were originally episodes of a greater work which related to the wars of Fingal. Concerning this hero innumerable traditions remain, to this day, in the Highlands of Scotland. The story of

Oscian, his son, is so generally known, that to describe one in whom the race of a great family ends, it has passed into a proverb; "Oscian the last "of the heroes."

There can be no doubt that these poems are to be ascribed to the Bards; a race of men well known to have continued throughout many ages in Ireland and the north of Scotland. Every chief or great man had in his family a Bard or poet, whose office it was to record in verse, the illustrious actions of that family. By the succession of these Bards, such poems were handed down from race to race; some in manuscript, but more by oral tradition. And tradition, in a country so free of intermixture with foreigners, and among a people so strongly attached to the memory of their ancestors, has preserved many of them in a great measure incorrupted to this day.

They are not set to music, nor sung. The versification in the original is simple; and to such as understand the language, very smooth and beautiful. Rhyme is seldom used: but the cadence, and the length of the line varied, so as to suit the sense. The translation is extremely literal. Even the arrangement of the words in the original has been imitated; to which must be imputed some inversions in the style, that otherwise would not have been chosen.

Of the poetical merit of these fragments nothing shall here be said. Let the public judge, and pronounce. It is believed, that, by a careful inquiry, many more remains of ancient genius, no less valuable than those now given to the world, might be found in the same country where these have been collected. In particular there is reason to hope that one work of considerable length, and which deserves to be styled an heroic poem, might be recovered and translated, if encouragement were given to such an undertaking. The subject is, an invasion of Ireland by Swarthan King of Lochlyn; which is the name of Denmark in the Erse language. Cuchulaid, the General or Chief of the Irish tribes, upon intelligence of the invasion, assembles his forces. Councils are held; and battles fought. But after several unsuccessful engagements, the Irish are forced to submit. At length, Fingal King of Scotland, called in this poem, 'The Desert of the hills,' arrives with his ships to assist Cuchulaid. He expels the Danes from the country; and returns home victorious. This poem is held to be of greater antiquity than any of the rest that are preserved: And the author speaks of himself as present in the expedition of Fingal. The three last poems in the collection are fragments which the translator obtained of this epic poem; and though very imperfect, they were judged not unworthy of being inserted. If the whole were recovered, it might serve to throw considerable light upon the Scottish and Irish antiquities.

# FRAGMENT

## I

## SHILRIC, VINVELA

### VINVELA

MY love is a son of the hill. He pursues the flying deer, His grey dogs are panting around him; his bow-string sounds in the wind. Whether by the fount of the rock, or by the stream of the mountain thou liest; when the rushes are nodding with the wind, and the mist is flying over thee, let me approach my love unperceived, and see him from the rock. Lovely I saw thee first by the aged oak; thou wert returning tall from the chace; the fairest among thy friends.

### SHILRIC

WHAT voice is that I hear? that voice like the summer-wind.— I sit not by the nodding rushes; I hear not the fount of the rock. Afar, Vinvela, afar I go to the wars of Fingal. My dogs attend me no more. No more I tread the hill. No more from on high I see thee, fair-moving by the stream of the plain; bright as the bow of heaven; as the moon on the western wave.

### VINVELA

THEN thou art gone, O Shilric! and I am alone on the hill. The deer are seen on the brow; void of fear they graze along. No more they dread the wind; no more the rustling tree. The hunter is far removed; he is in the field of graves. Strangers! sons of the waves! spare my lovely Shilric.

### SHILRIC

IF fall I must in the field, raise high my grave, Vinvela. Grey stones, and heaped-up earth, shall mark me to future times. When the hunter shall sit by the mound, and produce his food at noon, 'some warrior rests here,' he will say; and my fame shall live in his praise. Remember me, Vinvela, when low on earth I lie!

## VINVELA

YES!—I will remember thee—indeed my Shilric will fall. What shall I do, my love! when thou art gone for ever? Through these hills I will go at noon: I will go through the silent heath. There I will see where often thou sattest returning from the chace. Indeed, my Shilric will fall; but I will remember him.

## II

I SIT by the mossy fountain; on the top of the hill of winds. One tree is rustling above me. Dark waves roll over the heath. The lake is troubled below. The deer descend from the hill. No hunter at a distance is seen; no whistling cow-herd is nigh. It is mid-day: but all is silent. Sad are my thoughts as I sit alone. Didst thou but appear, O my love, a wanderer on the heath! thy hair floating on the wind behind thee; thy bosom heaving on the sight; thine eyes full of tears for thy friends, whom the mist of the hill had concealed! Thee I would comfort, my love, and bring thee to thy father's house.

BUT is it she that there appears, like a beam of light on the heath? bright as the moon in autumn, as the fun in a summer-storm?—She speaks: but how weak her voice! like the breeze in the reeds of the pool. Hark!

RETURNEST thou safe from the war? Where are thy friends, my love? I heard of thy death on the hill; I heard and mourned thee, Shilric!

YES, my fair, I return; but I alone of my race. Thou shalt see them no more: their graves I raised on the plain. But why art thou on the desert hill? why on the heath, alone?

ALONE I am, O Shilric! alone in the winter-house. With grief for thee I expired. Shilric, I am pale in the tomb.

SHE fleets, she sails away; as grey mist before the wind!—and, wilt thou not stay, my love? Stay and behold my tears? fair thou appearest, my love! fair thou wast, when alive!

BY the mossy fountain I will sit; on the top of the hill of winds. When mid-day is silent around, converse, O my love, with me! come on the wings of the gale! on the blast of the mountain, come! Let me hear thy voice, as thou passest, when mid-day is silent around.

## III

EVENING is grey on the hills. The north wind resounds through the woods. White clouds rise on the sky: the trembling snow descends. The river howls afar, along its winding course. Sad, by a hollow rock, the grey-hair'd Carryl fat. Dry fern waves over his head; his seat is in an aged birch. Clear to the roaring winds he lifts his voice of woe.

TOSSED on the wavy ocean is He, the hope of the isles; Malcolm, the support of the poor; foe to the proud in arms! Why hast thou left us behind? why live we to mourn thy fate? We might have heard, with thee, the voice of the deep; have seen the oozy rock.

SAD on the sea-beat shore thy spouse looketh for thy return. The time of thy promise is come; the night is gathering around. But no white sail is on the sea; no voice is heard except the blustering winds. Low is the soul of the war! Wet are the locks of youth! By the foot of some rock thou liest; washed by the waves as they come. Why, ye winds, did ye bear him on the desert rock? Why, ye waves, did ye roll over him?

BUT, Oh! what voice is that? Who rides on that meteor of fire! Green are his airy limbs. It is he! it is the ghost of Malcolm!— Rest, lovely soul, rest on the rock; and let me hear thy voice!—He is gone, like a dream of the night. I see him through the trees. Daughter of Reynold! he is gone. Thy spouse shall return no more. No more shall his hounds come from the hill, forerunners of their master. No more from the distant rock shall his voice greet thine ear. Silent is he in the deep, unhappy daughter of Reynold!

I WILL sit by the stream of the plain. Ye rocks! hang over my head. Hear my voice, ye trees! as ye bend on the shaggy hill. My voice shall preserve the praise of him, the hope of the isles.

## IV
## CONNAL, CRIMORA

### CRIMORA

WHO cometh from the hill, like a cloud tinged with the beam of the west? Whose voice is that, loud as the wind, but pleasant as the harp of Carryl? It is my love in the light of steel; but sad is his darkened brow. Live the mighty race of Fingal? or what disturbs my Connal?

### CONNAL

THEY live. I saw them return from the chace, like a stream of light. The sun was on their shields: In a line they descended the hill. Loud is the voice of the youth; the war, my love, is near. Tomorrow the enormous Dargo comes to try the force of our race. The race of Fingal he defies; the race of battle and wounds.

### CRIMORA

CONNAL, I saw his sails like grey mist on the fable wave. They came to land. Connal, many are the warriors of Dargo!

### CONNAL

BRING me thy father's shield; the iron shield of Rinval; that shield like the full moon when it is darkened in the sky.

### CRIMORA

THAT shield I bring, O Connal; but it did not defend my father. By the spear of Gauror he fell. Thou mayst fall, O Connal!

### CONNAL

FALL indeed I may: But raise my tomb, Crimora. Some stones, a mound of earth, shall keep my memory. Though fair thou art, my love, as the light; more pleasant than the gale of the hill; yet I will not stay. Raise my tomb, Crimora.

## CRIMORA

THEN give me those arms of light; that sword, and that spear of steel. I shall meet Dargo with thee, and aid my lovely Connal. Farewell, ye rocks of Ardven! ye deer! and ye streams of the hill!— We shall return no more. Our tombs are distant far.

## V

AUTUMN is dark on the mountains; grey mist rests on the hills. The whirlwind is heard on the heath. Dark rolls the river through the narrow plain. A tree stands alone on the hill, and marks the grave of Connal. The leaves whirl round with the wind, and strew the grave of the dead. At times are seen here the ghosts of the deceased, when the musing hunter alone stalks slowly over the heath.

WHO can reach the source of thy race, O Connal? and who recount thy Fathers? Thy family grew like an oak on the mountain, which meeteth the wind with its lofty head. But now it is torn from the earth. Who shall supply the place of Connal?

HERE was the din of arms; and here the groans of the dying. Mournful are the wars of Fingal! O Connal! it was here thou didst fall. Thine arm was like a storm; thy sword, a beam of the sky; thy height, a rock on the plain; thine eyes, a furnace of fire. Louder than a storm was thy voice, when thou confoundedst the field. Warriors fell by thy sword, as the thistle by the staff of a boy.

DARGO the mighty came on, like a cloud of thunder. His brows were contracted and dark. His eyes like two caves in a rock. Bright rose their swords on each side; dire was the clang of their steel.

THE daughter of Rinval was near; Crimora, bright in the armour of man; her hair loose behind, her bow in her hand. She followed the youth to the war, Connal her much beloved. She drew the string on Dargo; but erring pierced her Connal. He falls, like an oak on the plain; like a rock from the shaggy hill. What shall she do, hapless maid!—He bleeds; her Connal dies. All the night long she cries, and all the day, O Connal, my love, and my friend! With grief the sad mourner died.

EARTH here incloseth the loveliest pair on the hill. The grass grows between the stones of their tomb; I sit in the mournful shade. The wind sighs through the grass; and their memory rushes on my mind. Undisturbed you now sleep together; in the tomb of the mountain you rest alone.

## VI

SON of the noble Fingal, Oscian, Prince of men! what tears run down the cheeks of age? what shades thy mighty soul?

MEMORY, son of Alpin, memory wounds the aged. Of former times are my thoughts; my thoughts are of the noble Fingal. The race of the king return into my mind, and wound me with remembrance.

ONE day, returned from the sport of the mountains, from pursuing the sons of the hill, we covered this heath with our youth. Fingal the mighty was here, and Oscur, my son, great in war. Fair on our sight from the sea, at once, a virgin came. Her breast was like the snow of one night. Her cheek like the bud of the rose. Mild was her blue rolling eye: but sorrow was big in her heart.

FINGAL renowned in war! she cries, sons of the king, preserve me! Speak secure, replies the king, daughter of beauty, speak: our ear is open to all: our swords redress the injured. I fly from Ullin, she cries, from Ullin famous in war. I fly from the embrace of him who would debase my blood. Cremor, the friend of men, was my father; Cremor the Prince of Inverne.

FINGAL's younger sons arose; Carryl expert in the bow; Fillan beloved of the fair; and Fergus first in the race.— Who from the farthest Lochlyn? who to the seas of Molochasquir? who dares hurt the maid whom the sons of Fingal guard? Daughter of beauty, rest secure; rest in peace, thou fairest of women.

FAR in the blue distance of the deep, some spot appeared like the back of the ridge-wave. But soon the ship increased on our sight. The hand of Ullin drew her to land. The mountains trembled as he moved. The hills shook at his steps. Dire rattled his armour around him. Death and destruction were in his eyes. His stature like the roe of Morven. He moved in the lightning of steel.

OUR warriors fell before him, like the field before the reapers. Fingal's three sons he bound. He plunged his sword into the fairone's breast. She fell as a wreath of snow before the sun in spring. Her bosom heaved in death; her soul came forth in blood.

OSCUR my son came down; the mighty in battle descended. His armour rattled as thunder; and the lightning of his eyes was terrible. There, was the clashing of swords; there, was the voice of steel. They struck and they thrust; they digged for death with their swords. But death was distant far, and delayed to come. The fun began to decline; and the cow-herd thought of home. Then Oscur's keen steel found the heart of Ullin. He fell like a mountain-oak covered over with glistering frost: He shone like a rock on the plain.—Here the daughter of beauty lieth; and here the bravest of men. Here one day ended the fair and the valiant. Here rest the pursuer and the pursued.

SON of Alpin! the woes of the aged are many: their tears are for the past. This raised my sorrow, warriour; memory awaked my grief. Oscur my son was brave; but Oscur is now no more. Thou hast heard my grief, O son of Alpin; forgive the tears of the aged.

## VII

WHY openest thou afresh the spring of my grief, O son of Alpin, inquiring how Oscur fell? My eyes are blind with tears; but memory beams on my heart. How can I relate the mournful death of the head of the people! Prince of the warriors, Oscur my son, shall I see thee no more!

HE fell as the moon in a storm; as the sun from the midst of his course, when clouds rise from the waste of the waves, when the blackness of the storm inwraps the rocks of Ardannider. I, like an ancient oak on Morven, I moulder alone in my place. The blast hath lopped my branches away; and I tremble at the wings of the north. Prince of the warriors, Oscur my son! shall I see thee no more!

DERMID and Oscur were one: They reaped the battle together. Their friendship was strong as their steel; and death walked between them to the field. They came on the foe like two rocks falling from the brows of Ardven. Their swords were stained with the blood of the valiant: warriours fainted at their names. Who was a match for Oscur, but Dermid? and who for Dermid, but Oscur?

THEY killed mighty Dargo in the field; Dargo before invincible. His daughter was fair as the morn; mild as the beam of night. Her eyes, like two stars in a shower: her breath, the gale of spring: her breasts, as the new-fallen snow floating on the moving heath. The warriours saw her, and loved; their souls were fixed on the maid. Each loved her, as his fame; each must possess her or die. But her soul was fixed on Oscur; my son was the youth of her love. She forgot the blood of her father; and loved the hand that slew him.

SON of Oscian, said Dermid, I love; O Oscur, I love this maid. But her soul cleaveth unto thee; and nothing can heal Dermid. Here, pierce this bosom, Oscur; relieve me, my friend, with thy sword.

MY sword, son of Morny, shall never be stained with the blood of Dermid.

WHO then is worthy to slay me, O Oscur son of Oscian? Let

not my life pass away unknown. Let none but Oscur slay me. Send me with honour to the grave, and let my death be renowned.

DERMID, make use of thy sword; son of Morny, wield thy steel. Would that I fell with thee! that my death came from the hand of Dermid!

THEY fought by the brook of the mountain; by the streams of Branno. Blood tinged the silvery stream, and crudled round the mossy stones. Dermid the graceful fell; fell, and smiled in death.

AND fallest thou, son of Morny; fallest thou by Oscur's hand! Dermid invincible in war, thus do I see thee fall!—He went, and returned to the maid whom he loved; returned, but she perceived his grief.

WHY that gloom, son of Oscian? what shades thy mighty soul?

THOUGH once renowned for the bow, O maid, I have lost my fame. Fixed on a tree by the brook of the hill, is the shield of Gormur the brave, whom in battle I slew. I have wasted the day in vain, nor could my arrow pierce it.

LET me try, son of Oscian, the skill of Dargo's daughter. My hands were taught the bow: my father delighted in my skill.

SHE went. He stood behind the shield. Her arrow flew and pierced his breast*.

BLESSED be that hand of snow; and blessed thy bow of yew! I fall resolved on death: and who but the daughter of Dargo was worthy to slay me? Lay me in the earth, my fair-one; lay me by the side of Dermid.

OSCUR! I have the blood, the soul of the mighty Dargo. Well pleased I can meet death. My sorrow I can end thus.—She pierced her white bosom with steel. She fell; she trembled; and died.

---

* Nothing was held by the ancient Highlanders more essential to their glory, than to die by the hand of some person worthy or renowned. This was the occasion of Oscur's contriving to be slain by his mistress, now that he was weary of life. In those early times suicide was utterly unknown among that people, and no traces of it are found in the old poetry. Whence the translator suspects the account that follows of the daughter of Dargo killing herself, to be the interpolation of some later Bard.

BY the brook of the hill their graves are laid; a birch's unequal shade covers their tomb. Often on their green earthen tombs the branchy sons of the mountain feed, when mid-day is all in flames, and silence is over all the hills.

## VIII

BY the side of a rock on the hill, beneath the aged trees, old Oscian sat on the moss; the last of the race of Fingal. Sightless are his aged eyes; his beard is waving in the wind. Dull through, the leafless trees he heard the voice of the north. Sorrow revived in his soul: he began and lamented the dead.

HOW hast thou fallen like an oak, with all thy branches round thee! Where is Fingal the King? where is Oscur my son? where are all my race? Alas! in the earth they lie. I feel their tombs with my hands. I hear the river below murmuring hoarsely over the stones. What dost thou, O river, to me? Thou bringest back the memory of the past.

THE race of Fingal stood on thy banks, like a wood in a fertile soil, Keen were their spears of steel. Hardy was he who dared to encounter their rage. Fillan the great was there. Thou Oscur wert there, my son! Fingal himself was there, strong in the grey locks of years. Full rose his sinewy limbs; and wide his shoulders spread. The unhappy met with his arm, when the pride of his wrath arose.

THE son of Morny came; Gaul, the tallest of men. He stood on the hill like an oak; his voice was like the streams of the hill. Why reigneth alone, he cries, the son of the mighty Corval? Fingal is not strong to save: he is no support for the people. I am strong as a storm in the ocean; as a whirlwind on the hill. Yield, son of Corval; Fingal, yield to me.

OSCUR stood forth to meet him; my son would meet the foe. But Fingal came in his strength, and smiled at the vaunter's boast. They threw their arms round each other; they struggled on the plain. The earth is ploughed with their heels. Their bones crack as the boat on the ocean, when it leaps from wave to wave. Long did they toil; with night, they fell on the sounding plain; as two oaks, with their branches mingled, fall crashing from the hill. The tall son of Morny is bound; the aged overcame.

FAIR with her locks of gold, her smooth neck, and her breasts of snow; fair, as the spirits of the hill when at silent noon they glide along the heath; fair, as the rain-bow of heaven; came Min-vane the maid. Fingal! she softly saith, loose me my brother Gaul. Loose me the hope of my race, the terror of all but Fingal. Can I, replies the King, can I deny the lovely daughter of the hill? take thy brother, O Minvane, thou fairer than the snow of the north!

SUCH, Fingal! were thy words; but thy words I hear no more. Sightless I sit by thy tomb. I hear the wind in the wood; but no more I hear my friends. The cry of the hunter is over. The voice of war is ceased.

## IX

THOU askest, fair daughter of the isles! whose memory is preserved in these tombs? The memory of Ronnan the bold, and Connan the chief of men; and of her, the fairest of maids, Rivine the lovely and the good. The wing of time is laden with care. Every moment hath woes of its own. Why seek we our grief from afar? or give our tears to those of other times? But thou commandest, and I obey, O fair daughter of the isles!

CONAR was mighty in war. Caul was the friend of strangers. His gates were open to all; midnight darkened not on his barred door. Both lived upon the sons of the mountains. Their bow was the support of the poor.

CONNAN was the image of Conar's soul. Caul was renewed in Ronnan his son. Rivine the daughter of Conar was the love of Ronnan; her brother Connan was his friend. She was fair as the harvest-moon setting in the seas of Molochasquir. Her soul was settled on Ronnan; the youth was the dream of her nights.

RIVINE, my love! says Ronnan, I go to my king in Norway*. A year and a day shall bring me back. Wilt thou be true to Ronnan?

RONNAN! a year and a day I will spend in sorrow. Ronnan, behave like a man, and my soul shall exult in thy valour. Connan my friend, says Ronnan, wilt thou preserve Rivine thy sister? Durstan is in love with the maid; and soon shall the sea bring the stranger to our coast.

RONNAN, I will defend: Do thou securely go.—He went. He returned on his day. But Durstan returned before him.

GIVE me thy daughter, Conar, says Durstan; or fear and feel my power.

HE who dares attempt my sister, says Connan, must meet this edge of steel. Unerring in battle is my arm: my sword, as the lightning of heaven.

---

\* Supposed to be Fergus II. This fragment is reckoned not altogether so ancient as most of the rest.

RONNAN the warriour came; and much he threatened Durstan.

BUT, saith Euran the servant of gold, Ronnan! by the gate of the north shall Durstan this night carry thy fair-one away. Accursed, answers Ronnan, be this arm if death meet him not there.

CONNAN! saith Euran, this night shall the stranger carry thy sister away. My sword shall meet him, replies Connan, and he shall lie low on earth.

THE friends met by night, and they fought. Blood and sweat ran down their limbs as water on the mossy rock. Connan falls; and cries, O Durstan, be favourable to Rivine!—And is it my friend, cries Ronnan, I have slain? O Connan! I knew thee not.

HE went, and he fought with Durstan. Day began to rise on the combat, when fainting they fell, and expired. Rivine came out with the morn; and—O what detains my Ronnan!—She saw him lying pale in his blood; and her brother lying pale by his side. What could she say? what could she do? her complaints were many and vain. She opened this grave for the warriors; and fell into it herself, before it was closed; like the sun snatched away in a storm.

THOU hast heard this tale of grief, O fair daughter of the isles! Rivine was fair as thyself: shed on her grave a tear.

## X

IT is night; and I am alone, forlorn on the hill of storms. The wind is heard in the mountain. The torrent shrieks down the rock. No hut receives me from the rain; forlorn on the hill of winds.

RISE, moon! from behind thy clouds; stars of the night, appear! Lead me, some light, to the place where my love rests from the toil of the chace! his bow near him, unstrung; his dogs panting around him. But here I must sit alone, by the rock of the mossy stream. The stream and the wind roar; nor can I hear the voice of my love.

WHY delayeth my Shalgar, why the son of the hill, his promise? Here is the rock; and the tree; and here the roaring stream. Thou promisedst with night to be here. Ah! whither is my Shalgar gone? With thee I would fly my father; with thee, my brother of pride. Our race have long been foes; but we are not foes, O Shalgar!

CEASE a little while, O wind! stream, be thou silent a while! let my voice be heard over the heath; let my wanderer hear me. Shalgar! it is I who call. Here is the tree, and the rock. Shalgar, my love! I am here. Why delayest thou thy coming? Alas! no answer.

LO! the moon appeareth. The flood is bright in the vale. The rocks are grey on the face of the hill. But I see him not on the brow; his dogs before him tell not that he is coming. Here I must sit alone.

BUT who are these that lie beyond me on the heath? Are they my love and my brother?—Speak to me, O my friends! they answer not. My soul is tormented with fears.—Ah! they are dead. Their swords are red from the fight. O my brother! my brother! why hast thou slain my Shalgar? why, O Shalgar! hast thou slain my brother? Dear were ye both to me! speak to me; hear my voice, sons of my love! But alas! they are silent; silent for ever! Cold are their breasts of clay!

OH! from the rock of the hill; from the top of the mountain of winds, speak ye ghosts of the dead! speak, and I will not be afraid.—Whither are ye gone to rest? In what cave of the hill shall I find you?

I SIT in my grief. I wait for morning in my tears. Rear the tomb, ye friends of the dead; but close it not till I come. My life flieth away like a dream: why should I stay behind? Here shall I rest with my friends by the stream of the sounding rock. When night comes on the hill; when the wind is up on the heath; my ghost shall stand in the wind, and mourn the death of my friends. The hunter shall hear from his booth. He shall fear, but love my voice. For sweet shall my voice be for my friends; for pleasant were they both to me.

## XI

SAD! I am sad indeed: nor small my cause of woe!—Kirmor, thou hast lost no son; thou hast lost no daughter of beauty. Connar the valiant lives; and Annir the fairest of maids. The boughs of thy family flourish, O Kirmor! but Armyn is the last of his race.

RISE, winds of autumn, rise; blow upon the dark heath! streams of the mountains, roar! howl, ye tempests, in the trees! walk through broken clouds, O moon! show by intervals thy pale face! bring to my mind that sad night, when all my children fell; when Arindel the mighty fell; when Daura the lovely died.

DAURA, my daughter! thou wert fair; fair as the moon on the hills of Jura; white as the driven snow; sweet as the breathing gale. Armor renowned in war came, and sought Daura's love; he was not long denied; fair was the hope of their friends.

EARCH son of Odgal repined; for his brother was slain by Armor. He came disguised like a son of the sea; fair was his skiff on the wave; white white his locks of age; calm his serious brow. Fairest of women, he said, lovely daughter of Armyn! a rock not distant in the sea, bears a tree on its side; red shines the fruit afar. There Armor waiteth for Daura. I came to fetch his love. Come, fair daughter of Armyn!

SHE went; and she called on Armor. Nought answered, but the son of the rock. Armor, my love! my love! why tormentest thou me with fear? come, graceful son of Ardnart, come; it is Daura who calleth thee!—Earch the traitor fled laughing to the land. She lifted up her voice, and cried for her brother and her father. Arindel! Armyn! none to relieve your Daura?

HER voice came over the sea. Arindel my son descended from the hill; rough in the spoils of the chace. His arrows rattled by his side; his bow was in his hand; five grey dogs attended his steps. He saw fierce Earch on the shore; he seized and bound him to an oak. Thick fly the thongs of the hide around his limbs; he loads the wind with his groans.

ARINDEL ascends the surgy deep in his boat, to bring Daura to the land. Armor came in his wrath, and let fly the grey-feathered shaft. It sung; it sunk in thy heart, O Arindel my son! for Earch the traitor thou diedst. What is thy grief, O Daura, when round thy feet is poured thy brother's blood!

THE boat is broken in twain by the waves. Armor plunges into the sea, to rescue his Daura or die. Sudden a blast from the hill comes over the waves. He sunk, and he rose no more.

ALONE, on the sea-beat rock, my daughter was heard to complain. Frequent and loud were her cries; nor could her father relieve her. All night I stood on the shore. All night I heard her cries. Loud was the wind; and the rain beat hard on the side of the mountain. Before morning appeared, her voice was weak. It died away, like the evening-breeze among the grass of the rocks. Spent with grief she expired. O lay me soon by her side.

WHEN the storms of the mountain come; when the north lifts the waves on high; I sit by the sounding shore, and look on the fatal rock. Often by the setting moon I see the ghosts of my children. Indistinct, they walk in mournful conference together. Will none of you speak to me?—But they—do not regard their father.

## XII
## RYNO, ALPIN

### RYNO

THE wind and the rain are over: calm is the noon of day. The clouds are divided in heaven. Over the green hills flies the inconstant sun. Red through the stony vale comes down the stream of the hill. Sweet are thy murmurs, O stream! but more sweet is the voice I hear. It is the voice of Alpin the son of the song, mourning for the dead. Bent is his head of age, and red his tearful eye. Alpin, thou son of the song, why alone on the silent hill? why complainest thou, as a blast in the wood; as a wave on the lonely shore?

### ALPIN

MY tears, O Ryno! are for the dead; my voice, for the inhabitants of the grave. Tall thou art on the hill; fair among the sons of the plain. But thou shalt fall like Morar; and the mourner shalt sit on thy tomb. The hills shall know thee no more; thy bow shall lie in the hall, unstrung.

THOU wert swift, O Morar! as a roe on the hill; terrible as a meteor of fire. Thy wrath was as the storm of December. Thy sword in battle, as lightning in the field. Thy voice was like a stream after rain; like thunder on distant hills. Many fell by thy arm; they were consumed in the flames of thy wrath.

BUT when thou returnedst from war, how peaceful was thy brow! Thy face was like the sun after rain; like the moon in the silence of night; calm as the breast of the lake when the loud wind is laid.

NARROW is thy dwelling now; dark the place of thine abode. With three steps I compass thy grave, O thou who wast so great before! Four stones with their heads of moss are the only memorial of thee. A tree with scarce a leaf, long grass which whistles in the wind, mark to the hunter's eye the grave of the mighty Morar. Morar! thou art low indeed. Thou hast; no mother to mourn thee;

no maid with her tears of love. Dead is she that brought thee forth.
Fallen is the daughter of Morglan.

WHO on his staff is this? who is this, whose head is white
with age, whose eyes are red with tears, who quakes at every
step?—It is thy father, O Morar! the father of none but thee. He
heard of thy fame in battle; he heard of foes dispersed. He heard
of Morar's fame; why did he not hear of his wound? Weep, thou
father of Morar! weep; but thy son heareth thee not. Deep is the
sleep of the dead; low their pillow of dust. No more shall he hear
thy voice; no more shall he awake at thy call. When shall it be
morn in the grave, to bid the slumberer awake?

FAREWELL, thou bravest of men! thou conqueror in the field!
but the field shall see thee no more; nor the dark wood be light-
ened with the splendor of thy steel. Thou hast left no son. But the
song shall preserve thy name. Future times shall hear of thee; they
shall hear of the fallen Morar.

## XIII*

CUCHLAID sat by the wall; by the tree of the rustling leaf†. His spear leaned against the mossy rock. His shield lay by him on the grass. Whilst he thought on the mighty Carbre whom he slew in battle, the scout of the ocean came, Moran the son of Fithil.

RISE, Cuchulaid, rise! I see the ships of Garve. Many are the foe, Cuchulaid; many the sons of Lochlyn.

MORAN! thou ever tremblest; thy fears increase the foe. They are the ships of the Desert of hills arrived to assist Cuchulaid.

I SAW their chief, says Moran, tall as a rock of ice. His spear is like that fir; his shield like the rising moon. He sat upon a rock on the shore, as a grey cloud upon the hill. Many, mighty man! I said, many are our heroes; Garve, well art thou named‡, many are the sons of our king.

HE answered like a wave on the rock; who is like me here? The valiant live not with me; they go to the earth from my hand. The king of the Desert of hills alone can fight with Garve. Once we wrestled on the hill. Our heels overturned the wood. Rocks fell from their place, and rivulets changed their course. Three days we strove together; heroes stood at a distance, and feared. On the fourth, the King saith that I fell; but Garve saith, he stood. Let Cuchulaid yield to him that is strong as a storm.

NO. I will never yield to man. Cuchulaid will conquer or die. Go, Moran, take my spear; strike the shield of Caithbait which hangs before the gate. It never rings in peace. My heroes shall, hear on the hill. —

---

* This is the opening of the epic poem mentioned in the preface. The two following fragments are parts of some episodes of the same work.

† The aspen or poplar tree.

‡ Garve signifies a man of great size;

## XIV

## DUCHOMMAR, MORNA

### DUCHOMMAR

MORNA*, thou fairest of women, daughter of Cormac-Car-bre! why in the circle of stones, in the cave of the rock, alone? The stream murmureth hoarsely. The blast groaneth in the aged tree. The lake is troubled before thee. Dark are the clouds of the sky. But thou art like snow on the heath. Thy hair like a thin cloud of gold on the top of Cromleach. Thy breasts like two smooth rocks on the hill which is seen from the stream of Brannuin. Thy arms, as two white pillars in the hall of Fingal.

### MORNA

WHENCE the son of Mugruch, Duchommar the most gloomy of men? Dark are thy brows of terror. Red thy rolling eyes. Does Garve appear on the sea? What of the foe, Duchommar?

### DUCHOMMAR

FROM the hill I return, O Morna, from the hill of the flying deer. Three have I slain with my bow; three with my panting dogs. Daughter of Cormac-Carbre, I love thee as my soul. I have slain a deer for thee. High was his branchy head; and fleet his feet of wind.

### MORNA

GLOOMY son of Mugruch, Duchommar! I love thee not: hard is thy heart of rock; dark thy terrible brow. But Cadmor the son of Tarman, thou art the love of Morna! thou art like a sun-beam on the hill, in the day of the gloomy storm. Sawest thou the son of Tarman,

---

* The signification of the names in this fragment are; Dubhchomar, a black well-shaped man. Muirne or Morna a woman beloved by all. Cormac-cairbre, an un-equalled and rough warriour. Cromleach, a crooked hill. Mugruch, a surly gloomy man. Tarman, thunder. Moinie, soft in temper and person.

lovely on the hill of the chace? Here the daughter of Cormac-Carbre waiteth the coming of Cadmor,

### DUCHOMMAR

AND long shall Morna wait. His blood is on my sword. I met him by the mossy stone, by the oak of the noisy stream. He fought; but I flew him; his blood is on my sword. High on the hill I will raise his tomb, daughter of Cormac-Carbre. But love thou the son of Mugruch; his arm is strong as a storm.

### MORNA

AND is the son of Tarman fallen; the youth with the breast of snow! the first in the chace of the hill; the foe of the sons of the ocean! — Duchommar, thou art gloomy indeed; cruel is thy arm to me.— But give me that sword, son of Mugruch; I love the blood of Cadmor.

[He gives her the sword, with which she instantly stabs him.]

### DUCHOMMAR

DAUGHTER of Cormac-Carbre, thou hast pierced Duchommar! the sword is cold in my breast; thou hast killed the son of Mugruch. Give me to Moinie the maid; for much she loved Duchommar. My tomb she will raise on the hill; the hunter shall see it, and praise me — But draw the sword from my side, Morna; I feel it cold.—

[Upon her coming near him, he stabs her. As she fell, she plucked a stone from the side of the cave, and placed it betwixt them, that his blood might not be mingled with hers.]

## XV

WHERE* is Gealchossa my love, the daughter of Tuathal-Teachvar? I left her in the hall of the plain, when I fought with the hairy Ulfadha. Return soon, she said, O Lamderg! for here I wait in sorrow. Her white breast rose with sighs; her cheek was wet with tears. But she cometh not to meet Lamderg; or sooth his soul after battle. Silent is the hall of joy; I hear not the voice of the singer. Brann does not shake his chains at the gate, glad at the coming of his master. Where is Gealchossa my love, the daughter of Tuathal-Teachvar?

LAMDERG! says Firchios son of Aydon, Gealchossa may be on the hill, she and her chosen maids pursuing the flying deer.

FIRCHIOS! no noise I hear. No sound in the wood of the hill. No deer fly in my sight; no panting dog pursueth. I see not Gealchossa my love; fair as the full moon setting on the hills of Cromleach. Go, Firchios! go to Allad†, the grey-haired son of the rock. He liveth in the circle of stones; he may tell of Gealchossa.

ALLAD! saith Firchios, thou who dwellest in the rock; thou who tremblest alone; what saw thine eyes of age?

I SAW, answered Allad the old, Ullin the son of Carbre: He came like a cloud from the hill; he hummed a surly song as he came, like a storm in leafless wood. He entered the hall of the plain. Lamderg, he cried, most dreadful of men! fight, or yield to Ullin. Lamderg, replied Gealchossa, Lamderg is not here: he fights the hairy Ulfadha; mighty man, he is not here. But Lamderg never yields; he will fight the son of Carbre. Lovely art thou, O daughter of Tuathal-Teachvar! said Ullin. I carry thee to the house of Carbre; the valiant shall have Gealchossa. Three days from the top of Cromleach will I call Lamderg; to fight. The fourth, you belong to Ullin, if Lamderg die, or fly my sword.

---

* The signification of the names in this fragment are; Gealchossack, white-legged. Tuathal-Teachtmhar, the surly, but fortunate man. Lambhdearg, bloody-hand. Ulfadha, long beard. Firchios, the conqueror of men.

† Allad is plainly a Druid consulted on this occasion.

ALLAD! peace to thy dreams!—sound the horn, Firchios!—Ullin may hear, and meet me on the top of Cromleach.

LAMDERG rushed on like a storm. On his spear he leaped over rivers. Few were his strides up the hill. The rocks fly back from his heels; loud crashing they bound to the plain. His armour, his buckler rung. He hummed a surly song, like the noise of the falling stream. Dark as a cloud he stood above; his arms, like meteors, shone. From the summit of the hill, he rolled a rock. Ullin heard in the hall of Carbre.—

## FINIS

# FINGAL

# AN

# ANCIENT EPIC POEM

In SIX BOOKS
Together with several other POEMS, composed by
OSSIAN the Son of FINGAL
Translated from the Galic Language,

By JAMES MACPHERSON

*Fortia facta patrum.*
VIRGIL

LONDON
Printed for T. Becket and P. A. De Hondt, in the Strand

MDCCLXII

# PREFACE

THE love of novelty, which, in some degree, is common to all mankind, is more particularly the characteristic of that mediocrity of parts, which distinguishes more than one half of the human species. This inconstant disposition is never more conspicuous, than in what regards the article of amusement. We change our sentiments concerning it every moment, and the distance between our admiration and extreme contempt, is so very small, that the one is almost a sure presage of the other. The poets, whose business it is to please, if they want to preserve the fame they have once acquired, must very often forfeit their own judgments to this variable temper of the bulk of their readers, and accommodate their writings to this unsettled taste. A fame so fluctuating deserves not to be much valued.

Poetry, like virtue, receives its reward after death. The fame which men pursued in vain, when living, is often bestowed upon them when they are not sensible of it. This neglect of living authors is not altogether to be attributed to that reluctance which men shew in praising and rewarding genius. It often happens, that the man who writes differs greatly from the same man in common life. His foibles, however, are obliterated by death, and his better part, his writings, remain: his character is formed from them, and he that was no extraordinary man in his own time, becomes the wonder of succeeding ages.—From this source proceeds our veneration for the dead. Their virtues remain, but the vices, which were once blended with their virtues, have died with themselves.

This consideration might induce a man, diffident of his abilities, to ascribe his own compositions to a person, whose remote antiquity and whose situation, when alive, might well answer for faults which would be inexcusable in a writer of this age. An ingenious gentleman made this observation, before he knew any thing but the name of the epic poem, which is printed in the following collection. When he had read it, his sentiments were changed. He found it abounded too much with those ideas, that only belong to the most early state of society, to be the work of a modern poet. Of this, I am persuaded, the public will be as thoroughly convinced, as this gentleman was, when they shall see the poems; and that some will think, notwithstanding the disadvantages with which the works ascribed to Ossian appear, it would be a very uncommon instance of selfdenial in me to disown them, were they really of my composition.

I would not have dwelt so long upon this subject, especially as I have answered all reasonable objections to the genuineness of the poems in the Dissertation, were it not on account of the prejudices of the present age against the ancient inhabitants of Britain, who are thought to have been incapable of the generous sentiments to be met with in the poems of Ossian.—If we err in praising too much the times of our forefathers, it is also as repugnant to good sense, to be altogether blind to the imperfections of our own. If our fathers had not so much wealth, they had certainly fewer vices than the present age. Their tables, it is true, were not so well provided, neither were their beds so soft as those of modern times; and this, in the eyes of men who place their ultimate happiness in those conveniences of life, gives us a great advantage over them. I shall not enter farther into this subject, but only observe, that the general poverty of a nation has not the same influence, that the indigence of individuals, in an opulent country, has, upon the manners of the community. The idea of meanness, which is now connected with a narrow fortune, had its rise after commerce had thrown too much property into the hands of a few; for the poorer sort, imitating the vices of the rich, were obliged to have recourse to roguery and circumvention, in order to supply their extravagance, so that they were, not without reason, reckoned, in more than one sense, the worst of the people.

It is now two years since the first translations from the Galic language were handed about among people of taste in Scotland.

They became at last so much corrupted, through the carelessness of transcribers, that, for my own sake, I was obliged to print the genuine copies. Some other pieces were added, to swell the publication into a pamphlet, which was entitled, Fragments of Ancient Poetry.—The Fragments, upon their first appearance, were so much approved of, that several people of rank, as well as taste, prevailed with me to make a journey into the Highlands and western isles, in order to recover what remained of the works of the old bards, especially those of Ossian, the son of Fingal, who was the best, as well as most ancient, of those who are celebrated in tradition for their poetical genius.—I undertook this journey, more from a desire of complying with the request of my friends, than from any hopes I had of answering their expectations. I was not unsuccessful, considering how much the compositions of ancient times have been neglected, for some time past, in the north of Scotland. Several gentlemen in the Highlands and isles generously gave me all the assistance in their power; and it was by their means I was enabled to compleat the epic poem. How far it comes up to the rules of the epopæa, is the province of criticism to examine. It is only my business to lay it before the reader, as I have found it. As it is one of the chief beauties of composition, to be well understood, I shall here give the story of the poem, to prevent that obscurity which the introduction of characters utterly unknown might occasion.

Artho, supreme king of Ireland, dying at Temora the royal palace of the Irish kings, was succeeded by Cormac, his son, a minor. Cuchullin, the son of Semo, lord of the Isle of Mist, one of the Hebrides, being at that time in Ulster, and very famous for his great exploits, was, in a convention of the petty kings and heads of tribes assembled for that purpose at Temora, unanimously chosen guardian to the young king.—He had not managed the affairs of Cormac long, when news was brought, that Swaran, the son of Starno, king of Lochlin, or Scandinavia, intended to invade Ireland. Cuchullin immediately dispatched Munan, the son of Stirmal, an Irish chief, to Fingal, king of those Caledonians who inhabited the western coast of Scotland, to implore his aid. Fingal, as well from a principle of generosity, as from his connection with the royal family of Ireland, resolved on an expedition into that county; but before his arrival, the enemy had landed in Ulster.— Cuchullin in the mean time had gathered the flower of the Irish tribes to Tura, a castle of Ulster, and dispatched scouts along the coast, to give the most early intelligence of the enemy.—Such is the situation of affairs, when the poem opens.

Cuchullin, sitting alone beneath a tree, at the gate of Tura, for the other chiefs had gone on a hunting party to Cromla, a neighbouring hill, is informed of Swaran's landing by Moran, the son of Fithil, one of his scouts. He convenes the chiefs; a council is held, and disputes run high about giving battle to the enemy. Connal, the petty king of Togorma, and an intimate friend of Cuchullin, was for retreating till Fingal should arrive; but Calmar, the son of Matha, lord of Lara, a country in Connaught, was for engaging the enemy immediately.—Cuchullin, of himself willing to fight, went into the opinion of Calmar. Marching towards the enemy, he missed three of his bravest heroes, Fergus, Duchomar, and Caithbat. Fergus arriving, tells Cuchullin of the death of the two other chiefs; which introduces the affecting episode of Morna, the daughter of Cormac.—The army of Cuchullin is descried at a distance by Swaran, who sent the son of Arno to observe the motions of the enemy, while he himself ranged his forces in order of battle.—The son of Arno returning to Swaran, describes to him Cuchullin's chariot, and the terrible appearance of that hero. The armies engage, but night coming on, leaves the victory undecided. Cuchullin, according to the hospitality of the times, sends to Swaran a formal invitation to a feast, by his bard Carril, the son of Kinfena.—Swaran refuses to come. Carril relates to Cuchullin the story of Grudar and Brassoblis. A party, by Connal's advice, is sent to observe the enemy; which closes the action of the first day.

The ghost of Crugal, one of the Irish heroes who was killed in battle, appearing to Connal, foretels the defeat of Cuchullin in the next battle; and earnestly advises him to make peace with Swaran.

Connal communicates the vision; but Cuchullin is inflexible from
a principle of honour that he would not be the first to sue for
peace, and resolved to continue the war. Morning comes; Swaran
proposes dishonourable terms to Cuchullin, which are rejected.
The battle begins, and is obstinately fought for some time, until,
upon the flight of Grumal, the whole Irish army gave way. Cuchullin
and Connal cover their retreat: Carril leads them to a neighbouring hill, whither they are soon followed by Cuchullin himself, who
descries the fleet of Fingal making towards the coast; but, night
coming on, he lost sight of it again. Cuchullin, dejected after his
defeat, attributes his ill success to the death of Ferda his friend,
whom he had killed some time before. Carril, to shew that ill
success did not always attend those who innocently killed their
friends, introduces the episode of Comal and Galvina.

Cuchullin, pleased with Carril's story, insists with him for
more of his songs. The bard relates the actions of Fingal in
Lochlin, and death of Agandecca the beautiful sister of Swaran.
He had scarce-finished when Calmar the son of Matha, who had
advised the first battle, came wounded from the field, and told
them of Swaran's design to surprise the remains of the Irish army.
He himself proposes to withstand singly the whole force of the
enemy, in a narrow pass, till the Irish should make good their
retreat. Cuchullin, touched with the gallant proposal of Calmar,
resolves to accompany him, and orders Carril to carry off the few
that remained of the Irish. Morning comes, Calmar dies of his
wounds; and, the ships of the Caledonians appearing, Swaran
gives over the pursuit of the Irish, and returns to oppose Fingal's
landing. Cuchullin ashamed, after his defeat, to appear before
Fingal, retires to the cave of Tura. Fingal engages the enemy, puts
them to flight; but the coming on of night makes the victory not
decisive. The king, who had observed the gallant behaviour of his
grandson Oscar, gives him advices concerning his conduct in
peace and war. He recommends to him to place the example of
his fathers before his eyes, as the best model for his conduct; which
introduces the episode concerning Fainasóllis, the daughter of

the king of Craca, whom Fingal had taken under his protection, in his youth. Fillan and Oscar are dispatched to observe the motions of the enemy by night; Gaul the son of Morni desires the command of the army, in the next battle; which Fingal promises to give him. The song of the bards closes the third day.

The action of the poem being suspended by night, Ossian takes that opportunity to relate his own actions at the lake of Lego, and his courtship of Evirallin, who was the mother of Oscar, and had died some time before the expedition of Fingal into Ireland. Her ghost appears to him, and tells him that Oscar, who had been sent, the beginning of the night, to observe the enemy, was engaged with an advanced party, and almost overpowered. Ossian relieves his son; and an alarm is given to Fingal of the approach of Swaran. The king rises, calls his army together, and, as he had promised the preceding night, devolves the command on Gaul the son of Morni, while he himself, after charging his sons to behave gallantly and defend his people, retires to a hill, from whence he could have a view of the battle. The battle joins; the poet relates Oscar's great actions. But when Oscar, in conjunction with his father, conquered in one wing, Gaul, who was attacked by Swaran in person, was on the point of retreating in the other. Fingal sends Ullin his bard to encourage him with a war song, but notwithstanding Swaran prevails; and Gaul and his army are obliged to give way. Fingal, descending from the hill, rallies them again: Swaran desists from the pursuit, possesses himself of a rising ground, restores the ranks, and waits the approach of Fingal. The king, having encouraged his men, gives the necessary orders, and renews the battle. Cuchullin, who, with his friend Connal, and Carril his bard, had retired to the cave of Tura, hearing the noise, came to the brow of the hill, which overlooked the field of battle, where he saw Fingal engaged with the enemy. He, being hindered by Connal from joining Fingal, who was himself upon the point of obtaining a complete victory, sends Carril to congratulate that hero on his success.

In the mean time Fingal and Swaran meet; the combat is

described: Swaran is overcome, bound and delivered over as a prisoner to the care of Ossian and Gaul the son of Morni; Fingal, his younger sons, and Oscar, still pursue the enemy. The episode of Orla a chief of Lochlin, who was mortally wounded in the battle, is introduced. Fingal, touched with the death of Orla, orders the pursuit to be discontinued; and calling his sons together, he is informed that Ryno, the youngest of them, was killed. He laments his death, hears the story of Lamdarg and Gelchossa, and returns towards the place where he had left Swaran. Carril, who had been sent by Cuchullin to congratulate Fingal on his victory, comes in the mean time to Ossian. The conversation of the two poets closes the action of the fourth day.

Night comes on. Fingal gives a feast to his army, at which Swaran is present. The king commands Ullin his bard to give the *song of peace*; a custom always observed at the end of a war. Ullin relates the actions of Trenmor, great grandfather to Fingal, in Scandinavia, and his marriage with Inibaca, the daughter of a king of Lochlin who was ancestor to Swaran; which consideration, together with his being brother to Agandecca, with whom Fingal was in love in his youth, induced the king to release him, and permit him to return, with the remains of his army, into Lochlin, upon his promise of never returning to Ireland, in a hostile manner. The night is spent in settling Swaran's departure, in songs of bards, and in a conversation in which the story of Grumal is introduced by Fingal. Morning comes. Swaran departs; Fingal goes on a hunting party, and finding Cuchullin in the cave of Tura, comforts him, and sets sail, the next day, for Scotland; which concludes the poem.

The story of this poem is so little interlarded with fable, that one cannot help thinking it the genuine history of Fingal's expedition, embellished by poetry. In that case, the compositions of Ossian are not less valuable for the light they throw on the ancient state of Scotland and Ireland than they are for their poetical merit. Succeeding generations founded on them all their traditions concerning that period; and they magnified or varied them, in proportion as they were swayed by credulity or design. The bards of Ireland, by ascribing to Ossian compositions which are evidently their own, have occasioned a general belief, in that country, that Fingal was of Irish extraction, and not of the ancient Caledonians, as is said in the genuine poems of Ossian. The inconsistencies between those spurious pieces prove the ignorance of their authors. In one of them Ossian is made to mention himself as baptised by St. Patrick, in another he speaks of the famous crusade, which was not begun in Europe for many centuries after.

Though this anachronism quite destroys the authority of the bards with respect to Fingal; yet their desire to make him their countryman shews how famous he was in Ireland as well as in the north of Scotland.

Had the Senachies of Ireland been as well acquainted with the antiquities of their nation as they pretended, they might derive as much honour from Fingal's being a Caledonian, as if he had been an Irishman; for both nations were almost the same people in the days of that hero. The Celtæ, who inhabited Britain and Ireland before the invasion of the Romans, though they were divided into numerous tribes, yet, as the same language and customs, and the memory of their common origin remained among them, they considered themselves as one nation. After South Britain became a province of Rome, and its inhabitants begun to adopt the language and customs of their conquerors, the Celtæ beyond the pale of the empire, considered them as a distinct people, and consequently treated them as enemies. On the other hand, the strictest amity subsisted between the Irish and Scots Celtæ for many ages, and the customs and ancient language of both still remaining, leave no room to doubt that they were of old one and the same nation.

It was at first intended to prefix to Ossian's poems a discourse concerning the ancient inhabitants of Britain; but as a gentleman, in the north of Scotland, who has thoroughly examined the antiquities of this island, and is perfectly acquainted with all the branches of the Celtic tongue, is just now preparing for the press a work on that subject, the curious are referred to it.

# A DISSERTATION CONCERNING
## the ANTIQUITY, &c. of the POEMS of OSSIAN
## the SON of FINGAL

INQUIRIES into the antiquities of nations afford more pleasure than any real advantage to mankind. The ingenious may form systems of history on probabilities and a few facts; but at a great distance of time, their accounts must be vague and uncertain. The infancy of states and kingdoms is as destitute of great events, as of the means of transmitting them to posterity. The arts of polished life, by which alone facts can be preserved with certainty, are the production of a well formed community. It is then historians begin to write, and public transactions to be worthy remembrance. The actions of former times are left in obscurity, or magnified by uncertain traditions. Hence it is that we find so much of the marvellous in the origin of every nation; posterity being always ready to believe any thing, however fabulous, that reflects honour on their ancestors. The Greeks and Romans were remarkable for this weakness. They swallowed the most absurd fables concerning the high antiquities of their respective nations. Good historians, however, rose very early amongst them, and transmitted, with lustre, their great actions to posterity. It is to them that they owe that unrivalled fame they now enjoy, while the great actions of other nations are involved in fables, or lost in obscurity. The Celtic nations afford a striking instance of this kind. They, though once the masters of Europe from the mouth of the Oby, in Russia, to Cape Finistere, the western point of Gallicia in Spain, are very little mentioned in history. They trusted their fame to tradition and the songs of their bards, which, by the vicissitude of human affairs, are long since lost. Their ancient language is the only monument that remains of them; and the traces of it being found in places so widely distant of each other, serves only to shew the extent of their ancient power, but throws very little light on their history.

Of all the Celtic nations, that which possessed old Gaul is the most renowned; not perhaps on account of worth superior to the rest, but for their wars with a people who had historians to transmit the fame of their enemies, as well as their own, to posterity. Britain was first peopled by them, according to the testimony of the best authors; its situation in respect to Gaul makes the opinion probable; but what puts it beyond all dispute, is that the same customs and language prevailed among the inhabitants of both in the days of Julius Cæsar.

The colony from Gaul possessed themselves, at first, of that part of Britain which was next to their own country; and spreading northward, by degrees, as they increased in numbers, peopled the whole island. Some adventurers passing over from those parts of Britain that are within sight of Ireland, were the founders of the Irish nation: which is a more probable story than the idle fables of Milesian and Gallician colonies. Diodorus Siculus mentions it as a thing well known in his time, that the inhabitants of Ireland were originally Britons; and his testimony is unquestionable, when we consider that, for many ages, the language and customs of both nations were the same.

Tacitus was of opinion that the ancient Caledonians were of German extract. By the language and customs which always prevailed in the North of Scotland, and which are undoubtedly Celtic, one would be tempted to differ in opinion from that celebrated writer. The Germans, properly so called, were not the same with the ancient Celtæ. The manners and customs of the two nations were similar; but their language different. The Germans are the genuine descendants of the ancient Daæ, afterwards well known by the name of Daci, and passed originally into Europe by the way of the northern countries, and settled beyond the Danube, towards the vast regions of Transilvania, Wallachia, and Moldavia; and from thence advanced by degrees into Germany. The Celtæ, it is certain, sent many Colonies into that country, all of whom retained their own laws, language, and customs; and it is of them, if any colonies came from Germany into Scotland, that the ancient Caledonians were descended.

But whether the Caledonians were a colony of the Celtic Germans, or the same with the Gauls that first possessed themselves of Britain, is a matter of no moment at this distance of time. Whatever their origin was, we find them very numerous in the time of Julius Agricola, which is a presumption that they were long before settled in the country. The form of their government was a mixture of aristocracy and monarchy, as it was in all the countries where the Druids bore the chief sway. This order of men seems to have been formed on the same system with the Dactyli Idæi and Curetes of the ancients. Their pretended intercourse with heaven, their magic and divination were the same. The knowledge of the Druids in natural causes, and the properties of certain things, the fruit of the experiments of ages gained them a mighty reputation among the people. The esteem of the populace soon increased into a veneration for the order; which a cunning and ambitious tribe of men took care to improve, to such a degree, that they, in a manner, ingrossed the management of civil, as well as religious, matters. It is generally allowed that they did not abuse this extraordinary power; the preserving their character of sanctity was so essential to their influence, that they never broke out into violence or oppression. The chiefs were allowed to execute the laws, but the legislative power was entirely in the hands of the Druids. It was by their authority that the tribes were united, in times of the greatest danger, under one head. This temporary king, or Vergobretus, was chosen by them, and generally laid down his office at the end of the war. These priests enjoyed long this extraordinary privilege among the Celtic nations who lay beyond the pale of the Roman empire. It was in the beginning of the second century that their power among the Caledonians begun to decline. The poems that celebrate Trathal and Cormac, ancestors to Fingal, are full of particulars concerning the fall of the Druids, which account for the total silence concerning their religion in the poems that are now given to the public.

The continual wars of the Caledonians against the Romans hindered the nobility from initiating themselves, as the custom formerly was, into the order of the Druids. The precepts of their religion were confined to a few, and were not much attended to by a people inured to war. The Vergobretus, or chief magistrate, was chosen without the concurrence of the hierarchy, or continued in his office against their will. Continual power strengthened his interest among the tribes, and enabled him to send down, as hereditary to his posterity, the office he had only received himself by election.

On occasion of a new war against the *King of the World*, as the poems emphatically call the Roman emperor, the Druids, to vindicate the honour of the order, began to resume their ancient privilege of chusing the Vergobretus. Garmal, the son of Tarno, being deputed by them, came to the grandfather of the celebrated Fingal, who was then Vergobretus, and commanded him, in the name of the whole order, to lay down his office. Upon his refusal, a civil war commenced, which soon ended in almost the total extinction of the religious order of the Druids. A few that remained, retired to the dark recesses of their groves, and the caves they had formerly used for their meditations. It is then we find them in *the circle of stones*, and unheeded by the world. A total disregard for the order, and utter abhorrence of the Druidical rites ensued. Under this cloud of public hate, all that had any knowledge of the religion of the Druids became extinct, and the nation fell into the last degree of ignorance of their rites and ceremonies.

It is no matter of wonder then, that Fingal and his son Ossian make so little, if any, mention of the Druids; who were the declared enemies to their succession in the supreme magistracy. It is a singular case, it must be allowed, that there are no traces of religion in the poems ascribed to Ossian; as the poetical compositions of other nations are so closely connected with their mythology. It is hard to account for it to those who are not made acquainted with the manner of the old Scottish bards. That race of men carried their notions of martial honour to an extravagant pitch. Any aid given their heroes in battle, was thought to derogate from their fame; and the bards immediately transferred the glory of the action to him who had given that aid.

Had Ossian brought down gods, as often as Homer hath done, to assist his heroes, this poem had not consisted of elogiums on his friends, but of hymns to these superior beings. To this day, those that write in the Galic language seldom mention religion in their profane poetry; and when they professedly write of religion, they never interlard with their compositions, the actions of their heroes. This custom alone, even though the religion of the Druids had not been previously extinguished, may, in some measure, account for Ossian's silence concerning the religion of his own times.

To say, that a nation is void of all religion, is the same thing as to say, that it does not consist of people endued with reason. The traditions of their fathers, and their own observations on the works of nature, together with that superstition which is inherent in the human frame, have, in all ages, raised in the minds of men some idea of a superior being.—Hence it is, that in the darkest times, and amongst the most barbarous nations, the very populace themselves had some faint notion, at least, of a divinity. It would be doing injustice to Ossian, who, upon no occasion, shews a narrow mind, to think, that he had not opened his conceptions to that primitive and greatest of all truths. But let Ossian's religion be what it will, it is certain he had no knowledge of Christianity, as there is not the least allusion to it, or any of its rites, in his poems which absolutely fixes him to an æra prior to the introduction of that religion. The persecution begun by Dioclesian, in the year 303, is the most probable time in which the first dawning of Christianity in the north of Britain can be fixed.—The humane and mild character of Constantius Chlorus, who commanded then in Britain, induced the persecuted Christians to take refuge under him. Some of them, through a zeal to propagate their tenets, or through fear, went beyond the pale of the Roman empire, and settled among the Caledonians; who were the more ready to hearken to their doctrines, as the religion of the Druids had been exploded so long before.

These missionaries, either through choice, or to give more

weight to the doctrine they advanced, took possession of the cells and groves of the Druids; and it was from this retired life they had the name of *Culdees*, which in the language of the country signified *sequestered persons*. It was with one of the *Culdees* that Ossian, in his extreme old age, is said to have disputed concerning the Christian religion. This dispute is still extant, and is couched in verse, according to the custom of the times. The extreme ignorance on the part of Ossian, of the Christian tenets, shews, that that religion had only been lately introduced, as it is not easy to conceive, how one of the first rank could be totally unacquainted with a religion that had been known for any time in the country. The dispute bears the genuine marks of antiquity. The obsolete phrases and expressions peculiar to the times, prove it to be no forgery. If Ossian then lived at the introduction of Christianity, as by all appearance he did, his epoch will be the latter end of the third, and beginning of the fourth century. What puts this point beyond dispute, is the allusion in his poems to the history of the times.

The exploits of Fingal against Caracul, the son of the *King of the World*, are among the first brave actions of his youth. A complete poem, which relates to this subject, is printed in this collection.

In the year 210 the emperor Severus, after returning from his expeditions against the Caledonians, at York fell into the tedious illness of which he afterwards died. The Caledonians and Maiatæ, resuming courage from his indisposition, took arms in order to recover the possessions they had lost. The enraged emperor commanded his army to march into their country, and to destroy it with fire and sword. His orders were but ill executed, for his son, Caracalla, was at the head of the army, and his thoughts were entirely taken up with the hopes of his father's death, and with schemes to supplant his brother Geta.—He scarcely had entered the enemy's country, when news was brought him that Severus was dead.—A sudden peace is patched up with the Caledonians, and, as it appears from Dion Cassius, the country they had lost to Severus was restored to them.

The Caracul of Fingal is no other than Caracalla, who, as the son

of Severus, the Emperor of Rome, whose dominions were extended almost over the known world, was not without reason called
in the poems of Ossian, *the Son of the King of the World*. The space
of time between 211, the year Severus died, and the beginning of
the fourth century, is not so great, but Ossian the son of Fingal,
might have seen the Christians whom the persecution under
Dioclesian had driven beyond the pale of the Roman empire.

Ossian, in one of his many lamentations on the death of his
beloved son Oscar, mentions among his great actions, a battle
which he fought against Caros, king of ships, on the banks of the
winding Carun. It is more than probable, that the Caros mentioned here, is the same with the noted usurper Carausius, who
assumed the purple in the year 287, and seizing on Britain, defeated
the emperor Maximian Herculius, in several naval engagements,
which gives propriety to his being called in Ossian's poems, *the
King of Ships*. The *winding Carun* is that small river retaining still
the name of Carron, and runs in the neighbourhood of Agricola's
wall, which Carausius repaired to obstruct the incursions of the
Caledonians. Several other passages in the poems allude to the
wars of the Romans; but the two just mentioned clearly fix the
epoch of Fingal to the third century; and this account agrees
exactly with the Irish histories, which place the death of Fingal,
the son of Comhal, in the year 283, and that of Oscar and their
own celebrated Cairbre, in the year 296.

Some people may imagine, that the allusions to the Roman
history might have been industriously inserted into the poems, to
give them the appearance of antiquity. This fraud must then have
been committed at least three ages ago, as the passages in which
the allusions are made, are alluded to often in the compositions
of those times.

Every one knows what a cloud of ignorance and barbarism
overspread the north of Europe 300 years ago. The minds of men,
addicted to superstition, contracted a narrowness that destroyed
genius. Accordingly we find the compositions of those times trivial
and puerile to the last degree. But let it be allowed, that, amidst all

the untoward circumstances of the age, a genius might arise, it is not easy to determine what could induce him to give the honour of his compositions to an age so remote. We find no fact that he has advanced, to favour any designs which could be entertained by any man who lived in the fifteenth century. But should we suppose a poet, through humour, or for reasons which cannot be seen at this distance of time, would ascribe his own compositions to Ossian, it is next to impossible, that he could impose upon his countrymen, when all of them were so well acquainted with the traditional poems of their ancestors.

The strongest objection to the authenticity of the poems now given to the public under the name of Ossian, is the improbability of their being handed down by tradition through so many centuries. Ages of barbarism some will say, could not produce poems abounding with the disinterested and generous sentiments so conspicuous in the compositions of Ossian; and could these ages produce them, it is impossible but they must be lost, or altogether corrupted in a long succession of barbarous generations.

These objections naturally suggest themselves to men unacquainted with the ancient state of the northern parts of Britain. The bards, who were an inferior order of the Druids, did not share their bad fortune. They were spared by the victorious king, as it was through their means only he could hope for immortality to his fame. They attended him in the camp, and contributed to establish his power by their songs. His great actions were magnified, and the populace, who had no ability to examine into his character narrowly, were dazzled with his fame in the rhimes of the bards. In the mean time, men assumed sentiments that are rarely to be met with in an age of barbarism. The bards who were originally the disciples of the Druids, had their minds opened, and their ideas enlarged, by being initiated in the learning of that celebrated order. They could form a perfect hero in their own minds, and ascribe that character to their prince. The inferior chiefs made this ideal character the model of their conduct, and by degrees brought their minds to that generous spirit which

FINGAL AN ANCIENT EPIC POEM    115

breathes in all the poetry of the times. The prince, flattered by his bards, and rivalled by his own heroes, who imitated his character as described in the eulogies of his poets, endeavoured to excel his people in merit, as he was above them in station. This emulation continuing, formed at last the general character of the nation, happily compounded of what is noble in barbarity, and virtuous and generous in a polished people.

When virtue in peace, and bravery in war, are the characteristics of a nation, their actions become interesting, and their fame worthy of immortality. A generous spirit is warmed with noble actions, and becomes ambitious of perpetuating them. This is the true source of that divine inspiration, to which the poets of all ages pretended. When they found their themes inadequate to the warmth of their imaginations, they varnished them over with fables, supplied by their own fancy, or furnished by absurd traditions. These fables, however ridiculous, had their abettors; posterity either implicitly believed them, or through a vanity natural to mankind, pretended that they did. They loved to place the founders of their families in the days of fable, when poetry, without the fear of contradiction, could give what characters she pleased of her heroes. It is to this vanity that we owe the preservation of what remain of the works of Ossian. His poetical merit made his heroes famous in a country where heroism was much esteemed and admired. The posterity of these heroes, or those who pretended to be descended from them, heard with pleasure the eulogiums of their ancestors; bards were employed to repeat the poems, and to record the connection of their patrons with chiefs so renowned. Every chief in process of time had a bard in his family, and the office became at last hereditary. By the succession of these bards, the poems concerning the ancestors of the family were handed down from generation to generation; they were repeated to the whole clan on solemn occasions, and always alluded to in the new compositions of the bards. This custom came down near to our own times; and after the bards were discontinued, a great number in a clan retained by memory, or committed to writing, their compositions, and founded the antiquity of their families on the authority of their poems.

The use of letters was not known in the North of Europe till long after the institution of the bards: the records of the families of their patrons, their own, and more ancient poems were handed down by tradition. Their poetical compositions were admirably contrived for that purpose. They were adapted to music; and the most perfect harmony observed. Each verse was so connected with those which preceded or followed it, that if one line had been remembered in a stanza, it was almost impossible to forget the rest. The cadences followed in so natural a gradation, and the words were so adapted to the common turn of the voice, after it is raised to a certain key, that it was almost impossible, from a similarity of sound, to substitute one word for another. This excellence is peculiar to the Celtic tongue, and is perhaps to be met with in no other language. Nor does this choice of words clog the sense or weaken the expression. The numerous flections of consonants, and variation declension, make the language very copious.

The descendants of the Celtæ, who inhabited Britain and its isles, were not singular in this method of preserving the most precious monuments of their nation. The ancient laws of the Greeks were couched in verse, and handed down by tradition. The Spartans, through a long habit, became so fond of this custom, that they would never allow their laws to be committed to writing. The actions of great men, and the elogiums of kings and heroes were preserved in the same manner. All the historical monuments of the old Germans were comprehended in their ancient songs; which were either hymns to their gods, or elegies in praise of their heroes, and were intended to perpetuate the great events in their nation which were carefully interwoven them. This species of composition was not committed to writing, but delivered by oral tradition. The care they took to have the poems taught to their children, the uninterrupted custom of repeating them upon certain occasions, and the happy measure of the verse, served to preserve them for a long time uncorrupted. This oral chronicle of the

Germans was not forgot in the eighth century, and it probably would have remained to this day, had not learning, which thinks every thing, that is not committed to writing, fabulous, been introduced. It was from poetical traditions that Garcillasso composed his account of the Yncas of Peru. The Peruvians had lost all other monuments of their history, and it was from ancient poems which his mother, a princess of the blood of the Yncas, taught him in his youth, that he colleced the materials of his history. If other nations then, that had been often overrun by enemies, and had sent abroad and received colonies, could, for many ages, preserve, by oral tradition, their laws and histories uncorrupted, it is much more probable that the ancient Scots, a people so free of intermixture with foreigners, and so strongly attached to the memory of their ancestors, had the works of their bards handed down with great purity.

It will seem strange to some, that poems admired for many centuries in one part of this kingdom should be hitherto unknown in the other; and that the British, who have carefully traced out the works of genius in other nations, should so long remain strangers to their own. This, in a great measure, is to be imputed to those who understood both languages and never attempted a translation. They, from being acquainted but with detached pieces, or from a modesty, which perhaps the present translator ought, in prudence, to have followed, despaired of making the compositions of their bards agreeable to an English reader. The manner of those compositions is so different from other poems, and the ideas so confined to the most early state of society, that it was thought they had not enough of variety to please a polished age.

THIS was long the opinion of the translator of the following collection; and though he admired the poems, in the original, very early, and gathered part of them from tradition for his own amusement, yet he never had the smallest hopes of seeing them in an English dress. He was sensible that the strength and manner of both languages were very different, and that it was next to impossible to translate the Galic poetry into any thing of tolerable English verse; a prose translation he could never think of, as it must necessarily fall short of the majesty of an original. It was a gentleman, who has himself made a figure in the poetical world, that gave him the first hint concerning a literal prose translation. He tried it at his desire, and the specimen was approved. Other gentlemen were earnest in exhorting him to bring more to the light, and it is to their uncommon zeal that the world owes the Galic poems, if they have any merit.

It was at first intended to make a general collection of all the ancient pieces of genius to be found in the Galic language; but the translator had his reasons for confining himself to the remains of the works of Ossian. The action of the poem that stands the first, was not the greatest or most celebrated of the exploits of Fingal. His wars were very numerous, and each of them afforded a theme which employed the genius of his son. But, excepting the present poem, those pieces are irrecoverably lost, and there only remain a few fragments in the hands of the translator. Tradition has still preserved, in many places, the story of the poems, and many now living have heard them, in their youth, repeated.

The complete work, now printed, would, in a short time, have shared the fate of the rest. The genius of the highlanders has suffered a great change within these few years. The communication with the rest of the island is open, and the introduction of trade and manufactures has destroyed that leisure which was formerly dedicated to hearing and repeating the poems of ancient times. Many have now learned to leave their mountains, and seek their fortunes in a milder climate; and though a certain *amor patriæ* may sometimes bring them back, they have, during their absence, imbibed enough of foreign manners to despise the customs of their ancestors. Bards have been long disused, and the spirit of genealogy has greatly subsided. Men begin to be less devoted to their chiefs, and consanguinity is not so much regarded. When property is established, the human mind confines its views to the pleasure it procures. It does not go back to antiquity, or look forward to succeeding ages. The cares of life increase, and the actions of other times no longer amuse. Hence it is, that the taste for their ancient poetry is at a low ebb among the highlanders. They have not, however, thrown off the good qualities of their ancestors. Hospitality still subsists, and an uncommon civility to strangers. Friendship is inviolable, and revenge less blindly followed than formerly.

To say any thing, concerning the poetical merit of the poems, would be an anticipation on the judgment of the public. The poem which stands first in the collection is truly epic. The characters are strongly marked, and the sentiments breathe heroism. The subject of it is an invasion of Ireland by Swaran king of Lochlin, which is the name of Scandinavia in the Galic language. Cuchullin, general of the Irish tribes in the minority of Cormac king of Ireland, upon intelligence of the invasion, assembled his forces near Tura, a castle on the coast of Ulster. The poem opens with the landing of Swaran, councils are held, battles fought, and Cuchullin is, at last, totally defeated. In the mean time, Fingal, king of Scotland, whose aid was sollicited before the enemy landed, arrived and expelled them from the country. This war, which continued but six days and as many nights, is, including the episodes, the whole story of the poem. The scene is the heath of Lena near a mountain called Cromleach in Ulster.

All that can be said of the translation, is that it is literal, and that simplicity is studied. The arrangement of the words in the original is imitated, and the inversions of the style observed. As the translator claims no merit from his version, he hopes for the indulgence of the public where he fails. He wishes that the imperfect semblance he draws, may not prejudice the world against an original, which contains what is beautiful in simplicity, and grand in the sublime.

# FINGAL

## AN ANCIENT EPIC POEM
## IN SIX BOOKS

### BOOK I

UCHULLIN* sat by Tura's wall; by the tree of the rustling leaf.—His spear leaned against the mossy rock. His shield lay by him on the grass. As he thought of mighty Carbar†, a hero whom he slew in war; the scout‡ of the ocean came Moran§ the son of Fithil.

RISE, said the youth, Cuchullin, rise; I see the ships of Swaran. Cuchullin, many are the foe; many the heroes of the dark-rolling sea.

MORAN! replied the blue-eyed chief, thou ever tremblest, son

---

* Cuchullin the Son of Semo and grandson to Caithbat a druid celebrated in tradition for his wisdom and valour. Cuchullin when very young married Bragela the daughter of Sorglan, and passing over into Ireland, lived for some time with Connal, grandson by a daughter to Congal the petty king of Ulster. His wisdom and valour in a short time gained him such reputation, that in the minority of Cormac the supreme king of Ireland, he was chosen guardian to the young king, and sole manager of the war against Swaran king of Lochlin. After a series of great actions he was killed in battle somewhere in Connaught, in the twenty-seventh year of his age. He was so remarkable for his strength, that to describe a strong man it has passed into a proverb, 'He has the strength of Cuchullin.' They shew the remains of his palace at Dunscaich in the isle of Skye; and a stone to which he bound his dog Luath, goes still by his name.

† Cairbar or Cairbre signifies a strong man.

‡ Cuchullin having previous intelligence of the invasion intended by Swaran, sent scouts all over the coast of Ullin or Ulster, to give early notice of the first appearance of the enemy, at the same time that he sent Munan the son of Stirmal to implore the assistance of Fingal. He himself collected the flower of the Irish youth to Tura, a castle on the coast, to stop the progress of the enemy till Fingal should arrive from Scotland. We may conclude from Cuchullin's applying so early for foreign aid, that the Irish were not then so numerous as they have since been; which is a great presumption against the high antiquities of that people. We have the testimony of Tacitus that one legion only was thought sufficient, in the time of Agricola, to reduce the whole island under the Roman yoke; which would not probably have been the case had the island been inhabited for any number of centuries before.

§ Moran signifies many; and Fithil, or rather Fili, *an inferior bard.*

of Fithil: Thy fears have much increased the foe. Perhaps it is the king* of the lonely hills coming to aid me on green Ullin's plains.

I SAW their chief, says Moran, tall as a rock of ice. His spear is like that blasted fir. His shield like the rising moon.† He sat on a rock on the shore: like a cloud of mist on the silent hill.—Many, chief of men! I said, many are our hands of war. —Well art thou named, the Mighty Man, but many mighty men are seen from Tura's walls of wind.—He answered, like a wave on a rock, who in this land appears like me? Heroes stand not in my presence: they fall to earth beneath my hand. None can meet Swaran in the fight but Fingal, king of stormy hills. Once we wrestled on the heath of Malmor‡, and our heels overturned the wood. Rocks fell from their place; and rivulets, changing their course, fled murmuring from our strife. Three days we renewed our strife, and heroes stood at a distance and trembled. On the fourth, Fingal says, that the king of the ocean fell; but Swaran says, he stood. Let dark Cuchullin yield to him that is strong as the storms of Malmor.

No : replied the blue-eyed chief, I will never yield to man, Dark Cuchullin will be great or dead. Go, Fithil's son, and take my spear: strike the sounding shield of Cabait§. It hangs at Tura's rustling gate; the sound of peace is not its voice. My heroes shall hear on the hill.

HE went and struck the bossy shield. The hills and their rocks replied. The sound spread along the wood : deer start by the lake

---

* Fingal the son of Comtal and Morna the daughter of Thaddu. His grandfather was Trathal, and great grandfather Trenmor, both of whom are often mentioned in the poem.

† ———His ponderous shield
  Behind him cast ; the broad circumference
  Hung on his shoulders like the Moon.
  MILTON

‡ Meal-mór—*a great hill.*

§ Cabait, or rather Cathbait, grandfather to the hero, was so remarkable for his valour, that his shield was made use of to alarm his posterity to the battles of the family. We find Fingal making the same use of his own shield in the 4th book.—A horn was the most common instrument to call the army together before the invention of bagpipes.

of roes. Curach\* leapt from the sounding rock; and Connal of the
bloody spear. Crugal's† breast of snow beats high. The son of Favi
leaves the dark-brown hind. It is the shield of war, said Ronnar,
the spear of Cuchullin, said Lugar. Son of the sea put on thy arms!
Calmar lift thy sounding steel! Puno! horrid hero, rise: Cairbar
from thy red tree of Cromla. Bend thy white knee, O Eth; and
descend from the streams of Lena.—Ca-olt stretch thy white side
as thou movest along the whistling heath of Mora: thy side that is
white as the foam of the troubled sea, when the dark winds pour
it on the murmuring rocks of Cuthon‡.

Now I behold the chiefs in the pride of their former deeds; their
souls are kindled at the battles of old, and the actions of other
times. Their eyes are like flames of fire, and roll in search of the
foes of the land.—Their mighty hands are on their swords; and
lightning pours from their sides of steel.—They came like streams
from the mountains; each rushed roaring from his hill. Bright are
the chiefs of battle in the armour of their fathers. Gloomy and
dark their heroes followed, like the gathering of the rainy clouds
behind the red meteors of heaven.—The sounds of crashing arms
ascend. The gray dogs howl between.—Unequally bursts the song
of battle; and rocking Cromla§ echoes round. On Lena's dusky
heath they stood, like mist¶ that shades the hills of autumn: when
broken and dark it settles high, and lifts its head to heaven.

HAIL, said Cuchullin, sons of the narrow vales, hail ye
hunters of the deer. Another sport is drawing near: it is like the
dark rolling of that wave on the coast. Or shall we fight, ye sons

---

\* Cu-raoch signifies *the madness of battle.*

† Cruth-geal —*fair- complexioned.*

‡ Cu-thón—*the mournful sound of waves.*

§ Crom-leach signified a place of worship among the Druids. It is here the
proper name of a hill on the coast of Ullin or Ulster.

¶ *Greek Quotation* HOM.II.5.V.522
So when th' embattled clouds in dark array,
Along the skies their gloomy lines display;
The low hung vapours motionless and still
Rest on the summits of the shaded hill. POPE.

of war! or yield green Innisfail★ to Lochlin! O Connal† speak, thou first of men! thou breaker of the shields! thou hast often fought with Lochlin; shalt thou lift up thy father's spear?

CUCHULLIN! calm the chief replied, the spear of Connal is keen. It delights to shine in battle, and to mix with the blood of thousands. But tho' my hand is bent on war, my heart is for the peace of Erin‡. Behold, thou first in Cormac's war, the sable fleet of Swaran. His masts are as numerous on our coast as reeds in the lake of Lego. His ships are like forests cloathed with mist, when the trees yield by turns to the squally wind. Many are his chiefs in battle. Connal is for peace.—Fingal would shun his arm the first of mortal men: Fingal that scatters the mighty, as stormy winds the heath; when the streams roar thro' echoing Cona: and night settles with all her clouds on the hill.

FLY, thou chief of peace, said Calmar§ the son of Matha; fly, Connal, to thy silent hills, where the spear of battle never shone; pursue the dark-brown deer of Cromla: and stop with thine arrows the bounding roes of Lena. But, blue-eyed son of Semo, Cuchullin, ruler of the war, scatter thou the sons of Lochlin¶, and roar thro' the ranks of their pride. Let no vessel of the kingdom of Snow bound on the dark-rolling waves of Inis-tore±.

---

★ Ireland so called from a colony that settled there called Falans.—Innis-fail, *i.e.* the island of the Fa-il or Falans.

† Connal, the friend of Cuchullin, was the son of Cathbait prince of the Tongormaor the *island of blue waves*, probably one of the Hebrides. His mother was Fioncoma the daughter of Congal. He had a son by Foba of Conachar-nessar, who was afterwards king of Ulster. For his services in the war against Swaran he had lands conferred on him, which, from his name, were called Tir-chonnuil or Tir-connel, *i.e.* the land of Connal.

† Erin, a name of Ireland; from *car* or *tar* West, and *in* an island. This name was not always confined to Ireland, for there is the highest probability that the *Ierne* of the ancients was Britain to the North of the Forth.—For Ierne is said to be to the North of Britain, which could not be meant of Ireland. STABO, 1. 2. & 4. CASAUB. 1. I.

‡ Cálm-er, *a strong man.*

§ The Galic name of Scandinavia in general; in a more confined sense that of the peninsula of Jutland.

± Innis-tore, *the island of whales* the ancient name of the Orkney islands.

O YE dark winds of Erin rise! and roar ye whirlwinds of the heath! Amidst the tempest let me die, torn in a cloud by angry ghosts of men; amidst the tempest let Calmar die, if ever chace was sport to him so much as the battle of shields.

CALMAR! slow replied the chief, I never fled, O Matha's son. I was swift with my friends in battle, but small is the fame of Connal. The battle was won in my presence, and the valiant overcame. But, son of Semo, hear my voice, regard the ancient throne of Cormac. Give wealth and half the land for peace, till Fingal come with battle. Or, if war be thy choice, I lift the sword and spear. My joy shall be in the midst of thousands, and my soul brighten in the gloom of the fight.

TO me, Cuchullin replies, pleasant is the noise of arms: pleasant as the thunder of heaven before the shower of Spring. But gather all the shining tribes that I may view the sons of war. Let them move along the heath, bright as the sun-shine before a storm; when the west wind collects the clouds and the oaks of Morven echo along the shore.

BUT where are my friends in battle? The companions of my arm in danger? Where art thou, white-bosom'd Cathbat? Where is that cloud in war, Duchomar*: and hast thou left me, O Fergus†! in the day of the storm? Fergus, first in our joy at the feast; son of Rossa! arm of death! comest thou like a roe‡ from Malmor. Like a hart from the ecchoing; hills?—Hail thou son of Rossa! what shades the soul of war?

FOUR stones§, replied the chief, rise on the grave of Cathbat.—These hands have laid in earth Duchomar, that cloud in war.

---

\* Dubhchomar, *a black well shaped man.*

† Fear-guth,—*the man of the word;* or a commander of an army.

‡ Be thou like a roe or young hart on the mountains of Bether. SOLOMON'S Song.

§ This passage alludes to the manner of burial among the ancient Scots. They opened a grave six or eight feet deep : the bottom was lined with fine clay; and on this they laid the body of the deceased, and, if a warrior, his sword, and the head's of twelve arrows by his side. Above they laid another stratum of clay, in which they placed the horn of a deer, the symbol of hunting. The whole was covered with a fine mold, and four stones placed on end to mark the extent of the grave. These are the four stones alluded to here.

Cathbat, thou son of Torman, thou wert a sun-beam on the hill.—
And thou, O valiant Duchomar, like the mist of marshy Lano;
when it sails over the plains of autumn and brings death to the
people. Morna! thou fairest of maids! calm is thy sleep in the cave
of the rock. Thou hast fallen in darkness like a star, that shoots
athwart the desart, when the traveller is alone, and mourns the
transient beam. Say, said Semo's blue-eyed son, say how fell the
chiefs of Erin? Fell they by the sons of Lochlin, striving in the
battle of heroes? Or what confines the chiefs of Cromla to the dark
and narrow house\*?

CATHBAT, replied the hero, fell by the sword of Duchomar at
the oak of the noisy streams. Duchomar came to Tura's cave, and
spoke to the lovely Morna.

MORNA†, fairest among women, lovely daughter of Cormac-
cairbar. Why in the circle of stones; in the cave of the rock alone?
The stream murmurs hoarsely. The old tree's groan is in the wind.
The lake is troubled before thee, and dark are the clouds of the
sky. But thou art like snow on the heath; and thy hair like the mist
of Cromla; when it curls on the rocks, and it shines to the beam
of the west.—Thy breasts are like two smooth rocks seen from
Branno of the streams. Thy arms like two white pillars in the halls
of the mighty Fingal.

FROM whence, the white-armed maid replied, from whence,
Duchomar the most gloomy of men? Dark are thy brows and
terrible. Red are thy rolling eyes. Does Swaran appear on the sea?
What of the foe, Duchomar?

FROM the hill I return, O Morna, from the hill of the dark-
brown hinds. Three have I slain with my bended yew. Three with
my long bounding dogs of the chace.—Lovely daughter of Cormac,
I love thee as my soul.—I have slain one stately deer for thee.—
High was his branchy head; and fleet his feet of wind.

DUCHOMAR! calm the maid replied, I love thee not, thou
gloomy man.—Hard is thy heart of rock, and dark thy terrible

---

\* The grave.—The house appointed for all living. JOB.

† Muirne or Morna, *a woman beloved by all.*

brow. But Cathbat, thou son of Torman\* thou art the love of Morna.

THOU art like a sun-beam on the hill in the day of the gloomy storm. Sawest thou the son of Torman, lovely on the hill of his hinds? Here the daughter of Cormac waits the coming of Cathbat.

AND long shall Morna wait, Duchomar said, his blood is on my sword.—Long shall Morna wait for him. He fell at Branno's stream. High on Cromla I will raise his tomb, daughter of Cormac-cairbar; but fix thy love on Duchomar, his arm is strong as a storm.—

AND is the son of Torman fallen? said the maid of the tearful eye. Is he fallen on his ecchoing hill; the youth with the breast of snow? he that was first in the chace of the hill; the foe of the strangers of the ocean.—Duchomar thou art dark† indeed, and cruel is thy arm to Morna. But give me that sword, my foe; I love the blood of Caithbat.

HE gave the sword to her tears; but she pierced his manly breast.

HE fell, like the bank of a mountain-stream; stretched out his arm and said;

DAUGHTER of Cormac-cairbar, thou hast slain Duchomar. The sword is cold in my breast: Morna, I feel it cold. Give me to Moina‡ the maid; Duchomar was the dream of her night. She will raise my tomb; and the hunter shall see it and praise me. But draw the sword from my breast; Morna, the steel is cold.

SHE came, in all her tears, she came, and drew it from his breast. He pierced her white side with steel; and spread her fair locks on the ground. Her bursting blood sounds from her side: and her white arm is stained with red. Rolling in death she lay and Tura's cave answered to her sighs.—

PEACE, said Cuchullin, to the souls of the heroes; their deeds

---

\* Torman thunder. This is the true origin of the Jupiter Taramis of the ancients.

† She alludes to his name—*the dark man.*

‡ Moina, *soft in temper and person.*

were great in danger. Let them ride around\* me on clouds; and shew
their features of war: that my soul may be strong in danger; my arm
like the thunder of heaven.—But be thou on a moon-beam, O
Morna, near the window of my rest; when my thoughts are of peace;
and the din of arms is over.—Gather the strength of the tribes, and
move to the Wars of Erin.—Attend the car of my battles; and rejoice
in the noise of my course.—Place three spears by my side; and follow
the bounding of my steeds. That my soul may be strong in my
friends, when the battle darkens round the beams of my steel.

AS rushes a stream† of foam from the dark shady steep of
Cromla; when the thunder is rolling above, and dark-brown night
on half the hill. So fierce, so vast, and so terrible rushed on the
sons of Erin. The chief like a whale of ocean, whom all his billows
follow, poured valour forth as a stream, rolling his might along
the shore.

THE sons of Lochlin heard the noise as the sound of a winter-
stream. Swaran struck his bossy shield, and called the son of Arno.
What murmur rolls along the hill like the gathered flies of
evening? The sons of Innis-fail descend, or rustling winds‡ roar
in the distant wood. Such is the noise of Gormal before the white
tops of my waves arise. O son of Arno, ascend the hill and view the
dark face of the heath.

HE went, and trembling, swift returned. His eyes rolled wildly
round. His heart beat high against his side. His words were faultering, broken, slow.

---

\* It was the opinion then, as indeed it is to this day, of some of the highlanders,
that the souls of the deceased hovered round their living friends; and sometimes
appeared to them when they were about to enter on any great undertaking.

† *Greek Quotation* HOM.
As torrents roll encreas'd by numerous rills
With rage impetuous down the ecchoing hills;
Rush to the vales, and pour'd along the plain,
Roar thro' a thousand channels to the main. POPE.
*Latin Quotation* VIRG.

‡ As when the hollow rocks retain
The sound of blustering wind. MILTON.

RISE, son of ocean, rise chief of the dark-brown shields. I see the dark, the mountain-stream of the battle. The deep-moving strength of the sons of Erin.—The car, the car of battle comes, like the flame of death; the rapid car of Cuchullin, the noble son of Semo. It bends behind like a wave near a rock; like the golden mist of the heath. Its sides are embossed with stones, and sparkle like the sea round the boat of night. Of polished yew is its beam, and its seat of the smoothest bone. The sides are replenished with spears; and the bottom is the foot-stool of heroes. Before the right side of the car is seen the snorting horse. The high-maned, broad-breasted, proud, high-leaping strong steed of the hill. Loud and resounding is his hoof; the spreading of his mane above is like that stream of smoke on the heath. Bright are the sides of the steed, and his name is Sulin-Sifadda.

BEFORE the left side of the car is seen the snorting horse. The thin-maned, high-headed, strong-hooffed, fleet, bounding son of the hill: his name is Dufronnal among the stormy sons of the sword.—A thousand thongs bind the car on high. Hard polished bits shine in a wreath of foam. Thin thongs bright-studded with gems, bend on the stately necks of the steeds.—The steeds that like wreaths of mist fly over the streamy vales. The wildness of deer is in their course, the strength of the eagle descending on her prey. Their noise is like the blast of winter on the sides of the snowheaded Gormal.

WITHIN the car is seen the chief; the strong stormy son of the sword; the hero's name is Cuchullin, son of Semo king of shells. His red cheek is like my polished yew. The look of his blue-rolling eye is wide beneath the dark arch of his brow. His hair flies from his head like a flame, as bending forward he wields the spear. Fly, king of ocean, fly; he comes, like a storm, along the streamy vale.

WHEN did I fly, replied the king, from the battle of many spears? When did I fly, son of Arno, chief of the little soul? I met the storm of Gormal when the foam of my waves was high; I met the storm of the clouds and shall I fly from a hero? Were it Fingal himself my soul should not darken before him.—Rise to the battle, my thousands; pour round me like the ecchoing main. Gather round the bright steel of your king; strong as the rocks of my land; that meet the storm with joy, and stretch their dark woods to the wind.

AS autumn's* dark storms pour from two ecchoing hills, towards each other approached the heroes.—As two dark streams from high rocks meet, and mix and roar on the plain; loud, rough and dark in battle meet Lochlin and Innis-fail. Chief mixed his strokes with chief, and man with man; steel, clanging, sounded on steel, helmets are cleft on high. Blood bursts and smoaks around.—Strings murmur on the polished yews. Darts rush along the sky. Spears fall like the circles of light that gild the stormy face of the night.

AS the troubled noise of the ocean when roll the waves on high; as the last peal of the thunder of heaven, such is the noise of battle. Though Cormac's hundred bards were there to give the war to song; feeble were the voices of a hundred bards to send the deaths to future times. For many were the falls of the heroes; and wide poured the blood of the valiant.

MOURN, ye sons of the song, the death of the noble Sithallin†.—Let the sighs of Fiöna rise on the dark heaths of her

---

* The reader may compare this passage with a similar one in Homer. Iliad. 4. v. 446.

> Now shield with shield, with helmet helmet clos'd,
> To armour armour, lance to lance oppos'd,
> Host against host, with shadowy squadrons drew,
> The sounding darts in iron tempests flew;
> With streaming blood the slipp'ry fields are dy'd,
> And slaughter'd heroes swell the dreadful tide. POPE.

> Statius has very happily imitated Homer.
> *Jam clypeus clypeis, umbone repellitur umbo,*
> *Ense minax ensis pede pes, & cuspide cuspis, &c.*
> Arms on armour crashing, bray'd Horrible discord, and the madding wheels
> Of brazen chariots rag'd, & c. MILTON.

† Sithallin signifies *a handsome man,*—Fiona, *a fair maid;*—and Ardan, *pride.*

lovely Ardan.—They fell, like two hinds of the desert, by the hands
of the mighty Swaran; when, in the midst of thousands he roared;
like the shrill spirit of a storm, that sits dim, on the clouds of
Gormal, and enjoys the death of the mariner.

NOR slept thy hand by thy side, chief of the isle of mist*;
many were the deaths of thine arm, Cuchullin, thou son of Semo.
His sword was like the beam of heaven when it pierces the sons of
the vale; when the people are blasted and fall, and all the hills are
burning around.—Dusronnal† snorted over the bodies of heroes;
and Sifadda‡ bathed his hoof in blood. The battle lay behind them
as groves overturned on the desert of Cromla; when the blast has
passed the heath laden with the spirits of night.

WEEP on the rocks of roaring winds, O maid of Inistore§,
bend thy fair head over the waves, thou fairer than the ghost of
the hills; when it moves in a sun-beam at noon over the silence
of Morven. He is fallen! thy youth is low; pale beneath the sword
of Cuchullin. No more shall valour raise the youth to match the
blood of kings.—Trenar, lovely Trenar died, thou maid of Inistore.
His gray dogs are howling at home, and see his passing ghost. His
bow is in the hall unstrung. No sound is in the heath of his hinds.

AS roll a thousand waves to the rocks, so Swaran's host came
on; as meets a rock a thousand waves, so Inisfail met Swaran.
Death raises all his voices around, and mixes with the sound of
shields.—Each hero is a pillar of darkness, and the sword a beam

---

* The Isle of Sky ; not improperly called the *isle of mist* as its high hills, which
catch the clouds from the western ocean, occasion almost continual rains.

† One of Cuchullin's horses. Dubhstron gheal.

‡ Sith-fadda, *i.e. a long stride.*

§ The maid of Inistore was the daughter of Gorlo king of Inistore or Orkney
islands. Trenar was brother to the king of Iniscon, supposed to be one of the islands
of Shetland. The Orkneys and Shetland were at that time subject to the king of
Lochlin. We find that the dogs of Trenar are sensible at home of the death of their
master, the very instant he is killed.—It was the opinion of the times, that the souls
of heroes went immediately after death to the hills of their country, and the scenes
they frequented the most happy time of their life. It was thought too that dogs and
horses saw the ghosts of the deceased.

of fire in his hand. The field ecchoes from wing to wing, as a hundred hammers that rise by turns on the red son of the furnace. Who are these on Lena's heath that are so gloomy and dark? Who are these like two clouds★ and their swords like lightning above them? The little hills are troubled around, and the rocks tremble with all their moss.—Who is it but Ocean's son and the car-borne chief of Erin? Many are the anxious eyes of their friends, as they see them dim on the heath. Now night conceals the chiefs in her clouds, and ends the terrible fight. It was on Cromla's shaggy side that Dorglas placed the deer †; the early fortune of the chace, before the heroes left the hill.—A hundred youths collect the heath; ten heroes blow the fire; three hundred chuse the polish'd stones. The feast is smoaking wide.

CUCHULLIN, chief of Erin's war, resumed his mighty soul. He stood upon his beamy spear, and spoke to the son of songs; to Carril of other times, the gray-haired son of Kinfena‡. Is this feast spread for me alone and the king of Lochlin on Ullin's shore; far from the deer of his hills, and sounding halls of his feasts? Rise, Carril of other times, and carry my words to Swaran; tell him from the roaring of waters, that Cuchullin gives his feast. Here let him listen to the sound of my groves amidst the clouds of night.—For cold and bleak the blustering winds rush over the foam of his seas. Here let him praise the trembling harp, and hear the songs of heroes.

OLD Carril went, with softest voice, and called the king of

---

★ As when two black clouds
  With heaven's artillery fraught, come rattling on
  Over the Caspian. MILTON.

† The ancient manner of preparing feasts after hunting, is handed down by tradition.—A pit lined with smooth stones was made; and near it stood a heap of smooth flat stones of the flint kind. The stones as well as the pit were properly heated with heath. Then they laid some venison in the bottom, and a stratum of the stones above it; and thus they did alternately till the pit was full. The whole was covered over with heath to confine the steam. Whether this is probable I cannot say; but some pits are shewn, which the vulgar say, were used in that manner.

‡ Cean-feana, i.e. the head of the people.

dark-brown shields. Rise from the skins of thy chace, rise, Swaran king of groves.—Cuchullin gives the joy of shells; partake the feast of Erin's blue-eyed chief. He answered like the sullen sound of Cromla before a storm. Though all thy daughters, Inisfail! should extend their arms of snow; raise high the heavings of their breasts, and softly roll their eyes of love; yet, fixed as Lochlin's thousand rocks, here Swaran shall remain; till morn, with the young beams of my east, shall light me to the death of Cuchullin. Pleasant to my ear is Lochlin's wind. It rushes over my seas. It speaks aloft in all my shrowds, and brings my green forests to my mind; the green forests of Gormal that often ecchoed to my winds, when my spear was red in the chace of the boar. Let dark Cuchullin yield to me the ancient throne of Cormac, or Erin's torrents shall shew from their hills the red foam of the blood of his pride.

SAD is the sounds of Swaran's voice, said Carril of other times:—

Sad to himself alone, said the blue-eyed son of Semo. But, Carril, raise thy voice on high, and tell the deeds of other times. Send thou the night away in song; and give the joy of grief. For many heroes and maids of love, have moved on Inis-fail, And lovely are the songs of woe that are heard on Albion's rocks; when the noise of the chace is over, and the streams of Cona answer to the voice of Ossian*.

IN other days†, Carril replies, came the sons of Ocean to Erin. A thousand vessels bounded over the waves to Ullin's lovely plains. The sons of Inisfail arose to meet the race of dark-brown shields. Cairbar, first of men, was there, and Grudar, stately

---

* Ossian the son of Fingal and author of the poem. One cannot but admire the address of the poet in putting his own praise so naturally into the mouth of Cuchullin. The Com here mentioned is perhaps that small river that runs through Glenco in Argyleshire. One of the hills which environ that romantic valley is still called Scorna-fena, or the hill of Fingal's people.

† This episode is introduced with propriety. Calmar and Connal, two of the Irish heroes, had disputed warmly before the battle about engaging the enemy. Carril endeavours to reconcile them with the story of Cairbar and Grudar; who, tho' enemies before, fought side by side in the war. The poet obtained his aim, for we find Calmar and Connal perfectly reconciled in the third book.

youth. Long had they strove for the spotted bull, that lowed on Golbun's* ecchoing heath. Each claimed him as their own; and death was often at the point of their steel.

SIDE by side the heroes fought, and the strangers of Ocean fled. Whose name was fairer on the hill than the name of Cairbar and Grudar! But ah! why ever lowed the bull on Golbun's eechoing heath; they saw him leaping like the snow. The wrath of the chiefs returned.

ON Lubar's† grassy banks they fought, and Grudar like a sunbeam, fell. Fierce Cairbar came to the vale of the ecchoing Tura, where Brassolis‡, fairest of his sisters, all alone, raised the song of grief. She sung of the actions of Grudar, the youth of her secret soul.—She mourned him in the field of blood; but still she hoped for his return. Her white bosom is seen from her robe, as the moon from the clouds of night. Her voice was softer than the harp to raise the song of grief. Her soul was fixed on Grudar; the secret look of her eye was his.—When shalt thou come in thine arms, thou mighty in the war?—

TAKE, Brassolis, Cairbar came and said, take, Brassolis, this shield of blood. Fix it on high within my hall, the armour of my foe. Her soft heart beat against her side. Distracted, pale, she flew. She found her youth in all his blood; she died on Cromla's heath. Here rests their dust, Cuchullin; and these two lonely yews sprung from their tombs, and wish to meet on high. Fair was Brassolis on the plain, and Grudar on the hill. The bard shall preserve their names, and repeat them to future times.

PLEASANT is thy voice, O Carril, said the blue-eyed chief of Erin; and lovely are the words of other times. They are like the calm shower§ of spring; when the sun looks on the field, and the

---

* Golb-bhean, as well as Cromleach, signifies *a crooked hill.*

† Lubar—a river in Ulster. *Labhar* loud, noisy.

‡ Brassolis signifies *a woman with a white breast.*

§ Homer compares soft piercing words to the fall of snow.
  *Greek Quotation*
  But when he speaks, what elocution flows!
  Like the soft fleeces of descending snows. POPE.

light cloud flies over the hills. O strike the harp in praise of my love, the lonely sun-beam of Dunscaich. Strike the harp in the praise of Bragéla; she that I left in the Isle of Mist, the spouse of Semo's son. Dost thou raise thy fair face from the rock to find the sails of Cuchullin?—The sea is rolling far distant, and its white foam shall deceive thee for my sails. Retire, for it is night, my love, and the dark winds sigh in thy hair. Retire to the halls of my feasts, and think of the times that are past: for I will not return till the storm of war is ceased. O Connal, speak of wars and arms, and send her from my mind, for lovely with her raven-hair is the white-bosomed daughter of Sorglan.

CONNAL, slow to speak, replied, guard against the race of ocean; Send thy troop of night abroad, and watch the strength of Swaran.—-Cuchullin! I am for peace till, the race of the desert come; till Fingal come, the first of men, and beam, like the sun, on our fields.

THE hero struck the shield of his alarms—the warriors of the night moved on. The rest lay in the heath of the deer, and slept amidst the dusky wind.—The ghosts* of the lately dead were near, and swam on gloomy clouds. And far distant, in the dark silence of Lena, the feeble voices of death were heard.

---

* It was long the opinion of the ancient Scots, that a ghost was heard shrieking near the place where a death was to happen soon after. The accounts given, to this day, among the vulgar, of this extraordinary matter, are very poetical. The ghost comes mounted on a meteor, and surrounds twice or thrice the place destined for the person to die ; and then goes along the road through which the funeral is to pass, shrieking at intervals; at last, the meteor and ghost disappear above the burial place.

# FINGAL

## AN ANCIENT EPIC POEM
## IN SIX BOOKS

### BOOK II

ONNAL * lay by the sound of the mountain stream, beneath the aged tree. A stone, with its moss, supported his head. Shrill thro' the heath of Lena, he heard the voice of night. At distance from the heroes he lay, for the son of the sword feared no foe.

---

\* The scene of Connal's repose is familiar to those who have been in the highlands of Scotland. The poet removes him to a distance from the army, to add more horror to the description of Crugal's ghost by the loneliness of the place. It perhaps will not be disagreeable to the reader, to see how two other ancient poets handled a similar subject.

*Greek Quotaion* HOM. II. 23.
When lo! the shade, before his closing eyes,
Of sad Patroclus rose or seem'd to rise,
In the same robe he living wore, he came
In stature, voice, and pleasing look the same.
The form familiar hover'd o'er his head,
And sleeps Achilles thus? the phantom said. POPE.

*Latin Quotation* Æn. lib. 2.
When Hector's ghost before my sight appears :
A bloody shroud he seem'd, and bath'd in tears,
Such as he was, when, by Pelides slain.
Thessalian coursers drag'd him o'er the plain.
Swoln were his feet, as when the thongs were thrust
Through the bor'd holes, his body black with dust.
Unlike that Hector; who return'd from toils
Of war triumphant, in Æacian spoils:
Or him, who made the fainting Greeks retire,
And launch'd against their navy Phrygian fire.
His hair and beard stood stiffen'd with his gore;
And all the wounds he for his country bore. DRYDEN.

MY hero saw in his rest a dark-red stream of fire coming down from the hill. Crugal sat upon the beam, a chief that lately fell. He fell by the hand of Swaran, striving in the battle of heroes. His face is like the beam of the setting moon; his robes are of the clouds of the hill: his eyes are like two decaying flames. Dark is the wound of his breast.

CRUGAL, said the mighty Connal, son of Dedgal famed on the hill of deer. Why so pale and sad, thou breaker of the shields? Thou hast never been pale for fear.—What disturbs the son of the hill?

DIM, and in tears, he stood and stretched his pale hand over the hero.—Faintly he raised his feeble voice, like the gale of the reedy Lego.

MY ghost, O Connal, is on my native hills; but my corse is on the sands of Ullin. Thou shalt never talk with Crugal, or find his lone steps in the heath. I am light as the blast of Cromla, and I move like the shadow of mist, Connal, son of Colgar, I see the dark cloud of death : it hovers over the plains of Lena. The sons of green Erin shall fall. Remove from the field of ghosts.—Like the darkened moon* he retired, in the midst of the whistling blast. Stay, said the mighty Connal, stay my dark-red friend. Lay by that beam of heaven, son of the windy Cromla. What cave of the hill is thy lonely house? What green-headed hill is the place of thy rest? Shall we not hear thee in the storm? In the noise of the mountain-stream? When the feeble sons of the wind come forth, and ride on the blast of the desart.

THE soft-voiced Connal rose in the midst of his sounding arms, He struck his shield above Cuchullin. The son of battle waked.

WHY, said the ruler of the car, comes Connal through my night? My spear might turn against the sound; and Cuchullin mourn the death of his friend. Speak, Connal, son of Colgar, speak, thy counsel is like the sun of heaven.

---

* Greek Quotation HOM. II. 23. V. 100
  Like a thin smoke he sees the spirit fly,
  And hears a feeble, lamentable cry. POPE.

SON of Semo, replied the chief, the ghost of Crugal came from the cave of his hill.—The stars dim-twinkled through his form; and his voice was like the sound of a distant stream. He is a messenger of death.—He speaks of the dark and narrow house. Sue for peace, O chief of Dunscaich; or fly over the heath of Lena.

HE spoke to Connal, replied the hero, though stars dim-twinkled through his form. Son of Colgar, it was the wind that murmured in the caves of Lena.—Or if it was the form* of Crugal, why didst thou not force him to my sight. Hast thou enquired where is his cave? The house of the son of the wind? My sword might find that voice, and force his knowledge from him. And small is his knowledge, Connal, for he was here to day. He could not have gone beyond our hills, and who could tell him there of our death?

GHOSTS fly on clouds and ride on winds, said Connal's voice of wisdom. They rest together in their caves, and talk of mortal men.

THEN let them talk of mortal men; of every man but Erin's chief. Let me be forgot in their cave; for I will not fly from Swaran.—If I must fall, my tomb shall rise amidst the fame of future times. The hunter shall shed a tear on my stone; and sorrow dwell round the high-bosomed Bragéla. I fear not death, but I fear to fly, for Fingal saw me often victorious. Thou dim phantom of the hill, shew thyself to me! come on thy beam of heaven, and shew me my death in thine hand, yet I will not fly, thou feeble son of the wind. Go, son of Colgar, strike the shield of Caithbat, it hangs between the spears. Let my heroes rise to the sound in the midst of the battles of Erin. Though Fingal delays his coming with the race of the stormy hills; we shall fight, O Colgar's son, and die in the battle of heroes.

THE sound spreads wide; the heroes rise, like the breaking of a blue-rolling wave. They stood on the heath, like oaks with all

---

* The poet teaches us the opinions that prevailed in his time concerning the state of separate souls. From Connal's expression, 'That the stars dim-twinkled through the form of Crugal,' and Cuchullin's reply, we may gather that they both thought the soul was material; something like the of εἴδωλον the ancient Greeks.

their branches round them*; when they eccho to the stream of frost, and their withered leaves rustle to the wind.

HIGH Cromla's head of clouds is gray; the morning trembles on the half-enlightened ocean. The blue, gray mist swims slowly by, and hides the sons of Inis-fail.

RISE ye, said the king of the dark-brown shields, ye that came from Lochlin's waves. The sons of Erin have fled from our arms—pursue them over the plains of Lena.—And, Morla, go to Cormac's hall and bid them yield to Swaran; before the people shall fall into the tomb; and the hills of Ullin be silent.—They rose like a flock of sea-fowl when the waves expel them from the shore. Their sound was like a thousand streams that meet in Cona's vale, when after a stormy night, they turn their dark eddies beneath the pale light of the morning.

AS the dark shades of autumn fly over the hills of grass; so gloomy, dark, successive came the chiefs of Lochlin's ecchoing woods. Tall as the stag of Morven moved on the king of groves. His shining shield is on his side like a flame on the heath at night. When the world is silent and dark, and the traveller sees some ghost sporting in the beam.

A BLAST from the trouble of ocean removed the settled mist. The sons of Inisfail appear like a ridge of rocks on the shore.

GO, Morla, go, said Lochlin's king, and offer peace to these. Offer the terms we give to kings when nations bow before us. When the valiant are dead in war, and the virgins weeping on the field.

GREAT Morla came, the son of Swart, and stately strode the king of shields. He spoke to Erin's blue-eyed son, among the lesser heroes.

TAKE Swaran's peace, the warrior spoke, the peace he gives to kings when the nations bow before him. Leave Ullin's lovely plains

---

\* ————————————As when heaven's fire
Hath scath'd the forest oaks, or mountain pines
With singed tops, their stately growth tho' bare
Stand on the blasted heath. MILTON.

to us, and give thy spouse and dog. Thy spouse high-bosom'd, heaving fair. Thy dog that overtakes the wind. Give these to prove the weakness of thine arm, and live beneath our power.

TELL Swaran, tell that heart of pride, that Cuchullin never yields.—I give him the dark-blue rolling of ocean, or I give his people graves in Erin. But never shall a stranger have the lovely sun-beam of Dunscaich; or ever deer fly on Lochlin's hills before the nimble-footed Luäth.

VAIN ruler of the car, said Morla, wilt thou fight the king; that king whose ships of many groves could carry off thine Isle? So little is thy green-hilled Ullin to the king of stormy waves.

IN words I yield to many, Morla; but this sword shall yield to none. Erin shall own the sway of Cormac, while Connal and Cuchullin live. O Connal, first of mighty men, thou hast heard the words of Morla; shall thy thoughts then be of peace, thou breaker of the shields? Spirit of fallen Crugal! why didst thou threaten us with death ? Thy narrow house shall receive me in the midst of the light of renown.—Exalt, ye sons of Inisfail, exalt the spear and bend the bow; rush on the foe in darkness, as the spirits of stormy nights.

THEN dismal, roaring, fierce, and deep the gloom of battle rolled along; as mist* that is poured on the valley, when storms invade the silent sunshine of heaven. The chief moves before in arms, like an angry ghost before a cloud; when meteors inclose him with fire; and the dark winds are in his hand.—Carril, far on the heath, bids the horn of battle found. He raises the voice of the song, and pours his soul into the minds of heroes.

WHERE, said the mouth of the song, where is the fallen Crugal? He lies forgot on earth, and the hall of shells † is silent.—

---

\* ———————As evening mist
    Ris'n from a river o'er the marish glides
    And gathers round fast at the lab'rers heel.
    Homeward returning MILTON.

  † The ancient Scots, at well as the present highlanders, drunk in shells; hence it is that we so often meet, in the old poetry, with the chief of shells and the halls of shells.

Sad is the spouse of Crugal, for she is a stranger\* in the hall of her sorrow. But who is she, that, like a sun-beam, flies before the ranks of the foe? It is Degrena†, lovely fair, the spouse of fallen Crugal. Her hair is on the wind behind. Her eye is red; her voice is shrill. Green, empty is thy Crugal now, his form is in the cave of the hill. He comes to the ear of rest, and raises his feeble voice; like the humming of the mountain-bee, or collected flies of evening. But Degrena falls like a cloud of the morn; the sword of Lochlin is in her side. Cairbar, she is fallen, the rising thought of thy youth. She is fallen, O Cairbar, the thought of thy youthful hours.

FIERCE Cairbar heard the mournful sound, and rushed on like ocean's whale; he saw the death of his daughter; and roared in the midst of thousands‡. His spear met a son of Lochlin, and battle spread from wing to wing. As a hundred winds in Lochlin's groves, as fire in the firs of a hundred hills; so loud, so ruinous and vast the ranks of men are hewn down.—Cuchullin cut off heroes like thistles, and Swaran wasted Erin. Curach fell by his hand, and Cairbar of the bossy shield. Morglan lies in lasting rest; and Ca-olt trembles as he dies. His white breast is stained with his blood; and his yellow hair stretched in the dust of his native land. He often had spread the feast where he fell; and often raised the voice of the harp: when his dogs leapt around for joy; and the youths of the chace prepared the bow.

STILL Swaran advanced, as a stream that bursts from the desart. The little hills are rolled in its course; and the rocks half-sunk by its side.

BUT Cuchullin stood before him like a hill§, that catches the clouds of heaven.—The winds contend on its head of pines; and

---

\* Crugal had married Degrena but a little time before the battle, consequently she may with propriety be called a stranger in the hall of her sorrow.

† Deo-ghréna signifies *a sun-beam.*

‡ *Mediisque in millibus ardet.* VIRG.

§ Virgil and Milton have made use of a comparison similar to this; I shall lay both before the reader, and let him judge for himself which of these two great poets have best succeeded.

the hail rattles on its rocks. But, firm in its strength, it stands and shades the silent vale of Cona.

SO Cuchullin shaded the sons of Erin, and stood in the midst of thousands. Blood rises like the fount of a rock, from panting heroes around him. But Erin Falls on either wing like snow in the day of the sun.

O SONS of Inisfail, said Grumal, Lochlin conquers on the field. Why strive we as reeds against the wind? Fly to the hill of dark-brown hinds. He fled like the stag of Morven, and his spear is a trembling beam of light behind him. Few fled with Grumal, the chief of the little soul: they fell in the battle of heroes on Lena's ecchoing heath.

HIGH on his car, of many gems, the chief of Erin stood; he slew a mighty son of Lochlin, and spoke, in haste, to Connal.

O CONNAL, first of mortal men, thou hast taught this arm of death! Though Erin's sons have fled, shall we not fight the foe? O Carril, son of other times, carry my living friends to that bushy hill.—Here, Connal, let us stand like rocks, and save our flying friends.

CONNAL mounts the car of light. They stretch their shields like the darkened moon, the daughter of the starry skies, when she moves, a dun circle, through heaven. Sithfadda panted up the hill, and Stronnal haughty steed. Like waves behind a whale behind them rushed the foe.

Now on the rising side of Cromla stood Erin's few sad sons; like a grove through which the flame had rushed hurried on by

---

Latin Quotation
Like Eryx or like Athos great he shews
Or father Appenine when white with snows;
His head divine obscure in clouds he hides,
And shakes the sounding forest on his sides. DRYDEN.

On th' other side Satan alarm'd,
Collecting all his might, dilated stood
Like Teneriff or Atlas unremov'd:
His stature reach'd the sky. MILTON.

the winds of the stormy night.—Cuchullin stood beside an oak. He rolled his red eye in silence, and heard the wind in his bushy hair; when the scout of ocean came, Moran the son of Fithil.— The ships, he cried, the ships of the lonely isle! There Fingal comes the first of men, the breaker of the shields. The waves foam before his black prows. His masts with sails are like groves in clouds.

BLOW, said Cuchullin, all ye winds that rush over my isle of lovely mist. Come to the death of thousands, O chief of the hills of hinds. Thy sails, my friend, are to me like the clouds of the morning; and thy ships like the light of heaven; and thou thyself like a pillar of fire that giveth light in the night. O Connal, first of men, how pleasant are our friends! But the night is gathering around; where now are the ships of Fingal? Here let us pass the hours of darkness, and wish for the moon of heaven.

THE winds came down on the woods. The torrents rushied from the rocks. Rain gathered round the head of Cromla. And the red stars trembled between the flying clouds. Sad, by the side of a stream whose sound was ecchoed by a tree, sad by the side of a stream the chief of Erin sat. Connal son of Colgar was there, and Carril of other times.

UNHAPPY is the hand of Cuchullin, said the son of Semo, unhappy is the hand of Cuchullin since he flew his friend.— Ferda, thou son of Damman, I loved thee as myself.

How, Cuchullin, son of Semo, fell the breaker of the shields? Well I remember, said Connal, the noble son of Damman. Tall and fair he was like the rain-bow of the hill.

FERDA from Albion came, the chief of a hundred hills. In Muri's* hall he learned the sword, and won the friendship of Cuchullin. We moved to the chace together; and one was our bed in the heath.

DEUGALA was the spouse of Cairbar, chief of the plains of Ullin. She was covered with the light of beauty, but her heart was the house of pride. She loved that sun-beam of youth, the noble

---

* An academy in Ulster for teaching the use of arms.

son of Damman. Cairbar, said the white-armed woman, give me
half of the herd. No more I will remain in your halls. Divide the
herd, dark Cairbar.

LET Cuchullin, said Cairbar, divide my herd on the hill. His
breast is the seat of justice. Depart, thou light of beauty. I went
and divided the herd. One bull of snow remained. I gave that bull
to Cairbar. The wrath of Deugala rose.

SON of Damman, begun the fair, Cuchullin pains my soul. I
must hear of his death, or Lubar's stream shall roll over me. My pale
ghost shall wander near thee, and mourn the wound of my pride.
Pour out the blood of Cuchullin or pierce this heaving breast.

DEUGALA, said the fair-haired youth, how shall I slay the son
of Semo? He is the friend of my secret thoughts, and shall I lift
the sword? She wept three days before him, on the fourth he con-
sented to fight.

I WILL fight my friend, Deugala! but may I fall by his sword.
Could I wander on the hill and behold the grave of Cuchullin? We
fought on the hills of Muri. Our swords avoid a wound. They slide
on the helmets of steel; and sound on the slippery shields. Deugala
was near with a smile, and said to the son of Damman, thine arm
is feeble, thou sun-beam of youth. Thy years are not strong for
steel.—Yield to the son of Semo. He is like the rock of Malmor.

THE tear is in the eye of youth. He faultering said to me,
Cuchullin, raise thy bossy shield. Defend thee from the hand of
thy friend. My soul is laden with grief: for I must slay the chief of
men.

I SIGHED as the wind in the chink of a rock. I lifted high the
edge of my steel. The sun-beam of the battle fell; the first of
Cuchullin's friends. —

UNHAPPY is the hand of Cuchullin since the hero fell.

MOURNFUL is thy tale, son of the car, said Carril of other
times. It sends my soul back to the ages of old, and to the days of
other years.—Often have I heard of Comal who slew the friend he
loved; yet victory attended his steel; and the battle was consumed
in his presence.

COMAL was a son of Albion; the chief of an hundred hills. His deer drunk of a thousand streams. A thousand rocks replied to the voice of his dogs. His face was the mildness of youth. His hand the death of heroes. One was his love, and fair was she! The daughter of mighty Conloch. She appeared like a sun-beam among women. And her hair was like the wing of the raven. Her dogs were taught to the chace. Her bow-string sounded on the winds of the forest. Her soul was fixed on Comal. Often met their eyes of love. Their course in the chace was one, and happy were their words in secret.—But Gormal loved the maid, the dark chief of the gloomy Ardven. He watched her lone steps in the heath; the foe of unhappy Comal.

ONE day, tired of the chace, when the mist had concealed their friends, Comal and the daughter of Conloch met in the cave of Ronan*. It was the wonted haunt of Comal. Its sides were hung with his arms. A hundred shields of thongs were there; a hundred helms of sounding steel.

REST here, he said, my love Galvina; thou light of the cave of Ronan. A deer appears on Mora's brow. I go; but I will soon return. I fear, she said, dark Grumal my foe; he haunts the cave of Ronan. I will rest among the arms; but soon return, my love.

HE went to the deer of Mora. The daughter of Conloch would try his love. She cloathed her white sides with his armour, and strode from the cave of Ronan. He thought it was his foe. His heart beat high. His colour changed, and darkness dimmed his eyes. He drew the bow. The arrow flew. Galvina fell in blood. He run with wildness in his steps and called the daughter of Conloch, No answer in the lonely rock. Where are thou, O my love! He saw,

---

* The unfortunate death of this Ronan is the subject of the ninth fragment of ancient poetry published last year: it is not the work of Ossian, though it is writ in his manner, and bears the genuine marks of antiquity.—The concise expressions of Ossian are imitated, but the thoughts are too jejune and confined to be the production of that poet.—Many poems go under his name that have been evidently composed since his time; they are very numerous in Ireland, and some have come to the translator's hands. They are trivial and dull to the last degree; swelling into ridiculous bombast, or sinking into the lowest kind of prosaic style.

at length, her heaving heart beating around the arrow he threw. O Conloch's daughter, is it thou? He sunk upon her breast.

THE hunters found the hapless pair; he afterwards walked the hill. But many and silent were his steps round the dark dwelling of his love. The fleet of the ocean came. He fought, the strangers fled. He searched for his death over the field. But who could kill the mighty Comal! He threw away his dark-brown shield. An arrow found his manly breast. He sleeps with his loved Galvina at the noise of the sounding surge. Their green tombs are seen by the mariner, when he bounds on the waves of the north.

# FINGAL

## AN ANCIENT EPIC POEM
## IN SIX BOOKS

### BOOK III*

LEASANT are the words of the song, said Cuchullin, and lovely are the tales of other times. They are like the calm dew of the morning on the hill of roes, when the sun is faint on its side, and the lake is settled and blue in the vale. O Carril, raise again thy voice, and let me hear the song of Tura: which was sung in my halls of joy, when Fingal king of shields was there, and glowed at the deeds of his fathers.

FINGAL! thou man of battle, said Carril, early were thy deeds in arms. Loehlin was consumed in thy wrath, when thy youth strove with the beauty of maids. They smiled at the fair-blooming face of the hero; but death was in his hands. He was strong as the waters of Lora. His followers were like the roar of a thousand streams. They took the king of Lochlin in battle, but restored him to his ships. His big heart swelled with pride; and the death of the youth was dark in his soul.—For none ever, but Fingal, overcame the strength of the mighty Starno†.

HE sat in the hall of his shells in Lochlin's woody land. He called the gray-haired Snivan, that often sung round the circle‡ of Loda: when the stone of power heard his cry, and the battle turned in the field of the valiant.

---

* The second night, since the opening of the poem, continues; and Cuchullin, Connal, and Carril still sit in the place described in the preceding book. The story of Agandecca is introduced here with propriety, as great use is made of it in the course of the poem, and as it, in some measure, brings about the catastrophe.

† Starno was the father of Swaran as well as Agandecca.—His fierce and cruel character is well marked in other poems concerning the times,

‡ This passage most certainly alludes to the religion of Lochlin, and the stone of power here mentioned is the image of one of the deities of Scandanavia.

GO; gray-haired Snivan, Starno said, to Ardven's sea-surrounded rocks. Tell to Fingal king of the desart; he that is the fairest among his thousands, tell him I give him my daughter, the loveliest maid that ever heaved a breast of snow. Her arms are white as the foam of my waves. Her soul is generous and mild. Let him come with his bravest heroes to the daughter of the secret hall.

SNIVAN came to Albion's windy hills: and fair-haired Fingal went. His kindled soul flew before him as he bounded on the waves of the north.

WELCOME, said the dark-brown Starno, welcome, king of rocky Morven; and ye his heroes of might; sons of the lonely isle! Three days within my halls shall ye feast; and three days pursue my boars, that your fame may reach the maid that dwells in the secret hall.

THE king of snow* designed their death, and gave the feast of shells. Fingal, who doubted the foe, kept on his arms of steel. The sons of death were afraid, and fled from the eyes of the hero. The voice of sprightly mirth arose. The trembling harps of joy are strung. Bards sing the battle of heroes; or the heaving breast of love.—Ullin, Fingal's bard, was there; the sweet voice of the hill of Cona. He praised the daughter of the snow; and Morven's† high-descended chief.—The daughter of the snow overheard, and left the hall of her secret sigh. She came in all her beauty, like the moon from the cloud of the east.—Loveliness was around her as light. Her steps were like the music of songs. She saw the youth and loved him. He was the stolen sigh of her soul. Her blue eve rolled on him in secret: and she blest the chief of Morven.

THE third day with all its beams, shone bright on the wood of boars. Forth moved the dark-browed Starno; and Fingal, king of shields. Half the day they spent in the chace; and the spear of Fingal was red in the blood of Gormal.

---

* Starno is here poetically called the king of snow, from the great quantities of snow that fall in his dominions.

† All the North-west coast of Scotland probably went of old under the name of Morven, which signifies a ridge of very high hills.

IT was then the daughter of Starno, with blue eyes rolling in tears, came with her voice of love and spoke to the king of Morven.

FINGAL, high-descended chief, trust not Starno's heart of pride. Within that wood he has placed his chiefs; beware of the wood of death. But, remember, son of the hill, remember Agandecca: save me from the wrath of my father, king of the windy Morven!

THE youth, with unconcern, went on; his heroes by his side. The sons of death fell by his hand; and Gormal ecchoed around.

BEFORE the halls of Starno the sons of the chace convened. The king's dark brows were like clouds. His eyes like meteors of night. Bring hither, he cries, Agandecca to her lovely king of Morven, His hand is stained with the blood of my people; and her words have not been in vain.—

SHE came with the red eye of tears. She came with her loose raven locks. Her white breast heaved with sighs, like the foam of the streamy Lubar. Starno pierced her side with steel. She fell like a wreath of snow that slides from the rocks of Ronan; when the woods are still, and the eccho deepens in the vale.

THEN Fingal eyed his valiant chiefs, his valiant chiefs took arms. The gloom of the battle roared, and Lochlin fled or died.— Pale, in his bounding ship he closed the maid of the raven hair. Her tomb ascends on Ardven, and the sea roars round the dark dwelling of Agandecca.

BLESSED be her soul, said Cuchullin, and blessed be the mouth of the song.—Strong was the youth of Fingal, and strong is his arm of age. Lochlin shall fall again before the king of ecchoing Morven. Shew thy face from a cloud, O moon; light his white sails on the wave of the night. And if any strong spirit* of heaven sits on that low-hung cloud; turn his dark ships from the rock, thou rider of the storm!

---

* This is the only passage in the poem that has the appearance of religion.—But Cuchullin's apostrophe to this spirit is accompanied with a doubt; so that it is not easy to determine whether the hero meant a superior being, or the ghosts of deceased warriors, who were supposed in those times to rule the storms, and to transport themselves in a gust of wind from one country to another.

SUCH were the words of Cuchullin at the sound of the mountain-stream, when Calmar ascended the hill, the wounded son of Matha. From the field he came in his blood. He leaned on his bending spear. Feeble is the arm of battle! but strong the soul of the hero!

WELCOME! O son of Matha, said Connal, welcome art thou to thy friends! Why bursts that broken sigh from the breast of him that never feared before?

AND never, Connal, will he fear, chief of the pointed steel. My soul brightens in danger, and exults in the noise of battle. I am of the race of steel; my fathers never feared.

CORMAR was the first of my race. He sported through the storms of the waves. His black skiff bounded on ocean, and travelled on the wings of the blast. A spirit once embroiled the night. Seas swell and rocks resound. Winds drive along the clouds. The lightning flies on wings of fire. He feared and came to land: then blushed that he feared at all. He rushed again among the waves to find the son of the wind. Three youths guide the bounding bark; he stood with the sword unsheathed. When the low-hung vapour passed, he took it by the curling head, and searched its dark womb with his steel. The son of the wind forsook the air. The moon and stars returned.

SUCH was the boldness of my race; and Calmar is like his fathers. Danger flies from the uplifted sword. They best succeed who dare.

BUT now, ye sons of green-vallyed Erin, retire from Lena's bloody heath. Collect the sad remnant of our friends, and join the sword of Fingal. I heard the sound of Lochlin's advancing arms; but Calmar will remain and fight. My voice shall be such, my friends, as if thousands were behind me. But, son of Semo, remember me. Remember Calmar's lifeless corse. After Fingal has wasted the field, place me by some stone of remembrance, that future times may hear my fame; and the mother of Calmar rejoice over the stone of my renown.

NO : son of Matha, said Cuchullin, I will never leave thee. My joy is in the unequal field: and my soul increases in danger. Connal, and Carril of other times, carry off the sad sons of Erin; and when the battle is over, search for our pale corses in this narrow way. For near this oak we shall stand in the stream of the battle of thousands.

O FITHIL'S son, with feet of wind, fly over the heath of Lena. Tell to Fingal that Erin is inthralled, and bid the king of Morven hasten. O let him come like the sun in a storm, when he shines on the hills of grass.

MORNING is gray on Cromla; the sons of the sea ascend. Calmar stood forth to meet them in the pride of his kindling foul. But pale was the face of the warrior; he leaned on his father's spear. That spear which he brought from Lara's hall, when the soul of his mother was sad.—But slowly now the hero falls like a tree on the plains of Cona. Dark Cuchullin stands alone like a rock* in a sandy vale. The sea comes with its waves, and roars on its hardened sides. Its head is covered with foam, and the hills are echoing around.—Now from the gray mist of the ocean, the white-sailed ships of Fingal appear. High is the grove of their masts as they nod, by turns, on the rolling wave.

SWARAN saw them from the hill, and returned from the sons of Erin. As ebbs the resounding sea through the hundred isles of Inistore; so loud, so vast, so immense returned the sons of Lochlin against the king of the desart hill. But bending, weeping, sad, and slow, and dragging his long spear behind, Cuchullin sunk in Cromla's wood, and mourned his fallen friends. He feared the face of Fingal, who was wont to greet him from the fields of renown.

HOW many lie there of my heroes! the chiefs of Inisfail! they that were chearful in the hall when the sound of the shells arose, No more shall I find their steps in the heath, or hear their voice in

---

* *Greek Quotation* HOM. II. 15
   So some tall rock o'erhangs the hoary main,
   By winds assail'd, by billows beat in vain, Unmov'd it hears, above, the tempests blow,
   And sees the watry mountains break below. POPE.

the chace of the hinds. Pale, silent, low on bloody beds are they who were my friends! O spirits of the lately-dead, meet Cuchullin on his heath. Converse with him on the wind, when the rustling tree of Tura's cave resounds. There, far remote, I shall lie unknown. No bard shall hear of me. No gray stone shall rise to my renown. Mourn me with the dead, O Bragela! departed is my fame.

SUCH were the words of Cuchullin when he sunk in the woods of Cromla.

FINGAL, tall in his ship, stretched his bright lance before him. Terrible was the gleam of the steel: it was like the green meteor of death, setting in the heath of Malmor, when the traveller is alone, and the broad moon is darkened in heaven.

THE battle is over, said the king, and I behold the blood of my friends. Sad is the heath of Lena; and mournful the oaks of Cromla: the hunters have fallen there in their strength; and the son of Semo is no more.—Ryno and Fillan, my sons, sound the horn of Fingal's war. Ascend that hill on the shore, and call the children of the foe. Call them from the grave of Lamdarg, the chief of other times.

BE your voice like that of your father, when he enters the battles of his strength. I wait for the dark mighty man; I wait on Lena's shore for Swaran. And let him come with all his race; for strong in battle are the friends of the dead.

FAIR Ryno flew like lightning; dark Fillan as the shade of autumn. On Lena's heath their voice is heard; the sons of ocean heard the horn of Fingal's war. As the roaring eddy of ocean returning from the kingdom of snows; so strong, so dark, so sudden came down the sons of Lochlin. The king in their front appears in the dismal pride of his arms. Wrath burns in his dark-brown face: and his eyes roll in the fire of his valour.

FINGAL beheld the son of Starno; and he remembered Agandecca.—For Swaran with the tears of youth had mourned his white-bosomed sister. He sent Ullin of the songs to bid him to the feast of shells. For pleasant on Fingal's soul returned the remembrance of the first of his loves.

ULLIN came with aged steps, and spoke to Starno's son. O thou that dwellest afar, surrounded, like a rock, with thy waves, come to the feast of the king, and pass the day in rest. To morrow let us fight, O Swaran, and break the ecchoing shields.

TO-DAY, said Starno's wrathful son, we break the ecchoing shields: to-morrow my feast will be spread; and Fingal lie on earth.

AND to-morrow let his feast be spread, said Fingal with a smile; for to-day, O my sons, we shall break the ecchoing shields.— Ossian, stand thou near my arm. Gaul, lift thy terrible sword. Fergus, bend thy crooked yew. Throw, Fillan, thy lance through heaven.—Lift your shields like the darkened moon. Be your spears the meteors of death. Follow me in the path of my fame; and equal my deeds in battle.

AS a hundred winds on Morven; as the streams of a hundred hills; as clouds fly successive over heaven; or, as the dark ocean assaults the shore of the desert: so roaring, so vast, so terrible the armies mixed on Lena's ecchoing heath.

THE groan of the people spread over the hills; it was like the thunder of night, when the cloud bursts on Cona; and a thousand ghosts shriek at once on the hollow wind.

FINGAL rushed on in his strength, terrible as the spirit of Trenmor; when, in a whirlwind, he comes to Morven to see the children of his pride. —The oaks resound on their hills, and the rocks fall down before him. Bloody was the hand of my father when he whirled the lightning of his sword. He remembers the battles of his youth, and the field is wasted in his course.

RYNO went on like a pillar of fire.—Dark is the brow of Gaul. Fergus rushed forward with feet of wind; and Fillan like the mist of the hill.— Myself*, like a rock, came down, I exulted in the strength of the king. Many were the deaths of my arm; and dismal was the gleam of my sword. My locks were not then so gray; nor

---

* Here the poet celebrates his own actions, but he does it in such a manner that we are not displeased. The mention of the great actions of his youth immediately suggests to him the helpless situation of his age. We do not despise him for selfish praise, but feel his misfortunes.

trembled my hands of age. My eyes were not closed in darkness; nor failed my feet in the race.

WHO can relate the deaths of the people; or the deeds of mighty heroes; when Fingal, burning in his wrath, consumed the sons of Lochlin? Groans swelled on groans from hill to hill, till night had covered all. Pale, staring like a herd of deer, the sons of Lochlin convene on Lena. We sat and heard the sprightly harp at Lubar's gentle stream. Fingal himself was next to the foe; and listened to the tales of bards. His godlike race were in the song, the chiefs of other times. Attentive, leaning on his shield, the king of Morven sat. The wind whistled through his aged locks, and his thoughts are of the days of other years. Near him on his bending spear, my young, my lovely Oscar stood. He admired the king of Morven: and his actions were swelling in his soul.

SON of my son, begun the king, O Oscar, pride of youth, I saw the shining of thy sword and gloried in my race. Pursue the glory of our fathers, and be what they have been; when Trenmor lived, the first of men, and Trathal the father of heroes. They fought the battle in their youth, and are the song of bards.

O OSCAR! bend the strong in arm: but spare the feeble hand. Be thou a stream of many tides against the foes of thy people; but like the gale that moves the grass to those who ask thine aid.—So Trenmor lived; such Trathal was; and such has Fingal been. My arm was the support of the injured; and the weak rested behind the lightning of my steel.

OSCAR! I was young like thee, when lovely Fainasóllis came: that sun-beam! that mild light of love! the daughter of Craca's* king! I then returned from Cona's heath, and few were in my train. A white-sailed boat appeared far off; we saw it like a mist that rode on ocean's blast. It soon approached; we saw the fair. Her white breast heaved with sighs. The wind was in her loose dark hair: her rosy cheek had tears.

---

* What the Craca here mentioned was, is not, at this distance of time, easy to determine. The most probable opinion is, that it was one of the Shetland isles— There is a story concerning a daughter of the king of Craca in the sixth book.

DAUGHTER of beauty, calm I said, what sigh is in that breast? Can I, young as I am, defend thee, daughter of the sea? My sword is not unmatched in war, but dauntless is my heart.

To thee I fly, with sighs she replied, O prince of mighty men! To thee I fly, chief of the generous shells, supporter of the feeble hand! The king of Craca's ecchoing isle owned me the sun-beam of his race. And often did the hills of Cromala reply to the sighs of love for the unhappy Fainasóllis. Sora's chief beheld me fair; and loved the daughter of Craca. His sword is like a beam of light upon the warrior's side. But dark is his brow; and tempests are in his soul. I shun him on the rolling sea; but Sora's chief pursues.

REST thou, I said, behind my shield; rest in peace, thou beam of light! The gloomy chief of Sora will fly, if Fingal's arm is like his soul. In some lone cave I might conceal thee, daughter of the sea! But Fingal never flies; for where the danger threatens, I rejoice in the storm of spears.

I SAW the tears upon her cheek. I pitied Craca's fair.

NOW, like a dreadful wave afar, appeared the ship of stormy Borbar. His masts high-bended over the sea behind their sheets of snow. White roll the waters on either side. The strength of ocean sounds. Come thou, I said, from the roar of ocean, thou rider of the storm. Partake the feast within my hall. It is the house of strangers.

THE maid stood trembling by my side; he drew the bow: she fell. Unerring is thy hand, I said, but feeble was the foe.

WE fought, nor weak was the strife of death. He sunk beneath my sword. We laid them in two tombs of stones; the hapless lovers of youth.

SUCH have I been in my youth, O Oscar; be thou like the age of Fingal. Never search for the battle, nor shun it when it comes.

FILLAN and Oscar of the dark-brown hair; ye children of the race; fly over the heath of roaring winds; and view the sons of Lochlin. Far off I hear the noise of their fear, like the storms of ecchoing Cona. Go: that they may not fly my sword along the waves of the north.—For many chiefs of Erin's race lie here on the dark bed of death. The children of the storm are low; the sons of ecchoing Cromla.

THE heroes flew like two dark clouds: two dark clouds that are the chariots of ghosts; when air's dark children come to frighten hapless men.

IT was then that Gaul*, the son of Morni, stood like a rock in the night. His spear is glittering to the stars; his voice like many streams.

SON of battle, cried the chief, O Fingal, king of shells! let the bards of many songs sooth Erin's friends to rest. And, Fingal, sheath thy sword of death; and let thy people fight. We wither away without our fame; for our king is the only breaker of shields. When morning rises on our hills, behold at a distance our deeds. Let Lochlin feel the sword of Morni's son, that bards may sing of me. Such was the custom heretofore of Fingal's noble race. Such was thine own, thou king of swords, in battles of the spear.

O SON of Morni, Fingal replied, I glory in thy fame.—Fight; but my spear shall be near to aid thee in the midst of danger. Raise, raise the voice, sons of the song, and lull me into rest. Here will Fingal lie amidst the wind of night.—And if thou, Agandecca, art near, among the children of thy land; if thou fittest on a blast of wind among the high-shrouded masts of Lochlin; come to my dreams†, my fair one, and shew thy bright face to my soul.

MANY a voice and many a harp in tuneful sounds arose. Of Fingal's noble deeds they sung, and of the noble race of the hero. And sometimes on the lovely sound was heard the name of the now mournful Ossian.

---

* Gaul, the son of Morni, was chief of a tribe that disputed long, the pre-eminence, with Fingal himself. They were reduced at last to obedience, and Gaul, from an enemy, turned Fingal's best friend and greatest hero. His character is something like that of Ajax in the Iliad; a hero of more strength than conduct in battle. He was very fond of military fame, and here he demands the next battle to himself.—The poet, by an artifice, removes Fingal, that his return may be the more magnificent.

† The poet prepares us for the dream of Fingal in the next book.

OFTEN have I fought, and often won in battles of the spear. But blind, and tearful, and forlorn I now walk with little men. O Fingal, with thy race of battle I now behold thee not. The wild roes feed upon the green tomb of the mighty king of Morven.—Blest be thy soul, thou king of swords, thou most renowned on the hills of Cona!

# FINGAL

## AN ANCIENT EPIC POEM
## IN SIX BOOKS

### BOOK IV*

HO comes with her songs from the mountain, like the bow of the showery Lena? It is the maid of the voice of love. The white-armed daughter of Toscar. Often hast thou heard my song, and given the tear of beauty. Dost thou come to the battles of thy people, and to hear the actions of Oscar? When shall I cease to mourn by the streams of the ecchoing Cona? My years have passed away in battle, and my age is darkened with sorrow.

DAUGHTER of the hand of snow! I was not so mournful and blind; I was not so dark and forlorn when Everallin loved me. Everallin with the dark-brown hair, the white-bosomed love of Cormac. A thousand heroes sought the maid, she denied her love to a thousand; the sons of the sword were despised; for graceful in her eyes was Ossian.

I WENT in suit of the maid to Lego's sable surge; twelve of my people were there, the sons of the streamy Morven. We came to Branno friend of strangers: Branno of the sounding mail.— From whence, he said, are the arms of steel? Not easy to win is the maid that has denied the blue-eyed sons of Erin. But blest be thou, O son of Fingal, happy is the maid that waits thee. Tho'

---

\* Fingal being asleep, and the action suspended by night, the poet introduces the story of his courtship of Evirallin the daughter of Branno. The episode is necessary to clear up several passages that follow in the poem; at the same time that it naturally brings on the action of the book, which may be supposed to begin about the middle of the third night from the opening of the poem.—This book, as many of Ossian's other compositions, is addressed to the beautiful Malvina the daughter of Toscar. She appears to have been in love with Oscar, and to have affected the company of the father after the death of the son.

twelve daughters of beauty were mine, thine were the choice, thou son of fame!—Then he opened the hall of the maid, the dark-haired Everallin. Joy kindled in our breasts of steel and blest the maid of Branno.

ABOVE us on the hill appeared the people of stately Cormac. Eight were the heroes of the chief; and the heath flamed with their arms. There Colla, Durra of the wounds, there mighty Toscar, and Tago, there Frestal the victorious stood; Dairo of the happy deeds, and Dala the battle's bulwark in the narrow way.—The sword flamed in the hand of Cormac, and graceful was the look of the hero.

EIGHT were the heroes of Ossian; Ullin stormy son of war; Mullo of the generous deeds; the noble, the graceful Scelacha; Oglan, and Cerdal the wrathful, and Dumariccan's brows of death. And why should Ogar be the last; so wide renowned on the hills of Ardven ?

OGAR met Dala the strong, face to face, on the field of heroes. The battle of the chiefs was like the wind on ocean's foamy waves. The dagger is remembered by Ogar; the weapon which he loved; nine times he drowned it in Dela's side. The stormy battle turned. Three times I broke on Cormac's shield: three times he broke his spear. But, unhappy youth of love! I cut his head away.—Five times I shook it by the lock. The friends of Cormac fled.

WHOEVER would have told me, lovely maid, when then I strove in battle; that blind, forsaken, and forlorn I now should pass the night; firm ought his mail to have been, and unmatched his arm in battle.

NOW* on Lena's gloomy heath the voice of music died away. The unconstant blast blew hard, and the high oak shook its leaves around me; of Everallin were my thoughts, when she, in all the light of beauty, and her blue eyes rolling in tears, stood on a cloud before my sight, and spoke with feeble voice.

---

* The poet returns to his subject. If one could fix the time of the year in which the action of the poem happened, from the scene described here, I should be tempted to place it in autumn —The trees shed their leaves, and the winds are variable, both which circumstances agree with that season of the year.

O OSSIAN, rise and save my son; save Oscar prince of men, near the red oak of Lubar's stream, he fights with Lochlin's sons.—She sunk into her cloud again. I clothed me with my steel. My spear supported my steps, and my rattling armour rung. I hummed, as I was wont in danger, the songs of heroes of old. Like distant thunder * Lochlin heard; they fled; my son pursued.

I CALLED him like a distant stream. My son return over Lena. No further pursue the foe, though Ossian is behind thee.—He came; and lovely in my ear was Oscar's sounding steel. Why didst thou stop my hand, he said, till death had covered all? For dark and dreadful by the stream they met thy son and Fillan. They watched the terrors of the night. Our swords have conquered some. But as the winds of night pour the ocean over the white sands of Mora, so dark advance the sons of Lochlin over Lena's rustling heath. The ghosts of night shriek afar; and I have seen the meteors of death. Let me awake the king of Morven, he that smiles in danger; for he is like the sun of heaven that rises in a storm.

FINGAL had started from a dream, and leaned on Trenmor's shield; the dark-brown shield of his fathers; which they had lifted of old in the battles of their race.

MY hero had seen in his rest the mournful form of Agandecca; she came from the way of the ocean, and slowly, lonely, moved over Lena. Her face was pale like the mist of Cromla; and dark were the tears of her cheek. She often raised her dim hand from her robe; her robe which was of the clouds of the desart: she raised her dim hand over Fingal, and turned away her silent eyes.

WHY weeps the daughter of Starno, said Fingal, with a sigh? Why is thy face so pale, thou daughter of the clouds?

---

* Ossian gives the reader a high idea of himself. His very song frightens the enemy. This passage resembles one in the eighteenth Iliad, where the voice of Achilles frightens the Trojans from the body of Patroclus.

> Forth march'd the chief, and distant from the crowd
> High on the rampart rais'd his voice aloud.
> So high his brazen voice the hero rear'd,
> Hosts drop their arms and trembled as they fear'd. POPE.

SHE departed on the wind of Lena; and left him in the midst of the night.—She mourned the sons of her people that were to fall by Fingal's hand.

THE hero started from rest, and still beheld her in his soul.—The sound of Oscar's steps approached. The king saw the gray shield on his side. For the faint beam of the morning came over the waters of Ullin.

WHAT do the foes in their fear, said the rising king of Morven? Or fly they through ocean's foam, or wait they the battle of steel? But why should Fingal ask? I hear their voice on the early wind.—Fly over Lena's heath, O Oscar, and awake our friends to battle.

THE king stood by the stone of Lubar; and thrice reared his terrible voice. The deer started from the fountains of Cromla; and all the rocks shook on their hills. Like the noise of a hundred mountain-streams, that burst, and roar, and foam: like the clouds that gather to a tempest on the blue face of the sky; so met the sons of the desert, round the terrible voice of Fingal. For pleasant was the voice of the king of Morven to the warriors of his land: for often had he led them to battle, and returned with the spoils of the foe.

COME to battle, said the king, ye children of the storm. Come to the death of thousands. Comhal's son will see the fight.—My sword shall wave on that hill, and be the shield of my people. But never may you need it, warriors; while the son of Morni fights, the chief of mighty men.—He shall lead my battle; that his fame may rise in the song.

O YE ghosts of heroes dead! ye riders of the storm of Cromla! receive my falling people with joy, and bring them to your hills.—And may the blast of Lena carry them over my seas, that they may come to my silent dreams, and delight my soul in rest.

FILLAN and Oscar, of the dark-brown hair! fair Ryno, with the pointed steel! advance with valour to the fight; and behold the son of Morni. Let your swords be like his in the strife: and behold the deeds of his hands. Protect the friends of your father: and remember the chiefs of old. My children, I will see you yet, though here ye should fall in Erin. Soon shall our cold, pale ghosts meet in a cloud, and fly over the hills of Cona.

NOW like a dark and stormy cloud, edged round with the red lightning of heaven, and flying westward from the morning's beam, the king of hills removed. Terrible is the light of his armour, and two spears are in his hand.—His gray hair falls on the wind.— He often looks back on the war. Three bards attend the son of fame, to carry his words to the heroes.—High on Cromla's side he sat, waving the lightning of his sword, and as he waved we moved.

JOY rose in Oscar's face. His cheek is red. His eye sheds tears. The sword is a beam of fire in his hand. He came, and smiling, spoke to Ossian.

O RULER of the fight of steel! my father, hear thy son. Retire with Morven's mighty chief; and give me Ossian's fame. And if here I fall; my king, remember that breast of snow, that lonely sun-beam of my love, the white-handed daughter of Toscar. For with red cheek from the rock, and bending over the stream, her soft hair flies about her bosom as she pours the sigh for Oscar. Tell her I am on my hills a lightly-bounding son of the wind; that hereafter, in a cloud, I may meet the lovely maid of Toscar.

RAISE, Oscar, rather raise my tomb. I will not yield the fight to thee. For first and bloodiest in the war my arm shall teach thee how to fight. But, remember, my son, to place this sword, this bow, and the horn of my deer, within that dark and narrow house, whose mark is one gray stone. Oscar, I have no love to leave to the care of my son; for graceful Evirallin is no more, the lovely daughter of Branno.

SUCH were our words, when Gaul's loud voice came growing on the wind. He waved on high the sword of his father, and rushed to death and wounds.

AS waves white-bubbling over the deep come swelling, roaring on; as rocks of ooze meet roaring waves: so foes attacked and fought. Man met with man, and steel with steel. Shields sound, men fall. As a hundred hammers on the son of the furnace, so rose, so rung their swords.

GAUL rushed on like a whirlwind in Ardven. The destruction of heroes is on his sword. Swaran was like the fire of the desert in the ecchoing heath of Gormal. How can I give to the song the death of many spears? My sword rose high, and flamed in the strife of blood. And, Oscar, terrible wert thou, my best, my greatest son! I rejoiced in my secret soul, when his sword flamed over the slain. They fled amain through Lena's heath: and we pursued and flew. As stones that bound from rock to rock; as axes in eechoing woods; as thunder rolls from hill to hill in dismal broken peals; so blow succeeded to blow, and death to death, from the hand of Oscar* and mine.

BUT Swaran closed round Morni's son, as the strength of the tide of Inistore. The king half-rose from his hill at the sight, and half-assumed the spear. Go, Ullin, go, my aged bard, begun the king of Morven. Remind the mighty Gaul of battle; remind him of his fathers. Support the yielding fight with song; for song enlivens war. Tall Ullin went, with steps of age, and spoke to the king of swords.

SON† of the chief of generous steeds! high-bounding king of spears. Strong arm in every perilous toil. Hard heart that never yields. Chief of the pointed arms of death. Cut down the foe; let no white sail bound round dark Inistore. Be thine arm like thunder. Thine eyes like fire, thy heart of solid rock. Whirl round thy sword as a meteor at night, and lift thy shield like the flame of death. Son of the chief of generous steeds, cut down the foe; destroy.—The hero's heart beat high. But Swaran came with battle. He cleft the shield of Gaul in twain; and the sons of the desert fled.

---

* Ossian never fails to give a fine character of his beloved son. His speech to his father is that of a hero; it contains the submission due to a parent, and the warmth that becomes a young warrior. There is a propriety in dwelling here on the actions of Oscar, as the beautiful Malvina, to whom the book is addressed, was in love with that hero.

† The war-song of Ullin varies from the rest of the poem in the versification. It runs down like a torrent; and consists almost intirely of epithets. The custom of encouraging men in battle with extempore rhymes, has been carried down almost to our own times. Several of these war-songs are extant, but the most of them are only a group of epithets, without beauty or harmony, utterly destitute of poetical merit.

NOW Fingal arose in his might, and thrice he reared his voice. Cromla answered around, and the sons of the desert stood still.— They bent their red faces to earth, ashamed at the presence of Fingal. He came like a cloud of rain in the days of the sun, when slow it rolls on the hill, and fields expect the shower. Swaran beheld the terrible king of Morven, and stopped in the midst of his course. Dark he leaned on his spear, rolling his red eyes around. Silent and tall he seemed as an oak on the banks of Lubar, which had its branches blasted of old by the lightning of heaven.— It bends over the stream, and the gray moss whistles in the wind: so stood the king. Then slowly he retired to the rising heath of Lena. His thousands pour around the hero, and the darkness of battle gathers on the hill.

FINGAL, like a beam from heaven, shone in the midst of his people. His heroes gather around him, and he sends forth the voice of his power. Raise my standards* on high,—spread them on Lena's wind, like the flames of an hundred hills. Let them sound on the winds of Erin, and remind us of the fight. Ye sons of the roaring streams, that pour from a thousand hills, be near the king of Morven: attend to the words of his power. Gaul strongest arm of death! O Oscar, of the future fights; Connal, son of the blue blades of Sora; Dermid of the dark-brown hair, and Ossian king of many songs, be near your father's arm.

WE reared the sun-beam† of battle; the standard of the king. Each hero's soul exulted with joy, as, waving, it flew on the wind. It was studded with gold above, as the blue wide shell of the nightly sky. Each hero had his standard too; and each his gloomy men.

BEHOLD, said the king of generous shells, how Lochlin divides on Lena.—They stand like broken clouds on the hill, or

---

* Th' imperial ensign, which full high advanc'd,
   Shone like a meteor streaming to the wind. MILTON.
   † Fingal's standard was distinguished by the name of *sun-beam*; probably on account of its bright colour, and its being studded with gold. To begin a battle is expressed, in old composition, by *lifting of the sun-beam*.

an half consumed grove of oaks; when we see the sky through its branches, and the meteor passing behind. Let every chief among the friends of Fingal take a dark, troop of those that so high; nor let a son of the ecchoing groves bound on the waves of Inistore.

MINE, said. Gaul, be the seven chiefs that came from Lano's lake.—Let Inistore's dark king, said Oscar, come to the sword of Ossian's son.— To mine the king of Iniscon, said Connal, heart of steel! Or Mudan's chief or I, said brown-haired Dermid, shall sleep on clay-cold earth. My choice, though now so weak and dark, was Terman's battling king; I promised with my hand to win the hero's dark-brown shield.—Blest and victorious be my chiefs, said Fingal of the mildest look; Swaran, king of roaring waves, thou art the choice of Fingal.

NOW, like an hundred different winds that pour through, many vales; divided, dark the sons of the hill advanced, and Cromla ecchoed around.

HOW can I relate the deaths when we closed in the strife of our steel? O daughter of Toscar! bloody were our hands! The gloomy ranks of Lochlin fell like the banks of the roaring Cona.— Our arms were victorious on Lena: each chief fulfilled his promise. Beside the murmur of Branno thou didst often sit, O maid; when thy white bosom rose frequent, like the down of the swan when slow she sails the lake, and sidelong winds are blowing.— Thou hast seen the sun\* retire red and flow behind his cloud; night gathering round on the mountain, while the unfrequent blast† roared in narrow vales. At length the rain beats hard; and

---

\* Latin Quotation VIRG.
Above the rest the sun, who never lies, Foretels the change of weather in the skies. For if he rise, unwilling to his race, Clouds on his brow and spots upon his face; Or if thro' mists he shoots his fallen beams, Frugal of light, in loose and straggling streams, Suspect a drifting day. DRYDEN.

† Latin Quotation VIRG.
For ere the rising winds begin to roar,
The working seas advance to wash the shore;
Soft whispers run along the leafy wood,
And mountains whittle to the murm'ring flood. DRYDEN.

thunder rolls in peals. Lightning glances on the rocks. Spirits ride on beams of fire. And the strength of the mountain-streams* comes roaring down the hills. Such was the noise of battle, maid of the arms of snow. Why, daughter of the hill, that tear? the maids of Lochlin have cause to weep. The people of their country fell, for bloody were the blue blades of the race of my heroes. But I am sad, forlorn, and blind; and no more the companion of heroes. Give, lovely maid, to me thy tears, for I have seen the tombs of all my friends.

IT was then by Fingal's hand a hero fell, to his grief.—Gray-haired he rolled in the dust, and lifted his faint eyes to the king. And is it by me thou hast fallen, said the son of Comhal, thou friend of Agandecca! I have seen thy tears for the maid of my love in the halls of the bloody Starno. Thou hast been the foe of the foes of my love, and hast thou fallen by my hand? Raise, Ullin, raise the grave of the son of Mathon; and give his name to the song of Agandecca; for dear to my soul hast thou been, thou darkly-dwelling maid of Ardven.

CUCHULLIN, from the cave of Cromla, heard the noise of the troubled war. He called to Connal chief of swords, and Carril of other times. The gray-haired heroes heard his voice, and took their aspen spears.

THEY came, and saw the tide of battle, like the crowded waves of the ocean; when the dark wind blows from the deep, and rolls the billows through the sandy vale.

CUCHULLIN kindled at the fight, and darkness gathered on his brow. His hand is on the sword of his fathers: his red-rolling eyes on the foe. He thrice attempted to rush to battle, and thrice did Connal stop him: Chief of the isle of mist, he said, Fingal subdues the foe. Seek not a part of the fame of the king; himself is like the storm.

THEN, Carril, go, replied the chief, and greet the king of

---

* Latin Quotation VIRG.
   The rapid rains, descending from the hills,
   To rolling torrents swell the creeping rills. DRYDEN.

Morven. When Lochlin falls away like a stream after rain, and the
noise of the battle is over. Then be thy voice sweet in his ear to
praise the king of swords. Give him the sword of Caithbat, for
Cuchullin is worthy no more to lift the arms of his fathers.

BUT, O ye ghosts of the lonely Cromla! ye souls of chiefs that
are no more! be ye the companions of Cuchullin, and talk to him
in, the cave of his sorrow. For never more shall I be renowned
among the mighty in the land. I am like a beam that has shone,
like a mist that fled away; when the blast of the morning came,
and brightened the shaggy side of the hill. Connal! talk of arms no
more: departed is my fame.—My sighs shall be on Cromla's wind;
till my footsteps cease to be seen.—And thou, white-bosom'd
Bragela, mourn over the fall of my fame; for, vanquished, I will
never return to thee, thou sun-beam of Dunscaich.

# FINGAL

## AN ANCIENT EPIC POEM
## IN SIX BOOKS

### BOOK V*

OW Connal, on Cromla's windy side, spoke to the chief of the noble car. Why that gloom, son of Semo? Our friends are the mighty in battle. And renowned art thou, O warrior! many were the deaths of thy steel. Often has Bragela met with blue-rolling eyes of joy often has she met her hero, returning in the midst of the valiant; when his sword was red with slaughter, and his foes silent in the fields of the tomb. Pleasant to her ears were thy bards, when thine actions rose in the song.

BUT behold the king of Morven; he moves below like a pillar of fire. His strength is like the stream of Lubar, or the wind of the ecchoing Cromla; when the branchy forests of night are over-turned.

HAPPY are thy people, O Fingal, thine arm shall fight their battles: thou art the first in their dangers; the wisest in the days of their peace. Thou speakest and thy thousands obey; and armies' tremble at the sound of thy steel. Happy are thy people, Fingal, chief of the lonely hills.

WHO is that so dark and terrible coming in the thunder of his course? who is it but Starno's son to meet the king of Morven?

---

* The fourth day still continues. The poet by putting the narration in the mouth of Connal, who still remained with Cuchullin on the side of Cromla, gives propriety to the praises of Fingal. The beginning of this book, in the original, is one of the most beautiful parts of the poem. The verisification is regular and full, and agrees very well with the sedate character of Connal.—No poet has adapted the cadence of his verse more to the temper of the speaker, than Ossian has done. It is more than probable that the whole poem was originally designed to be sung to the harp, as the versification is so various, and so much suited to the different passions of the human mind.

Behold the battle of the chiefs: it is like the storm of the ocean, when two spirits meet far distant, and contend for the rolling of the wave. The hunter hears the noise on his hill; and sees the high billows advancing to Ardven's shore.

SUCH were the words of Connal, when the heroes met in the midst of their falling people. There was the clang of arms! there, every blow, like the hundred hammers of the furnace! Terrible is the battle of the kings, and horrid the look of their eyes. Their dark-brown shields are cleft in twain; and their steel flies, broken, from their helmets. They fling their weapons down. Each rushes* to his hero's grasp. Their sinewy arms bend round each other: they turn from side to side, and strain and stretch their large spreading limbs below. But when the pride of their strength arose, they shook the hill with their heels; rocks tumble from their places on high; the green-headed bushes are overturned. At length the strength of Swaran fell; and the king of the groves is bound.

THUS have I seen on Cona; but Court I behold no more, thus have I seen two dark hills removed from their place by the strength of the bursting stream. They turn from side to side, and their tall oaks meet one another on high. Then they fall together with all their rocks and trees. The streams are turned by their sides, and the red ruin is seen afar.

SONS of the king of Morven, said the noble Fingal, guard the king of Lochlin; for he is strong as his thousand waves. His hand is taught to the battle, and his race of the times of old. Gaul, thou first of my heroes, and Ossian king of songs, attend the friend of Agandecca, and raise to joy his grief.—But, Oscar, Fillan, and Ryno, ye children of the race! pursue the rest of Lochlin over the heath of

---

\* This passage resembles one in the twenty third Iliad.
  Close lock'd above their heads and arms are mixt;
  Below their planted feet at distance fixt;
  Now to the grasp each manly body bend;
  The humid sweat from ev'ry pore descends;
  Their bones resound with blows: sides, shoulders, thighs,
  Swell to each gripe, and bloody tumours rise. POPE.

Lena; that no vessel may hereafter bound on the dark-rolling waves of Inistore.

THEY flew like lightning over the heath. He slowly moved as a cloud of thunder when the sultry plain of summer is silent. His sword is before him as a sun-beam, terrible as the streaming meteor of night. He came toward a chief of Lochlin, and spoke to the son of the wave.

WHO is that like a cloud at the rock of the roaring stream? He cannot bound over its course; yet stately is the chief! his bossy shield is on his side; and his spear like the tree of the desart. Youth of the dark-brown hair, art thou of Fingal's foes?

I AM a son of Lochlin, he cries, and strong is my arm in war. My spouse is weeping at home, but Orla* will never return.

OR fights or yields the hero, said Fingal of the noble deeds? foes do not conquer in my presence; but my friends are renowned in the hall. Son of the wave, follow me, partake the feast of my shells, and pursue the deer of my desart.

NO: said the hero, I assist the feeble: my strength shall remain with the weak in arms. My sword has been always unmatched, O warrior: let the king of Morven yield.

I NEVER yielded, Orla, Fingal never yielded to man. Draw thy sword and chuse thy foe. Many are my heroes.

AND does the king refuse the combat, said Orla of the dark-brown hair? Fingal is a match for Orla: and he alone of all his race.

BUT, king of Morven, if I shall fall; as one time the warrior must die; raise my tomb in the midst, and let it be the greatest on Lena. And send, over the dark-blue wave, the sword of Orla to the spouse of his love; that she may shew it to her son, with tears, to kindle his soul to war.

SON of the mournful tale, said Fingal, why dost thou awaken

---

* The story of Orla is so beautiful and affecting in the original, that many are in possession of it in the north of Scotland, who never heard a syllable more of the poem. It varies the action, and awakes the attention of the reader when he expected nothing but languor in the conduct of the poem, as the great action was over in the conquest of Swaran.

my tears? One day the warriors must die, and the children see their useless arms in the hall. But, Orla, thy tomb shall rise, and thy white-bosomed spouse weep over thy sword.

THEY fought on the heath of Lena, but feeble was, the arm of Orla. The sword of Fingal descended, and cleft his shield in twain. It fell and glittered on the ground, as the moon on the stream of night.

KING of Morven, said the hero, lift thy sword, and pierce my breast. Wounded and faint from battle my friends have left me here. The mournful tale shall come to my love on, the banks of the streamy Loda; when she is alone in the wood; and the rustling blast in the leaves.

NO; said the king of Morven, I will never wound thee, Orla. On the banks of Loda let her see thee escaped from the hands of war. Let thy gray-haired father, who, perhaps, is blind with age, hear the sound of thy voice in his hall.—With joy let the hero rise, and search for his son with his hands.

BUT never will he find him, Fingal; said the youth of the streamy Loda.—On Lena's heath I shall die; and foreign bards will talk of me. My broad belt covers my wound of death. And now I give it to the wind.

THE dark blood poured from his side, he fell pale on the heath of Lena. Fingal bends over him as he dies, and calls his younger heroes.

OSCAR and Fillan, my sons, raise high the memory of Orla. Here let the dark-haired hero rest far from the spouse of his love. Here let him rest in his narrow house far from the sound of Loda.

THE sons of the feeble will find his bow at home, but will not be able to bend it. His faithful dogs howl on his hills, and his boars, which he used to pursue, rejoice. Fallen is the arm of battle; the mighty among the valiant is low!

EXALT the voice, and blow the horn, ye sons of the king of Morven: let us go back to Swaran, and send the night away on song. Fillan, Oscar, and Ryno, fly over the heath of Lena. Where,

Ryno, art thou, young son of fame? Thou art not wont to be the last to answer thy father.

RYNO, said Ullin first of bards, is with the awful forms of his fathers. With Trathal king of shields, and Trenmor of the mighty deeds. The youth is low,—the youth is pale,—he lies on Lena's heath.

AND fell the swiftest in the race, said the king, the first to bend the bow? Thou scarce hast been known to me; why did young Ryno fall? But sleep thou softly on Lena, Fingal shall soon behold thee. Soon shall my voice be heard no more, and my footsteps cease to be seen. The bards will tell of Fingal's name; the stones will talk of me. But, Ryno, thou art low indeed,—thou hast not received thy fame. Ullin, strike the harp for Ryno; tell what the chief would have been. Farewel, thou first in every field. No more shall I direct thy dart. Thou that hast been so fair; I behold thee not—Farewel.

THE tear is on the cheek of the king, for terrible was his son in war. His son! that was like a beam of fire by night on the hill; when the forests sink down in its course, and the traveller trembles at the sound.

WHOSE fame is in that dark-green tomb, begun the king of generous shells? four stones with their heads of moss stand there; and mark the narrow house of death. Near it let my Ryno rest, and be the neighbour of the valiant. Perhaps some chief of fame is here to fly with my son on clouds. O Ullin, raise the songs of other times. Bring to memory the dark dwellers of the tomb. If in the field of the valiant they never fled from danger, my son shall rest with them, far from his friends, on the heath of Lena.

HERE, said the mouth of the song, here rest the first of heroes. Silent is Lamderg* in this tomb, and Ullin king of swords. And who, soft smiling from her cloud, shews me her face of love? Why, daughter, why so pale art thou, first of the maids of Cromla?

---

* Lamh-dhearg signifies *bloody hand*. Gelchossa, *white legged*, Tuathal, *surly*. Ulfadda, *long-beard*. Ferchios, *the conquerer of men*.

Dost thou sleep with the foes in battle, Gelchossa, white-bosomed daughter of Tuathal?—Thou hast been the love of thousands, but Lamderg was thy love. He came to Selma's mossy towers, and, striking his dark buckler, spoke:

WHERE is Gelchossa, my love, the daughter of the noble Tuathal? I left her in the hall of Selma, when I fought with the gloomy Ulfadda. Return soon, O Lamderg, she said, for here I am in the midst of sorrow. Her white breast rose with sighs. Her cheek was wet with tears. But I see her not coming to meet me; and to sooth my soul after battle. Silent is the hall of my joy; I hear not the voice of the bard.—Bran* does not shake his chains at the gate, glad at the coming of Lamderg. Where is Gelchossa, my love, the mild daughter of the generous Tuathal?

LAMDERG! says Ferchios the son of Aidon, Gelchossa may be on Cromla; she and the maids of the bow pursuing the flying deer.

FERCHIOS! replied the chief of Cromla, no noise meets the ear of Lamderg. No sound is in the woods of Lena. No deer fly in my fight. No panting dog pursues. I see not Gelchossa my love, fair as the full moon setting on the hills of Cromla. Go, Ferchios, go to Allad† the gray-haired son of the rock. His dwelling is in the circle of stones. He may know of Gelchossa.

THE son of Aidon went; and spoke to the ear of age. Allad! thou that dwellest in the rock: thou that tremblest alone, what saw thine eyes of age?

I SAW, answered Allad the old, Ullin the son of Cairbar. He came like a cloud from Cromla; and he hummed a surly song like a blast in a leafless wood. He entered the hall of Selma.—Lamderg, he said, most dreadful of men, fight or yield to Ullin. Lamderg,

---

\* Bran is a common name of gray-hounds to this day. It is a custom in the north of Scotland, to give the names of the heroes mentioned in this poem, to their dogs; a proof that they are familiar to the car, and their fame generally known.

† Allad is plainly a druid: he is called the son of the rock, from his dwelling in a cave; and the circle of stones here mentioned is the pale of the druidical temple. He is here consulted as one who had a supernatural knowledge of things; from the druids, no doubt, came the ridiculous notion of the second fight, which prevailed in the highlands and isles.

replied Gelchossa, the son of battle, is not here. He fights Ulfada mighty chief. He is not here, thou first of men. But Lamderg never yielded. He will fight the son of Cairbar.

LOVELY art thou, said terrible Ullin, daughter of the generous Tuathal. I carry thee to Cairbar's halls. The valiant shall have Gelchossa. Three days I remain on Cromla, to wait that son of battle, Lamderg. On the fourth Gelchossa is mine, if the mighty Lamderg flies.

ALLAD! said the chief of Cromla, peace to thy dreams in the cave. Ferchios, sound the horn of Lamderg that Ullin may hear on Cromla. Lamderg*, like a roaring storm, ascended the hill from Selma. He hummed a surly song as he went, like the noise of a falling stream. He stood like a cloud on the hill, that varies its form to the wind. He rolled a stone, the sign of war. Ullin heard in Cairbar's hall. The hero heard, with joy, his foe, and took his father's spear. A smile brightens his dark-brown cheek, as he places his sword by his side. The dagger glittered in his hand. He whistled as he went.

GELCHOSSA saw the silent chief, as a wreath of mist ascending the hill.—She struck her white and heaving breast; and silent, tearful, feared for Lamderg.

CAIRBAR, hoary chief of shells, said the maid of the tender hand; I must bend the bow on Cromla; for I see the dark-brown hinds.

SHE hasted up the hill. In vain! the gloomy heroes fought.— Why should I tell the king of Morven how wrathful heroes fight!— Fierce Ullin fell. Young Lamderg came all pale to the daughter of generous Tuathal.

WHAT blood, my love, the soft-haired woman said, what blood runs down my warrior's side?—It is Ullin's blood, the chief replied, thou fairer than the snow of Cromla! Gelchossa, let me rest here a little while. The mighty Lamderg died.

---

* The reader will find this passage altered from what it was in the fragments of ancient poetry.—It is delivered down very differently by tradition, and the translator has chosen that reading which favours least of bombast.

AND sleepest thou so soon on earth, O chief of shady Cromla? three days she mourned beside her love.—The hunters found her dead. They raised this tomb above the three. Thy son, O king of Morven, may rest here with heroes.

AND here my son will rest, said Fingal, the noise of their fame has reached my ears. Fillan and Fergus! bring hither Orla; the pale youth of the stream of Loda. Not unequalled shall Ryno lie in earth when Orla is by his side. Weep, ye daughters of Morven; and ye maids of the streamy Loda. Like a tree they grew on the hills; and they have fallen like the oak* of the desert; when it lies across a stream, and withers in the wind of the mountain.

OSCAR! chief of every youth! thou seest how they have fallen. Be thou, like them, on earth renowned. Like them the song of bards. Terrible were their forms in battle; but calm was Ryno in the days of peace. He was like the bow† of the shower seen far distant on the stream; when the sun is setting on Mora, and silence on the hill of deer. Rest, youngest of my sons, rest, O Ryno, on Lena. We too shall be no more; for the warrior one day must fall.

SUCH was thy grief, thou king of hills, when Ryno lay on earth. What must the grief of Ossian be, for thou thyself art gone. I hear not thy distant voice on Cona. My eyes perceive thee not. Often forlorn and dark I sit at thy tomb; and feel it with my hands. When I think I hear thy voice; it is but the blast of the desert.— Fingal has long since fallen asleep, the ruler of the war.

THEN Gaul and Ossian sat with Swaran on the soft green banks of Lubar. I touched the harp to please the king. But gloomy

---

* *Greek Quotation* HOM. II. 16.
——as the mountain oak
Nods to the ax, till with a groaning sound
It sinks, and spreads its honours on the ground. POPE.
† ——a bow
Conspicuous with three lifted colours gay.
—What mean those colour'd streaks in heav'n,
Distended as the brow of God appeas'd,
Or serve they as a flow'ry verge to bind
The fluid skirts of that same watry cloud? MILTON

was his brow. He rolled his red eyes towards Lena. The hero mourned his people.

I LIFTED my eyes to Cromla, and I saw the son of generous Semo.—Sad and slow he retired from his hill towards the lonely cave of Tura. He saw Fingal victorious, and mixed his joy with grief. The sun is bright on his armour, and Connal slowly followed. They sunk behind the hill like two pillars of the fire of night: when winds pursue them over the mountain, and the flaming heath resounds. Beside a stream of roaring foam his cave is in a rock. One tree bends above it; and the rushing winds eccho against its sides. Here rests the chief of Dunscaich, the son of generous Semo. His thoughts are on the battles he lost; and the tear is on his cheek. He mourned the departure of his fame that fled like the mist of Cona. O Bragela, thou art too far remote to cheer the soul of the hero. But let him see thy bright form in his soul; that his thoughts may return to the lonely sun-beam of Dunscaich.

WHO comes with the locks of age? It is the son of the songs. Hail, Carril of other times, thy voice is like the harp in the halls of Tura. Thy, words are pleasant as the shower that falls on the fields of the sun. Carril of the times of old, why comest thou from the son of the generous Semo?

OSSIAN king of swords, replied the bard, thou best raisest the song. Long hast thou been known to Carril, thou ruler of battles. Often have I touched the harp to lovely Evirallin. Thou too hast often accompanied my voice in Branno's hall of generous shells. And often, amidst our voices, was heard the mildest Evirallin. One day she sung of Cormac's fall, the youth that died for her love. I saw the tears on her cheek, and on thine, thou chief of men. Her soul was touched for the unhappy, though she loved him not. How fair among a thousand maids was the daughter of the generous Branno!

BRING not, Carril, I replied, bring not her memory to my mind. My soul must melt at the remembrance. My eyes must have their tears. Pale in the earth is she the softly-blushing fair of my love.

BUT sit thou on the heath, O Bard, and let us hear thy voice.
It is pleasant as the gale of spring that sighs on the hunter's ear;
when he wakens from dreams of joy, and has heard the music of
the spirits* of the hill.

---

\* ——Others more mild
Retreated in a silent valley, sing
With notes angelical.——
——The harmony,
What could it less when spirits immortal sing?
Suspended hell, and took with ravishment
The thronging audience. MILTON.

# FINGAL

## AN ANCIENT EPIC POEM
## IN SIX BOOKS

### BOOK VI*

HE clouds of night came rolling down and rest on Cromla's dark-brown steep. The stars of the north arise over the rolling of the waves of Ullin; they shew their heads of fire through the flying mist of heaven. A distant wind roars in the wood; but silent and dark is the plain of death.

STILL on the darkening Lena arose in my ears the tuneful voice of Carril. He sung of the companions of our youth, and the days of former years; when we met on the banks of Lego, and sent round the joy of the shell. Cromla, with its cloudy steeps, answered to his voice. The ghosts of those he sung came in their rustling blasts. They were seen to bend with joy towards the sound of their praise.

BE thy soul blest, O Carril, in the midst of thy eddying winds. O that thou wouldst come to my hall when I am alone by night!— And thou dost come, my friend, I hear often thy light hand on my harp; when it hangs on the distant wall, and the feeble sound touches my ear. Why dost thou not speak to me in my grief, and tell when I shall behold my friends? But thou passest away in thy murmuring blast; and thy wind whittles through the gray hair of Ossian.

NOW on the side of Mora the heroes gathered to the feast. A

---

* This book opens with the fourth night, and ends on the morning of the sixth day. The time of five days, five nights, and a part of the sixth day is taken up in the poem. The scene lies in the heath of Lena, and the mountain Cromla on the coast of Ulster.

thousand aged oaks are burning to the wind.—The strength* of the shells goes round. And the souls of warriors brighten with joy. But the king of Lochlin is silent, and sorrow reddens in the eyes of his pride. He often turned toward Lena and remembered that he fell.

FINGAL leaned on the shield of his fathers. His gray locks slowly waved on the wind, and glittered to the beam of night. He saw the grief of Swaran, and spoke to the first of Bards.

RAISE, Ullin, raise the song of peace, and sooth my soul after battle, that my ear may forget the noise of arms. And let a hundred harps be near to gladden the king of Lochlin. He must depart from us with joy.—None ever went sad from Fingal. Oscar! the lightning of my sword is against the strong in battle; but peaceful it lies by my side when warriors yield in war.

TRENMOR†, said the mouth of the songs, lived in the days of other years. He bounded over the waves of the north: companion of the storm. The high rocks of the land of Lochlin, and its groves of murmuring sounds appeared to the hero through the mist;— he bound his white-bosomed sails.—Trenmor pursued the boar that roared along the woods of Gormal. Many had fled from its presence; but the spear of Trenmor slew it.

THREE chiefs that beheld the deed, told of the mighty stranger. They told that he stood like a pillar of fire in the bright arms of his valour. The king of Lochlin prepared the feast, and called the blooming Trenmor. Three days he feasted at Gormal's windy towers; and got his choice in the combat.

---

* By the strength of the shell is meant the liquor the heroes drunk: of what kind it was, cannot be ascertained at this distance of time. The translator has met with several ancient poems that mention waxlights and wine as common in the halls of Fingal. The names of both are borrowed from the Latin, which plainly shews that our ancestors had them from the Romans, if they had them at all. The Caledonians in their frequent incursions to the province might become acquainted with those conveniencies of life, and introduce them into their own country, among the booty which they carried from South Britain.

† Trenmor was great grandfather to Fingal. The story is introduced to facilitate the dismission of Swaran.

THE land of Lochlin had no hero that yielded not to Trenmor. The shell of joy went round with songs in praise of the king of Morven; he that came over the waves, the first of mighty men.

NOW when the fourth gray morn arose, the hero launched his ship; and walking along the silent shore waited for the rushing wind. For loud and distant he heard the blast murmuring in the grove.

COVERED over with arms of steel a son of the woody Gormal appeared. Red was his cheek and fair his hair. His skin like the snow of Morven. Mild rolled his blue and smiling eye when he spoke to the king of swords.

STAY, Trenmor, stay thou first of men, thou hast not conquered Lonval's son. My sword has often met the brave. And the wise shun the strength of my bow.

THOU fair-haired youth, Trenmor replied, I will not fight with Lonval's son. Thine arm is feeble, sun-beam of beauty. Retire to Gormal's dark-brown hinds.

BUT I will retire, replied the youth, with the sword of Trenmor; and exult in the sound of my fame. The virgins shall gather with smiles around him who conquered Trenmor. They shall sigh with the sighs of love, and admire the length of thy spear; when I shall carry it among thousands, and lift the glittering point to the sun.

THOU shalt never carry my spear, said the angry king of Morven.—Thy mother shall find thee pale on the shore of the ecchoing Gormal; and, looking over the dark-blue deep, see the sails of him that slew her son.

I WILL not lift the spear, replied the youth, my arm is not strong with years. But with the feathered dart, I have learned to pierce a distant foe. Throw down that heavy mail of steel; for Trenmor is covered all over.—I first, will lay my mail on earth.— Throw now thy dart, thou king of Morven.

HE saw the heaving of her breast. It was the sister of the king.—She had seen him in the halls of Gormal; and loved his face of youth.—The spear dropt from the hand of Trenmor: he bent his red cheek to the ground, for he had seen her like a beam of light that meets the sons of the cave, when they revisit the fields of the sun, and bend their aching eyes.

CHIEF of the windy Morven, begun the maid of the arms of snow; let me rest in thy bounding ship, far from the love of Corlo. For he, like the thunder of the desart, is terrible to Inibaca. He loves me in the gloom of his pride, and shakes ten thousand spears.

REST thou in peace, said the mighty Trenmor, behind the shield of my fathers. I will not fly from the chief, though he shakes ten thousand spears.

THREE days he waited on the shore; and sent his horn abroad. He called Corlo to battle from all his ecchoing hills. But Corlo came not to battle. The king of Lochlin descended. He feasted on the roaring shore; and gave the maid to Trenmor.

KING of Lochlin, said Fingal, thy blood flows in the veins of thy foe. Our families met in battle, because they loved the strife of spears. But often did they feast in the hall; and send round the joy of the shell.—Let thy face brighten with gladness, and thine ear delight in the harp. Dreadful as the storm of thine ocean, thou hast poured thy valour forth; thy voice has been like the voice of thousands when they engage in battle. Raise, to-morrow, thy white sails to the wind, thou brother of Agandecca. Bright as the beam of noon she comes on my mournful soul. I have seen thy tears for the fair one, and spared thee in the halls of Starno; when my sword was red with slaughter, and my eye full of tears for the maid.—Or dost thou chuse the fight? The combat which thy fathers gave to Trenmor is thine: that thou mayest depart renowned like the sun setting in the west.

KING of the race of Morven, said the chief of the waves of Lochlin; never will Swaran fight with thee, first of a thousand heroes! I have seen thee in the halls of Starno, and few were thy years beyond my own.—When shall I, I said to my soul, lift the spear like the noble Fingal? We have fought heretofore, O warrior, on the side of the shaggy Malmor; after my waves had carried me to thy halls, and the feast of a thousand shells was spread. Let the bards send him who overcame to future years, for noble was the strife of heathy Malmor.

BUT many of the ships of Lochlin have lost their youths on Lena. Take these, thou king of Morven, and be the friend of Swaran. And when thy sons shall come to the mossy towers of Gormal; the feast of shells shall be spread, and the combat offered on the vale.

NOR ship, replied the king, shall Fingal take, nor land of many hills. The desart is enough to me with all its deer and woods. Rise on thy waves again, thou noble friend of Agandecca. Spread thy white sails to the beam of the morning, and return to the ecchoing hills of Gormal.

BLEST be thy soul, thou king of shells, said Swaran of the dark-brown shield. In peace thou art the gale of spring. In war the mountain-storm. Take now my hand in friendship, thou noble king of Morven.

LET thy bards mourn those who fell. Let Erin give the sons of Lochlin to earth; and raise the mossy stones of their fame. That the children of the north hereafter may behold the place where their fathers fought. And some hunter may say, when he leans on a mossy tomb, here Fingal and Swaran fought, the heroes of other years. Thus hereafter shall he say, and our fame shall last for ever.

SWARAN, said the king of the hills, to-day our fame is greatest. We shall pass away like a dream. No sound will be in the fields of our battles. Our tombs will be lost in the heath. The hunter shall not know the place of our rest. Our names may be heard in the song, but the strength of our arms will cease.

O OSSIAN, Carril, and Ullin, you know of heroes that are no more. Give us the song of other years. Let the night pass away on the sound, and morning return with joy.

WE gave the song to the kings, and a hundred harps accompanied our voice. The face of Swaran brightened like the full moon of heaven, when the clouds vanish away, and leave her calm and broad in the midst of the sky.

IT was then that Fingal spoke to Carril the chief of other times. Where is the son of Semo; the king of the isle of mist? has he retired, like the meteor of death, to the dreary cave of Tura?

CUCHULLIN, said Carril of other times, lies in the dreary cave of Tura. His hand is on the sword of his strength. His thoughts on the battles which he lost. Mournful is the king of spears, for he has often been victorious. He sends the sword of his war to rest on the side of Fingal. For, like the storm of the desert, thou hast scattered all his foes. Take, O Fingal, the sword of the hero; for his fame is departed like mist when it flies before the rustling wind of the vale.

NO: replied the king, Fingal shall never take his sword. His arm is mighty in war; and tell him his fame shall never fail. Many have been overcome in battle, that have shone afterwards like the sun of heaven.

O SWARAN, king of the resounding woods, give all thy grief away.—The vanquished, if brave, are renowned; they are like the sun in a cloud when he hides his face in the south, but looks again on the hills of grass.

GRUMAL was a chief of Cona. He fought the battle on every coast. His soul rejoiced in blood; his ear in the din of arms. He poured his warriors on the sounding Craca; and Craca's king met him from his grove; for then within the circle of Brumo★ he spoke to the stone of power.

FIERCE was the battle of the heroes, for the maid of the breast of snow. The fame of the daughter of Craca had reached Grumal at the streams of Cona; he vowed to have the white-bosomed maid, or die on the ecchoing Craca. Three days they strove together, and Grumal on the fourth was bound.

FAR from his friends they placed him in the horrid circle of Brumo; where often, they said, the ghosts of the dead howled round the stone of their fear. But afterwards he shone like a pillar

---

★ This passage alludes to the religion of the king of Craca. See a note on a similar subject in the third book.

of the light of heaven. They fell by his mighty hand, and Grumal had his fame.

RAISE, ye bards of other times, raise high the praise of heroes; that my soul may settle on their fame; and the mind of Swaran cease to be sad.

THEY lay in the heath of Mora; the dark winds rustle over the heroes.—A hundred voices at once arose, a hundred harps were strung; they sung of other times, and the mighty chiefs of former years.

WHEN now shall I hear the bard; or rejoice at the fame of my fathers? The harp is not strung on Morven; nor the voice of music raised on Cona. Dead with the mighty is the bard; and fame is in the desart no more.

MORNING trembles with the beam of the east, and glimmers on gray-headed Cromla. Over Lena is heard the horn of Swaran, and the sons of the ocean gather around.—Silent and sad they mount the wave, and the blast of Ullin is behind their sails. White, as the mist of Morven, they float along the sea.

CALL, said Fingal, call my dogs, the long-bounding sons of the chace. Call white-breasted Bran; and the surly strength of Luath.—Fillan, and Ryno—but he is not here; my son rests on the bed of death. Fillan and Fergus, blow my horn, that the joy of the chace may arise; that the deer of Cromla may hear and start at the lake of roes.

THE shrill sound spreads along the wood. The sons of heathy Cromla arise.—A thousand dogs fly off at once, gray-bounding through the divided heath. A deer fell by every dog, and three by the white-breasted Bran. He brought them, in their flight, to Fingal, that the joy of the king might be great.

ONE deer fell at the tomb of Ryno; and the grief of Fingal returned. He saw how peaceful lay the stone of him who was the first at the chace.—No more shalt thou rise, O my son, to partake of the feast of Cromla. Soon will thy tomb be hid, and the grass grow rank on thy grave. The sons of the feeble shall pass over it, and shall not know that the mighty lie there.

OSSIAN and Fillan, sons of my strength, and Gaul king of the blue blades of war, let us ascend the hill to the cave of Tura, and find the chief of the battles of Erin.—Are these the walls of Tura, gray and lonely they rise on the heath? The king of shells is sad, and the halls are desolate. Come let us find the king of swords, and give him all our joy.

BUT is that Cuchullin, O Fillan, or a pillar of smoke on the heath? The wind of Cromla is on my eyes, and I distinguish not my friend.

FINGAL! replied the youth, it is the son of Semo. Gloomy and sad is the hero; his hand is on his sword. Hail to the son of battle, breaker of the shields!

HAIL to thee, replied Cuchullin, hail to all the sons of Morven. Delightful is thy presence, O Fingal, it is like the sun on Cromla; when the hunter mourns his absence for a season, and sees him between the clouds. Thy sons are like stars that attend thy course, and give light in the night.

IT is not thus thou hast seen me, O Fingal, returning from the wars of the desert; when the kings of the world* had fled, and joy returned to the hill of hinds.

MANY are thy words, Cuchullin, said Connan† of the small renown. Thy words are many, son of Semo, but where are thy deeds in arms? Why did we come, over the ocean, to aid thy feeble sword? Thou flyest to thy cave of sorrow, and Connan fights thy battles; Resign to me these arms of light; yield them, thou son of Erin.

NO hero, replied the chief, ever fought the arms of Cuchullin; and had a thousand heroes fought them it were in vain, thou

---

* This is the only passage in the poem, wherein the wars of Fingal against the Romans are alluded to:—The Roman emperor is distinguished in old composition by the title of *king of the world*.

† Connan was of the family of Morni. He is mentioned in several other poems, and always appears with the same character. The poet passed him over in silence till now, and his behaviour here deserves no better usage.

gloomy youth. I fled not to the cave of sorrow, as long as Erin's warriors lived.

YOUTH of the feeble arm, said Fingal, Connan, say no more. Cuchullin is renowned in battle, and terrible over the desart. Often have I heard thy fame, thou stormy chief of Inisfail. Spread now thy white sails for the isle of mist, and see Bragela leaning on her rock. Her tender eye is in tears, and the winds lift her long hair from her heaving breast. She listens to the winds of night to hear the voice of thy rowers*; to hear the song of the sea, and the sound of thy distant harp.

AND long shall she listen in vain; Cuchullin shall never return. How can I behold Bragela to raise the sigh of her breast? Fingal, I was always victorious in the battles of other spears!

AND hereafter thou shalt be victorious, said Fingal king of shells. The fame of Cuchullin shall grow like the branchy tree of Cromla. Many battles await thee, O chief, and many shall be the wounds of thy hand.

BRING hither, Oscar, the deer, and prepare the feast of shells; that our souls may rejoice after danger, and our friends delight in our presence.

WE sat, we feasted, and we sung. The soul of Cuchullin rose. The strength of his arm returned; and gladness brightened on his face.

ULLIN gave the song, and Carril raised the voice. I, often, joined the bards, and sung of battles of the spear.—Battles! where I often fought; but now I fight no more. The fame of my former actions is ceased; and I sit forlorn at the tombs of my friends.

THUS they passed the night in the song; and brought back the morning with joy. Fingal arose on the heath, and shook his glittering spear in his hand.—He moved first toward the plains of Lena, and we followed like a ridge of fire.

---

* The practice of singing when they row is universal among the inhabitants of the northwest coast of Scotland and the isles. It deceives time, and inspirits the rowers.

SPREAD the sail, said the king of Morven, and catch the winds that pour from Lena.—We rose on the wave with songs, and rushed, with joy, through the foam of the ocean*.

---

* It is allowed by the best critics that an epic poem ought to end happily. This rule, in its most material circumstances, is observed by the three most deservedly celebrated poets, Homer, Virgil, and Milton; yet, I know not how it happens, the conclusions of their poems throw a melancholy damp on the mind. One leaves his reader at a funeral; another at the untimely death of a hero; and a third in the solitary scenes of an unpeopled world.

*Greek Quotation* HOMER.
Such honours Ilion to her hero paid,
And peaceful slept the mighty Hector's shade. POPE.

*Latin Quotation* VIRGIL.
He rais'd his arm aloft; and at the word
Deep in his bosom drove the shining sword.
The streaming blood distain'd his arms around,
And the disdainful soul came rushing thro' the wound. DRYDEN.

They, hand in hand, with wand'ring sleps and slow,
Through Eden took their solitary way. MILTON.

# HUGH BLAIR (1718–1800)

Hugh Blair was the main supporter of James Mapherson's Ossianic translations. Throughout the controversy over the poems and their authenticity, Blair remained an ardent backer of Macpherson and his endeavour to disseminate knowledge about the ancient Caledonians.

Blair was a churchman and academic. He began his career as a Minister of the Church of Scotland, where he was affiliated with the moderate party, and became a very popular preacher. A successful academic career was meanwhile built up, ultimately enabling him to give patronage to such up-and-coming writers as Robert Burns. Blair's public status and personal sociability assisted him in becoming firm friends with several members of the Scottish Enlightenment literati.

Blair met Macpherson in 1759, and was instrumental in the publishing of *Fragments of Ancient Poetry*. Deploying his enthusiasm and rhetorical talent on writing an anonymous preface to the poems, Blair suggested the existence of a complete Gaelic epic in the Highlands. That same year, in December, he started to deliver lectures on English language and literature, and in 1760 he became Professor of Rhetoric at the University of Edinburgh. This was the first dedicated chair of English in any university. Two years later, Blair became Professor of Rhetoric and *Belles Lettres* at the same university.

The extracts below are from Blair's *A Critical Dissertation on the Poems of Ossian, the Son of Fingal* which was published in 1763. The dissertation is an extended version of one of Blair's lectures on primitive poetry and Ossian. In it, Blair discusses the merits of ancient poetry (its sincerity, passion and unrestrained emotions) and, in particular, the virtues of the Ossianic poems which combined fiery sublime emotions with noble tenderness. He therefore presents Ossian as a bard on a par with Homer but with special 'northern' genteel qualities. He attests that the very style of the poems confirms their authenticity.

The second editon of the *Dissertation* (1765) contained an added discussion of *Temora* and was a response to the growing distrust of the Ossianic poems, which Blair noted as coming primarily from English commentators. It was accompanied by an appendix, reproduced below, in which Blair defends his continuing belief in Macpherson. It also included testimonial evidence in favour of the poems.

Blair was the established academic authority on the poetry of Ossian, and as such was a key pillar supporting Macpherson's endeavour. Blair's *Dissertation* accompanied every edition of the Ossianic poetry after 1765. It was widely published across Europe and made Blair famous as a literary critic. Yet, Blair did not persuade many of the poems' doubters, and the authenticity debate continued.

EXTRACTS FROM BLAIR'S

*A Critical Dissertation on the Poems of Ossian, the Son of Fingal*

2nd LONDON EDITION, 1765

The compositions of Ossian are so strongly marked with characters of antiquity, that although there were no external proof to support that antiquity, hardly any reader of judgment and taste, could hesitate in referring them to a very remote aera. There are four great stages through which men successively pass in the progress of society. The first and earliest is the life of hunters; pasturage succeeds to this, as the ideas of property begin to take root; next agriculture; and lastly, commerce. Throughout Ossian's poems, we plainly find ourselves in the first of these periods of society; during which, hunting was the chief employment of men, and the principal method of their procuring subsistence. Pasturage was not indeed wholly unknown; for we hear of dividing the herd in the case of a divorce*; but the allusions to herds and to cattle are not many; and of agriculture, we find no traces. No cities appear to have been built in the territories of Fingal. No arts are mentioned

---

* Vol. i., p.44.

except that of navigation and of working in iron*. Everything presents to us the most simple and unimproved manners. At their feasts, the heroes prepared their own repast; they sat round the light of the burning oak; the wind lifted their locks, and whistled through their open halls. Whatever was beyond the necessaries of life, was known to them only as the spoil of the Roman province; 'the gold of the stranger; the lights of the stranger; the steeds of the stranger, the children of the rein.'

This representation of Ossian's times, must strike us the more, as geniune and authentick, when it is compared with a poem of later date, which Mr Macpherson has preserved in one of his notes. It is that wherein five bards are represented as passing the evening in the house of a chief, and each of them separately giving his description of the night†. The night scenery is beautiful; and the author has plainly imitated the style and manner of Ossian: But he has allowed some images to appear which betray a later period of society. For we meet with windows clapping, the herds of goats and cows seeking shelter, the shepherd wandering, corn on the plain, and the wakeful hind rebuilding the shocks of corn which had been overturned by the tempest. Whereas in Ossian's works, from beginning to end, all is consistent; no modern allusion drops

---

* Their skill in navigation need not at all surprize us; Living in the western islands, along the coast, or in a country which is every where intersected with arms of the sea, one of the first objects of their attention, from the earliest time, must have been how to traverse the waters. Hence that knowledge of the flars, so necessary for guiding them by night, of which we find several traces in Ossian's works; particularly in the beautiful description of Cathmor's shield, in the 7th book of Temora. Among all the northern maritime nations, navigation was very early studied. Piratical incursions were the chief means they employed for acquiring beoty; and were among the first exploits which distinguished them in the world. Even the savage Americans were at their first discovery found to possess the most surprizing skill and dexterity in navigating their immense lakes and rivers.

The description of Cuchullin's chariot, in the 1st book of Fingal, has been objected to by some, as representing greater magnificence than is consistent with the supposed poverty of that age. But this chariot is plainly only a horse-litter; and the gems mentioned in the description, are no other than the shining stones or pebbles, known to be frequently found along the western coast of Scotland.

† Vol. i., p.350.

from him; but every where, the same face of rude nature appears; a country wholly uncultivated, thinly inhabited, and recently peopled. The grass of the rock, the flower of the heath, the thistle with its beard, are the chief ornaments of his landscapes. 'The desart,' says Fingal, 'is enough to me, with all its woods and deer.'*

The circle of ideas and transactions, is no wider than suits such an age: Nor any greater diversity introduced into characters, than the events of that period would naturally display. Valour and bodily strength are the admired qualities. Contentions arise, as is usual among savage nations, from the slightest causes. To be affronted at a tournament, or to be omitted in the invitation to a feast, kindles a war. Women are often carried away by force; and the whole tribe, as in the Homeric times, rise to avenge the wrong. The heroes show refinement of sentiment indeed on several occasions, but none of manners. They speak of their past actions with freedom, boast of their exploits, and sing their own praise. In their battles, it is evident that drums, trumpets, or bagpipes, were not known or used. They had no expedient for giving the military alarms but striking a shield,  or raising a loud cry: And hence the loud and terrible voice of Fingal is often mentioned, as a necessary qualification of a great general; like the βoήν ἀγαθος Μενέλαος of Homer. Of military discipline or skill, they appear to have been entirely destitute. Their armies seem not to have been numerous; their battles were disorderly; and terminated, for the most part, by a personal combat, or wrestling of the two chiefs; after which, 'the bard sung the song of peace, and the battle ceased along the field.'†

The manner of composition bears all the marks of the greatest antiquity. No artful transitions; nor full and extended connection of parts; such as we find among the poets of later times, when order and regularity of composition were more studied and known; but a style always rapid and vehement; in narration concise even to abruptness, and leaving several circumstances to be supplied by the reader's imagination. The language has all that figurative cast,

---

* Vol. i., p.116.
† Vol. i., p.197.

which, as I before shewed, partly a glowing and undisciplined imagination, partly the sterility of language and the want of proper terms, have always introduced into the early speech of nations; and in several respects, it carries a remarkable resemblance to the style of the Old Testament. It deserves particular notice, as one of the most geniune and decisive characters of antiquity, that very few general terms or abstract ideas, are to be met with in the whole collection of Ossian's works. The ideas of men, at first, were all particular. They had not words to express general conceptions. These were the consequence of more profound reflection and longer acquaintance with the arts of thought and of speech. Ossian, accordingly, almost never expresses himself in the abstract. His ideas extended little farther than to the objects he saw around him. A public, a community, the universe, were conceptions beyond his sphere. Even a mountain, a sea, or a lake, which he has occasion to mention, though only in a simile, are for the most part particularized; it is the hill of Cromla, the storm of the sea of Malmor, or the reeds of the lake of Lego. A mode of expression, which whilst it is characteristical of ancient ages, is at the same time highly favourable to descriptive poetry. For the same reasons, personification is a poetical figure not very common with Ossian. Inanimate objects, such as winds, trees, flowers, he sometimes personifies with great beauty. But the personifications which are so familiar to later poets of Fame, Time, Terror, Virtue, and the rest of that class, were unknown to our Celtic bard. These were modes of conception too abstract for his age.

All these are marks so undoubted, and some of them too, so nice and delicate, of the most early times, as put the high antiquity of these poems out of question. Especially when we consider, that if there had been any imposture in this case, it must have been contrived and executed in the Highlands of Scotland, two or three centuries, ago; as up to this period, both by manuscripts, and by the testimony of a multitude of living witnesses, concerning the uncontrovertible tradition of these poems, they can clearly be traced. Now this is a period when that country enjoyed no advantages for a composition of this kind, which it may not be supposed to have enjoyed in as great, if not in a greater degree, a thousand years before. To suppose that two or three hundred years ago, when we well know the Highlands to have been in a state of gross ignorance and barbarity, there should have arisen in that country a poet, of such exquisite genius, and of such deep knowledge of mankind, and of history, as to divest himself of the ideas and manners of his own age, and to give us a just and natural picture of a state of society ancienter by a thousand years; one who could support this counterfeited antiquity through such a large collection of poems, without the least inconsistency; and who possessed of all this genius and art, had at the same time the self-denial of concealing himself, and of ascribing his own works to an antiquated bard, without the imposture being detected; is a supposition that transcends all bounds of credibility.

There are, besides, two other circumstances to be attended to, still of greater weight, if possible, against this hypothesis. One is the total absence of religious ideas from this work; for which the translator has, in his preface, given a very probable account, on the footing of its being the work of Ossian. The druidical superstition was, in the days of Ossian, on the point of its final extinction; and for particular reasons, odious to the family of Fingal; whilst the Christian faith was not yet established. But had it been the work of one, to whom the ideas of christianity were familiar from his infancy; and who had superadded to them also the bigotted superstition of a dark age and country; it is impossible but in some passage or other, the traces of them would have appeared. The other circumstance is, the entire silence which reigns with respect to all the great clans or families, which are now established in the Highlands. The origin of these several clans is known to be very ancient: And it is as well known, that there is no passion by which a native Highlander is more distinguished, than by attachment to his clan, and jealousy for its honour. That a Highland bard, in forging a work relating to the antiquities of his country, should have inserted no circumstance which pointed out the rise of his own clan, which ascertained its antiquity, or increased its glory, is of all suppositions that can be formed, the most improbable; and the silence on this head, amounts to a demonstration that the author lived before any of the present great clans were formed or known.

Assuming it then, as we well may, for certain, that the poems now under consideration, are genuine venerable monuments of very remote antiquity; I proceed to make some remarks upon their general spirit and strain. The two great characteristics of Ossian's poetry are, tenderness and sublimity. It breathes nothing of the gay and chearful kind; an air of solemnity and seriousness is diffused over the whole. Ossian is perhaps the only poet who never relaxes, or lets himself down into the light and amusing strain; which I readily admit to be no small disadvantage to him, with the bulk of readers. He moves perpetually in the high region of the grand and the pathetick. One key note is struck at the beginning, and supported to the end; nor is any ornament introduced, but what is perfectly concordant with the general tone or melody. The events recorded, are all serious and grave; the scenery throughout, wild and romantic. The extended heath by the sea shore; the mountain shaded with mist; the torrent rushing through a solitary valley; the scattered oaks, and the tombs of warriors overgrown with moss; all produce a solemn attention in the mind, and prepare it for great and extraordinary events. We find not in Ossian, an imagination that sports itself, and dresses out gay trifles to please the fancy. His poetry, more perhaps than that of any other writer, deserves to be stiled, *The Poetry of the Heart*. It is a heart penetrated with noble sentiments, and with sublime and tender passions; a heart that glows, and kindles the fancy; a heart that is full, and pours itself forth. Ossian did not write, like modern poets, to please readers and critics. He sung from the love of poetry and song. His delight was to think of the heroes among whom he had flourished; to recall the affecting incidents of his life; to dwell upon his past wars and loves and friendships; till, as he expresses it himself, 'there comes a voice to Ossian and awakes his soul. It is the voice of years that are gone; they roll before me with all their deeds'; and under this true poetic inspiration, giving vent to his genius, no wonder we should so often hear, and acknowledge in his strains, the powerful and ever-pleasing voice of nature.

——Arte, natura potentior omni.——

Est Deus in nobis, agitante calescimus illo.

It is necessary here to observe, that the beauties of Ossian's writings cannot be felt by those who have given them only a single or a hasty perusal. His manner is so different from that of the poets, to whom we are most accustomed; his style is so concise, and so much crowded with imagery; the mind is kept at such a stretch in accompanying the author; that an ordinary reader is at first apt to be dazzled and fatigued, rather than pleased. His poems require to be taken up at intervals, and to be frequently reviewed; and then it is impossible but his beauties must open to every reader who is capable of sensibility. Those who have the highest degree of it, will relish them the most.

## APPENDIX

THE substance of the preceding Dissertation was originally delivered, soon after the first publication of Fingal, in the course of my lectures in the university of Edinburgh; and, at the desire of several of the hearers, was afterwards enlarged and given to the publick.

As the degree of antiquity belonging to the poems of Ossian, appeared to be a point which might bear dispute, I endeavoured, from internal evidence, to show that these poems must be referred to a very remote period; without pretending to ascertain precisely the date of their composition. I had not the least suspicion, when this Dissertation was first published, that there was any occasion for supporting their authenticity, as genuine productions of the Highlands of Scotland, as translations from the Galic language; not forgeries of a supposed translator. In Scotland, their authenticity was never called in question. I myself had particular reasons to be fully satisfied concerning it. My knowledge of Mr Macpherson's personal honour and integrity, gave me full assurance of his being incapable of putting such a gross imposition, first, upon his friends, and then upon the publick; and if this had not been sufficient, I knew, besides, that the manner in which these poems were brought to light, was entirely inconsistent with any fraud. An accidental conversation with a gentleman distinguished in the literary world, gave occasion to Mr Macpherson's translating literally one or two small pieces of the old Galic poetry. These being shown to me and some others rendered us very desirous of becoming more acquainted with that poetry. Mr Macpherson, afraid of not doing justice to compositions which he admired in the original, was very backward to undertake the task of translating; and the publication of The fragments of ancient poems, was with no small importunity extorted from him. The high reputation which these presently acquired, made it he thought unjust that the world should be deprived of the possession of more, if more of the same kind could be recovered: And Mr Macpherson was warmly urged by several gentlemen of rank and taste, to disengage himself from other occupations, and to undertake a journey through the Highlands and Islands, on purpose to make a collection of those curious remains of ancient genius. He complied with their desire, and spent several months in visiting those remote parts of the country; during which time he corresponded frequently with his friends in Edinburgh, informed them of his progress, of the applications which he made in different quarters, and of the success which he met with; several letters of his, and of those who assisted him in making discoveries passed through my hands; his undertaking was the object of considerable attention; and returning at last, fraught with the poetical treasures of the north, he set himself to translate under the eye of some who were acquainted with the Galic language, and looked into his manuscripts; and by a large publication made an appeal to all the natives of the Highlands and Islands of Scotland, whether he had been faithful to his charge, and done justice to their well known and favourite poems.

Such a transaction certainly did not afford any favourable opportunity for carrying on an imposture. Yet in England, it seems, an opinion has prevailed with some, that an imposture has been carried on; that the poems which have been given to the world are not translations of the works of any old Galic Bard, but modern compositions, formed, as it is said, upon a higher plan of poetry and sentiment than could belong to an age and a country reputed barbarous: And I have been called upon and urged to produce some evidence for satisfying the world that they are not the compositions of Mr Macpherson himself, under the borrowed name of Ossian.

If the question had been concerning manuscripts brought from some distant or unknown region, with which we had no intercourse; or concerning translations from an Asiatic or American language which scarce any body understood, suspicions might naturally have arisen, and an author's assertions have been anxiously and scrupulously weighed. But in the case of a literal translation, professed to be given of old traditionary poems of our own country; of poems asserted to be known in the original to many thousand inhabitants of Great Britain, and illustrated too by many of their current tales and stories concerning them, such extreme scepticism is altogether out of place. For who would have been either so hardy or so stupid, as to attempt a forgery which could not have failed of being immediately detected? Either the author must have had the influence to engage, as confederates in the fraud, all the natives of the Highlands and Islands, dispersed as they are throughout every corner of the British dominions; or, we should, long ere this time, have heard their united voice exclaiming, 'These are not our poems, nor what we were ever accustomed to hear from our bards or our fathers.' Such remonstrances would, at least, have reached those who dwell in a part of the country which is adjacent to the Highlands; and must have come loud to the ears of such, especially, as were known to be the promoters of Mr Macpherson's undertaking. The silence of a whole country in this case, and of a country, whose inbabitants are well known to be attached, in a remarkable degree, to all their own antiquities, is of as much weight as a thousand positive testimonies. And surely, no person of common understanding would have adventured, as Macpherson has done in his dissertation on Temora, to engage in a controversy with the whole Irish nation concerning these poems, and to insist upon the honour of them being due to Scotland, if they had been mere forgeries of his own; which the Scots, in place of supporting so ridiculous a claim, must have instantly rejected.

But as reasoning alone is apt not to make much impression, where suspicions have been entertained concerning a matter of fact, it was thought proper to have recourse to express testimonies. I have accordingly applied to several persons of credit and honour, both gentlemen of fortune, and clergymen of the established church, who are natives of the Highlands or Islands of Scotland, and well acquainted with the language of the country, desiring to know their real opinion of the translations published by Mr Macpherson. Their original letters to me in return, are in my possession. I shall give a fair and faithful account of the result of their testimony: And I have full authority to use the names of those gentlemen for what I now advance.

I must begin with affirming, that though among those with whom I have corresponded, some have had it in their power to be more particular and explicit in their testimony than others; there is not, however, one person, who insinuates the most remote suspicion that Mr Macpherson has either forged; or adulterated any one of the Poems he has published. If they make any complaints of him, it is on account of his having omitted other poems which they think of equal merit with any which he has published. They all, without exception, concur in holding his translations to be genuine, and proceed upon their authenticity as a fact acknowledged throughout all those Northern Provinces; assuring me that any one would be exposed to ridicule among them, who should call it in question. I must observe, that I had no motive to direct my choice of the persons to whom I applied for information preferably to others, except their being pointed out to me, as the

persons in their different counties who were most likely to give
light on this head.

With regard to the manner in which the originals of these
poems have been preserved and transmitted, which has been represented as so mysterious and inexplicable, I have received the
following plain account: That until the present century, almost
every great family in the Highlands had their own bard, to whose
office it belonged to be master of all the poems and songs of the
country; that among these poems the works of Ossian are easily
distinguished from those of later bards by several peculiarities in
his style and manner; that Ossian has been always reputed the
Homer of the Highlands, and all his compositions held in singular
esteem and veneration; that the whole country is full of traditionary
stories derived from his poems, concerning Fingal and his race of
heroes, of whom there is not a child but has heard, and not a dis-
trict in which there are not places pointed out famous for being
the scene of some of their feats of arms; that it was wont to be the
great entertainment of the Highlanders, to pass the winter evenings
in discoursing of the times of Fingal, and rehearsing these old
poems, of which they have been all along enthusiastically fond;
that when assembled at their festivals, or on any of their publick
occasions, wagers were often laid who could repeat most of them,
and to have store of them in their memories, was both an honourable and a profitable acquisition, as it procured them access
into the families of their great men; that with regard to their
antiquity, they are beyond all memory or tradition; insomuch that
there is a word commonly used in the Highlands to this day, when
they would express any thing which is of the most remote or unknown antiquity, importing, that it belongs to the age of Fingal.

I am farther informed, that after the use of letters was introduced into that part of the country, the bards and others began
early to commit several of these poems to writing; that old manuscripts of them, many of which are now destroyed or lost, are
known and attested to have been in the posesion of some great
families; that the most valuable of those which remained, were

collected by Mr Macpherson during his journey through that country; that though the poems of Ossian, so far as they were handed down by oral tradition, were no doubt liable to be interpolated, and to have their parts disjoined and put out of their natural order, yet by comparing together the different oral editions of them (if we may use that phrase) in different corners of the country, and by comparing these also with the manuscripts which he obtained, Mr Macpherson had it in his power to ascertain, in a great measure, the genuine original, to restore the parts to their proper order, and to give the whole to the publick in that degree of correctness, in which it now appears.

I am also acquainted, that if enquires had been made 50 or threescore years ago, many more particulars concerning these poems might have been learned, and many more living witnesses have been produced for attesting their authenticity; but that the manners of the inhabitants of the Highland counties have of late undergone a great change. Agriculture, trades, and manufactures, begin to take place of hunting, and the shepherd's life. The introduction of the busy and laborious arts has considerably abated that poetical enthusiasm which is better suited to a vacant and indolent state. The fondness of reciting their old poems decays; the custom of teaching them to their children is fallen into desuetude; and few are now to be found, except old men, who can rehearse from memory any considerable parts of them.

For these particulars, concerning the state of the Highlands and the transmission of Ossian's poems, I am indebted to the reverend and very learned and ingenious Mr John Macpherson, minister of Slate in the Island of Sky, and to the reverend Mr Donald Macleod minister of Glenelg in Invernessshire, Mr Angus Macneil minister of the Island of South Uist, Mr Neil Macleod minister of Ross, in the Island of Mull, and Mr Alexander Macaulay chaplain to the 88th Regiment.

The honourable colonel Hugh Mackay of Bighouse in the Shire of Sutherland, Donald Campbell of Airds in Argyleshire, Esq; AEneas Mackintosh of Mackintosh in Invernessshire, Esq; and

Ronald Macdonell of Keappoch in Lochaber, Esq; captain in the 87th regiment commanded by colonel Fraser, all concur in testifying that Mr Macpherson's collection consists of genuine Highland poems; known to them to be such, both from the general report of the country where they live, and from their own remembrance of the originals. Colonel Mackay asserts very positively, upon personal knowledge, that many of the poems published by Mr Macpherson are true and faithful translations. Mr Campbell declares that he has heard many of them, and captain Macdonell that he has heard parts of every one of them, recited in the original language.

James Grant of Rothiemurchus, Esq; and Alexander Grant, of Delrachny, Esq; both in the Shire of Inverness, desire to be named as vouchers for the poem of Fingal in particular. They remember to have heard it often in their younger days, and are positive that Mr Macpherson has given a just translation of it.

Lauchlan Macpherson of Strathmashie in Invernessshire, Esq; gives a very full and explicit testimony, from particular knowledge, in the following words: That in the year 1760, he accompanied Mr Macpherson during some part of his journey through the Highlands in search of the poems of Ossian; that he assisted him in collecting them; that he took down from oral tradition, and transcribed from old manuscripts by far the greatest part of those pieces Mr Macpherson has published; that since the publication he has carefully compared the translation with the copies of the originals in his hands; and that he finds it amazingly literal, even to such a degree as often to preserve the cadence of the Galic versification. He affirms, that among the manuscripts which were at that time in Mr Macpherson's possession, he saw one of as old a date as the year 1410.

Sir James Macdonald of Macdonald, in the Island of Sky, Baronet, assured me, that after having made, at my desire, all the enquires he could in his part of the country, he entertained no doubt that Mr Macpherson's collection consisted entirely of authentick Highland poems; that he had lately heard several parts of them repeated in the original, in the Island of Sky, with some variations from the printed translation, such as might naturally be expected from the circumstances of oral tradition; and some parts, in particular the episode of Fairasollis in the third book of Fingal, which agree literally with the translation; and added, that he had heard recitations of other poems not translated by Mr Macpherson, but generally reputed to be of Ossian's composition, which were of the same spirit and strain with such as are translated, and which he esteemed not inferiour to any of them in sublimity of description, dignity of sentiment, or any other of the beauties of poetry. This last particular must have great weight; as it is well known how much the judgment of Sir James Macdonald deserves to be relied upon, in every thing that relates to literature and taste.

The late reverend Mr Alexander Macfarlane, minister of Arrachar in Dumbartonshire, who was remarkably eminent for his profound knowledge in Galic learning and antiquities, wrote to me soon after the publication of Mr Macpherson's work, terming it, a masterly translation; informing me that he had often heard several of these poems in the original, and remarked many passages so particularly striking beyond any thing he had ever read in any human composition, that he never expected to see a strength of genius able to do them that justice in a translation, which Mr Macpherson has done.

Norman Macleod of Macleod, in the Island of Sky, Esq; Walter Macfarlane of Macfarlane in Dumbartonshire, Esq; Mr Alexander Macmillan, deputy keeper of his Majesty's signet, Mr Adam Fergusson, professor of moral philosophy in the University of Edinburgh, and many other gentlemen natives of the Highland counties, whom I had occasion to converse with upon this subject, declare, that though they cannot now repeat from memory any of these poems in the original, yet from what they have heard in their youth, and from the impression of the subject still remaining on their minds, they firmly believe those which Mr Macpherson has published, to be the old poems of Ossian current in the country.

Desirous, however, to have this translation particularly compared with the oral editions of any who had parts of the original distinctly on their memory, I applied to several clergymen to make enquiry in their respective parishes concerning such persons; and to compare what they rehearsed with the printed version. Accordingly, from the reverend Mr John Macpherson minister of Slate in Sky, Mr Neil Macleod minister of Ross in Mull, Mr Angus Macneil minister of South Uist, Mr Donald Macqueen minister of Kilmuir in Sky, and Mr Donald Macleod minister of Glenelg, I have had reports on this head, containing distinct and explicit testimonies to almost the whole epic poem of Fingal, from beginning to end, and to several also of the lesser poems, as rehearsed in the original, in their presence, by persons whose names and places of abode they mention, and compared by themselves with the printed translation. They affirm that in many places, what was rehearsed in their presence agreed literally and exactly with the translation. In some places they found variations from it, and variations even among different rehearsers of the same poem in the original; as words and stanzas omitted by some which others repeated, and the order and connection in some places changed. But they remark, that these variations are on the whole not very material; and that Mr Macpherson seemed to them to follow the most just and authentic copy of the sense of his author. Some of these clergymen, particulary Mr Neil Macleod, can themselves repeat from memory several passages of Fingal; the translation of which they assure me is exact. Mr Donald Macleod acquaints me, that it was in his house Mr Macpherson had the description of Cuchullin's horses and chariot, in the first book of Fingal, given him by Allan Macaskill school-master. Mr Angus Macneil writes, that Mr Macdonald, a parishioner of his, declares, that he has often seen and read a great part of an ancient manuscript, once in the possession of the family of Clanronald, and afterwards carried to Ireland, containing many of these poems; and that he rehearsed before him several passages out of Fingal, which agreed exactly with Mr Macpherson's translation; that Neil Macmurrich, whose predecessors had for many generations been bards to the family of Clanronald, declared also in his presence, that he had often seen and read the same old manuscript; that he himself, gave to Mr Macpherson a manuscript containing some of the poems which are now translated and published, and rehearsed before Mr Macneil, in the original, the whole of the poem entitled Dar-thula, with very little variation from the printed translation. I have received the same testimony concerning this poem, Dar-thula, from Mr Macpherson minister of Slate; and in a letter communicated to me from Lieutenant Duncan Macnicol, of the 88th regiment, informing me of its being recited in the original, in their presence, from beginning to end: On which I lay the more stress, as any person of taste who turns to that poem will see, that it is one of the most highly finished in the whole collection, and most distinguished for poetical and sentimental beauties; insomuch, that whatever genius could produce Dar-thula, must be judged fully equal to any performance contained in Mr Macpherson's publication. I must add here, that though they who have compared the translation with what they have heard rehearsed of the original, bestow high praises both upon Mr Macpherson's genius and his fidelity; yet I find it to be their general opinion, that in many places he has not been able to attain to the strength and sublimity of the original which he copied.

I have authority to say, in the name of Lieutenant Colonel Archibald Macnab of the 88th regiment, or regiment of Highland Voluntiers commanded by colonel Campbell, that he has undoubted evidence of Mr Macpherson's collection being genuine, both from what he well remembers to have heard in his youth, and from his having heard very lately a considerable part of the poem of Temora rehearsed in the original, which agreed exactly with the printed version.

By the reverend Mr Alexander Pope minister of Reay, in the shire of Caithness, I am informed, that twenty-four years ago, he had begun to make a collection of some of the old poems current in his part of the country; on comparing which, with Mr Macpher-

son's work, he found in his collection the poem intitled, the battle of Lora, some parts of Lathmon, and the account of the death of
Oscar. From the above mentioned Lieutenant Duncan Macnicol,
testimonies have been also received to a great part of Fingal, to
part of Temora, and Carric-thura, as well as to the whole of Dar-
thula, as recited in his presence in the original, compared, and
found to agree with the translation.

I myself read over the greatest part of the English version of
the six books of Fingal, to Mr Kenneth Macpherson of Stornoway
in the Island of Lewis, merchant, in presence of the reverend Mr
Alexander Macaulay chaplain to the 88th regiment. In going along
Mr Macpherson vouched what was read to be well known to him
in the original, both the descriptions and the sentiments. In some
places, though he remembered the story, he did not remember the
words of the original; in other places, he remembered and repeated the Galic lines themselves, which, being interpreted to me by
Mr Macaulay, were found, upon comparison, to agree often literally with the printed version, and sometimes with slight variations
of a word or an epithet. This testimony carried to me, and must
have carried to any other who had been present, the highest
conviction; being precisely a testimony of that nature which an
Englishman well acquainted with Milton, or any favourite author,
would give to a foreigner, who shewed him a version of this author
into his own language, and wanted to be satisfied from what the
Englishman could recollect of the original, whether it was really
a translation of Paradise Lost, or a spurious work under that title
which had been put into his hands.

The above mentioned Mr Alexander Macaulay, Mr Adam Fergusson professor of moral philosophy, and Mr Alexander Fraser,
governor to Francis Stuart, Esq; inform me, that at several different times they were with Mr Macpherson, after he had returned from
his journey through the Highlands, and whilst he was employed
in the work of translating; that they looked into his manuscripts,
several of which had the appearance of being old; that they were
fully satisfied of their being genuine Highland poems; that they

compared the translation in many places with the original; and they attest it to be very just and faithful, and remarkably literal.

It has been thought worth while to bestow this attention on establishing the authenticity of the works of Ossian, now in possession of the publick: Because whatever rank they are allowed to hold as works of genius; whatever different opinions may be entertained concerning their poetical merit, they are unquestionably valuable in another view; as monuments of the taste and manners of an ancient age, as useful materials for enlarging our knowledge of the human mind and character; and must, beyond all dispute, be held as at least, one of the greatest curiosities, which have at any time enriched the republick of letters. More testimonies to them might have been produced by a more enlarged correspondence with the Highland counties: But I apprehend, if any apology is necessary, it is for producing so many names, in a question, where the consenting silence of a whole country, was to every unprejudiced person, the strongest proof, that spurious compositions, in the name of that country, had not been obtruded upon the world.

FINIS

# SAMUEL JOHNSON (1709–1784) AND JAMES BOSWELL (1740–1795)

Of all the opponents of James Macpherson's Ossianic translations, the English writer and lexicographer Samuel Johnson remains the most formidable. Johnson's critical stance on the poems was rooted in his distrust and dislike of oral culture in general, and the Highlands and its cultural heritage in particular. The extracts below illustrate Johnson's strong belief that the poems were 18th-century forgeries, since in his view the ancient Highlands lacked the requisite sophistication to have produced such works. The material also demonstrates his insistence on wanting to see written Gaelic original manuscripts, which he did not believe existed.

Some of the extracts are drawn from the writings of James Boswell, who was Johnson's close friend and biographer. Boswell, a Scottish lawyer, recorded his friend's life in great detail. It is interesting to note that Boswell had been one of the early supporters of Macpherson. He had given financial aid for Macpherson to publish *Fingal*, and had met up with Macpherson on several occasions when Macpherson first arrived in London. Boswell later claimed that it was after reading *Fingal*, which was presented as a complete epic, that he came to doubt the veracity of the poems. There can be little doubt that Boswell's close friendship with Johnson, whose intellect he admired, must also have influenced his thinking on the poems.

The extracts give an insight into Boswell and Johnson's three-month-long journey through Scotland in 1773, during which they examined the Highland landscape and its culture. Whereas the younger and more enthusiastic Boswell attached a romantic and emotional Jacobitism to the landscape and its people, the infirm and irascible Johnson professed to being unimpressed with the region. Johnson's account of this journey was published as *A Journey to the Western Islands of Scotland* (1775). In it, he affirmed his suspicions of Macpherson.

Some of the most astonishing passages below deal with Macpherson's reaction to Johnson's account. Macpherson demanded an apology for the numerous insults it contained, and when Johnson refused and kept pressing for Gaelic manuscripts, the row became increasingly heated and bitter. Johnson ended up buying a large oak staff to defend himself in case he was attacked by Macpherson.

The extracts below are from Boswell's biography *The Life of Johnson* (1791), his *Journal of a Tour to the Hebrides* (1785) and Johnson's *A Journey to the Western Islands of Scotland* (1775).

### EXTRACTS FROM BOSWELL'S
## *The Life of Samuel Johnson*

Dr Blair had been presented to him by Dr James Fordyce. At this time the controversy concerning the pieces published by Mr James Macpherson, as translations of *Ossian*, was at its height. Johnson had all along denied their authenticity; and, what was still more provoking to their admirers, maintained that they had no merit. The subject having been introduced by Dr Fordyce, Dr Blair, relying on the internal evidence of their antiquity, asked Dr Johnson whether he thought any man of a modern age could have written such poems? Johnson replied, 'Yes, Sir, many men, many women, and many children.' Johnson, at this time, did not know that Dr Blair had just published a *Dissertation*, not only defending their authenticity, but seriously ranking them with the poems of *Homer* and *Virgil*; and when he was afterwards informed of this circumstance, he expressed some displeasure at Dr Fordyce's having suggested the topick, and said, 'I am not sorry that they got thus much for their pains. Sir, it was like leading one to talk of a book when the authour is concealed behind the door.'

...

Mr Macpherson's menaces made Johnson provide himself with the sample implement of defence [*oak stick*]; and had he been attacked, I have no doubt that, old as he was, he would have made his corporal prowess be felt as much as his intellectual.

...

That he was to some degree of excess a *true-born Englishman*, so as to have ever entertained an undue prejudice against both the country and the people of Scotland, must be allowed. But it was a prejudice of the head, and not of the heart... His disbelief of the authenticity of the poems ascribed to Ossian, a Highland bard, was confirmed in the course of his journey, by a very strict examination of the evidence offered for it; and although their authenticity was made too much a national point by the Scotch, there were many respectable persons in that country, who did not concur in this; so that his judgement upon the question ought not to be decried, even by those who differ from him. As to myself, I can only say, upon a subject now become very uninteresting, that when the fragments of Highland poetry first came out, I was much pleased with their wild peculiarity, and was one of those who subscribed to enable their editor, Mr Macpherson, then a young man, to make a search in the Highlands and Hebrides for a long poem in the Erse Language, which was reported to be preserved somewhere in those regions. But when there came forth an Epick Poem in six books, with all the common circumstances of former compositions of that nature; and when, upon an attentive examination of it, there was found a perpetual recurrence of the same images which appear in the fragments; and when no ancient manuscript, to authenticate the work, was deposited in any publick library, though that was insisted on as a reasonable proof, *who* could forbear to doubt?

...

(*Letter from Johnson to Boswell*, 1775) 'You then are going wild about Ossian. Why do you think any part can be proved? The dusky manuscript of Egg is probably not 50 years old; if it be an hundred, it proves nothing. The tale of Clanranald has no proof. Has Clanranald told it? Can he prove it? There are, I believe, no Erse manuscripts. None of the old families had a single letter in Erse that we heard of. You say it is likely that they could write. The learned, if any learned there were, could; but knowing by that learning, some written language, in that language they wrote, as letters had never been applied to their own. If there are manuscripts, let them be shewn, with some proof that they are not forged for the occasion. You say many can remember parts of Ossian. I believe all those parts are versions of the English; at least there is no proof of their antiquity.

'Macpherson is said to have made some translations himself; and having taught a boy to write it, ordered him to say that he had learnt it of his grandmother. The boy, when he grew up, told the story. This Mrs Williams heard at Mr Strahan's table. Do not be credulous; you know how little a Highlander can be trusted. Macpherson is, so far as I know, very quiet. Is not that proof enough? Everything is against him. No visible manuscript; no inscription in the language: no correspondence among friends: no transaction of business, of which a single scrap remains in the ancient families. Macpherson's pretence is, that the character was Saxon. If he had not talked unskillfully of *manuscripts*, he might have fought with oral tradition much longer.

*The Journal of a Tour to the Hebrides, with Samuel Johnson*

Dr Johnson proceeded 'I look upon McPherson's *Fingal* to be as gross an imposition as ever the world was troubled with. Had it been really an ancient work, a true specimen how men thought at that time, it would have been a curiosity of the first rate. As a modern production, it is nothing'. —He said, he could never get the meaning of an *Erse* song explained to him. They told him, the chorus was generally unmeaning. 'I take it, (said he,) Erse songs are like a song which I remember: it was composed in Queen Elizabeth's time, on the Earl of Essex; and the burthen was

'Radaratoo, radarate, radara tadara tandore.'

'But surely, said Mr McQueen, there were words to it, which had meaning. —Johnson. 'Why, yes, sir; I recollect a stanza, and you shall have it:

'O! then bespoke the prentices all,
Living in London, both proper and tall,
For Essex's sake they would fight all.

Radaratoo, radarate, radara, tadara, tandore*.'

When Mr McQueen began again to expatiate on the beauty of Ossian's poetry, Dr Johnson entered into no further controversy, but, with a pleasant smile, only cried, 'Ay, ay; Radaratoo radarate.'

### EXTRACT FROM JOHNSON'S
### A Journey to the Western Islands of Scotland (London, 1775)

The Earse has many dialects, and the words used in some Islands are not always known in others. In literate nations, though the pronunciation, and sometimes the words of common speech may differ, as now in England, compared with the South of Scotland, yet there is a written diction, which pervades all dialects, and is understood in every province. But where the whole language is colloquial, he that has only one part, never gets the rest, as he cannot get it but by change of residence.

In an unwritten speech, nothing that is not very short is transmitted from one generation to another. Few have opportunities of hearing a long composition often enough to learn it, or have inclination to repeat it so often as is necessary to retain it; and what is once forgotten is lost for ever. I believe there cannot be recovered, in the whole Earse language, five hundred lines of which there is any evidence to prove them a hundred years old. Yet I hear that the father of Ossian boasts of two chests more of ancient poetry, which he suppresses, because they are too good for the English.

---

* This drolt quotation, I have since found, was from a song in honour of the Earl of Essex, called 'Queen Elizabeth's Champion,' which is preserved in a collection of Old Ballads, in three volumes, published in London in different years, between 1720 and 1730. The full verse is as follows:

Oh! then bespoke the prentices all,
Living in London, both proper and tall,
In a kind letter sent straight to the Queen,
For Essex's sake they would fight all.

'Raderer too, tandaro te,
Raderer, tandorer, tan do re.'

# MALCOLM LAING (1762–1818)

Malcolm Laing was a historian, advocate and politician who published an annotated edition of Ossianic poetry which was intended to demolish the case for their authenticity. Born in Kirkwall, Orkney, in 1762, Laing was educated at the University of Edinburgh and was based in the city for much of his career. In the 1790s he spoke out in the High Court in defence of political reformers charged with sedition. Thereafter, his legal work became less significant and he increasingly turned his hand to history writing.

In 1802 he published *The history of Scotland, from the union of the crowns on the accession of King James VI to the throne of England, to the union of the kingdoms in the reign of Queen Anne, with two dissertations, historical and critical, on the Gowrie conspiracy, and on the supposed authenticity of Ossian's poems*. His dissertation put forward a very negative interpretation of Macpherson's work, and in so doing paved the way for his 1805 edition of *The poems of Ossian, containing the poetical works of James Macpherson in prose and verse, with notes and illustrations*. A handsomely produced and popular edition, it contained a substantial preface along with extensive notes and references. Laing's intention was to establish once and for all that Macpherson was a fraud who had used his own notable talents as a poet and classicist to fabricate the poems. At the same time, it attempts to indict Macpherson with having plagiarised his Ossianic poetry from a range of sources including Milton's *Paradise Lost*, the Bible and Homer.

Laing's negative attitude towards Macpherson has been identified by the historian William Ferguson as stemming from the traditions of his native Northern Isles, where an affinity with the Scandinavian world to the east could be matched by an antipathy and mistrust of the Celtic to the west. This cultural attitude predisposed Laing towards the work of the vituperative anti-Celticist John Pinkerton, noted for his hatred of all things Ossianic. Upon a correspondence being established between the two men, Laing set about his own anti-Ossianic project with Pinkerton's blessing.

In later years, Laing went on to became a radical Whig MP, representing Orkney and Shetland from 1807 to 1812. He was plagued
by chronic illness, which forced his retirement from politics and
writing, and he died in 1818 in Kirkwall. Below is an extract from
Laing's preface to his 1805 edition of the poems of Ossian.

### EXTRACTS FROM MALCOLM LAING'S PREFACE
### TO THE OSSIANIC POEMS

It is now almost unnecessary to add, that these are all detached
ballads unconnected with each other; and that no trace of an epic
poem has ever been discovered in the Highlands of Scotland, either
before or since the publication of Ossian. Above 20 years before
Macpherson published, Dr Ferguson, and Mr Pope minister of Reay
in Caithness, could find nothing but the ballads of Magnus, Erragon, Lammon-more, and the Death of Oscar; and Jerom Stone*,
a school-master at Dunkeld, who died in 1756, collected these and
seven other Irish ballads, but no part of Macpherson's Ossian was
then discovered. For the space of forty-three years since the first
appearance of Ossian, the Highlands have been ransacked by
every traveller, and every chieftain of information or research; by
Sir James Foulis and Sir Adolphus Oughton, both collectors, who
had acquired the language in order to peruse the originals; by Mr
Hill, Dr Young, Mr Dempster, and the editors of the Perth Collection of Gaelic poems; by the Highland Societies, both of London
and of Edinburgh; and the result of every enquiry is this, that
much has been fabricated by Macpherson, Clark, Kennedy, and
Smith, but that nothing has been discovered, except the Irish ballads. During a period of sixty-seven years, before, and since the
appearance of Ossian, no part of the pretended originals has been
found in the Highlands, either floating on tradition, or preserved
in manuscripts.

---

* Report, 23–5–7. Appendix, 53. 63. Jerom Stone's collection was purchased
from his brother by Mr Chalmers, and presented to the Highland Society. It contains
ten such ballads as Magnus, Erragon, the Death of Conloch, of Oscar, and of Fraoch,
with six modern poems; of all of which, an index is now before me.

# REPORT OF THE COMMITTEE OF THE HIGHLAND SOCIETY OF SCOTLAND, APPOINTED TO INQUIRE INTO THE NATURE AND AUTHENTICITY OF THE POEMS OF OSSIAN (1805)

THE Highland Society of Scotland was founded in 1784 in Edinburgh. It was designed to improve the living conditions of the Highlands and to preserve its language, poetry and music. The society supported a bard, ran piping competitions and sponsored Gaelic classes. Among the prominent forces behind the society were the politician and agricultural improver Sir John Sinclair (1754–1835) and the popular writer Henry Mackenzie (1745–1831).

Following the death of James Macpherson in 1796, Mackenzie suggested that a committee be set up to look into the authenticity of Macpherson's Ossianic works. Mackenzie became the convenor for the committee which contacted informants and collected manuscripts. On board were Dr Donald Smith (1756–1805) and Reverend Donald MacIntosh (1743–1808), both of whom could read Gaelic.

The committee's report was published in 1805 and remains a key source for anyone interested in exploring the Ossianic controversy and Gaelic literature. The report came with a large number of letters and testimonies. Those originally written in Gaelic were published in Gaelic and came with English translations. The extracts below include the questionnaire that was sent out to people in the Highlands, a letter by the minister Mr Gallie who had assisted Macpherson in his translations and the conclusion the Committee reached with regard to the authenticity of the poems.

## EXTRACTS FROM THE REPORT OF THE HIGHLAND COMMITTEE OF SCOTLAND

In execution of the business assigned it, your Committee conceived it to be foreign to its duty to enter into any elaborate argument or discussion on the authenticity of those poems, or to examine, with critical or historical labour, the opinions of different writers who have made this matter a subject of controversy. It conceived the purpose of its nomination to be, to employ the influence of the Society, and the extensive communication which it possesses with every part of the Highlands, in collecting what materials or information it was still practicable to collect, regarding the authenticity and nature of the poems ascribed to Ossian, and particularly of that celebrated collection published by Mr James Macpherson.

For the purpose above mentioned, the Committee, soon after its appointment, circulated the following set of Queries, through such parts of the Highlands and Islands, and among such persons resident there, as seemed most likely to afford the information required.

### QUERIES

I. Have you ever heard repeated or sung, any of the poems ascribed to Ossian, translated and published by Mr Macpherson? By whom have you heard them so repeated, and at what time or times? Did you ever commit any of them to writing, or can you remember them so well as now to set them down? In either of these cases, be so good to send the Gaelic original to the Committee.

II. The same answer is requested concerning any other ancient poems of the same kind, and relating to the same traditionary persons or stories with those in Mr Macpherson's collection.

III. Are any of the persons, from whom you heard any such poems, now alive? Or are there, in your part of the country, any persons who remember and can repeat or recite such poems? If there are, be so good to examine them as to the manner of their getting or learning such compositions; and set down, as accurately as possible, such as they can now repeat or recite; and transmit such their account, and such compositions as they repeat, to the Committee.

IV. If there are, in your neighbourhood, any persons from whom Mr Macpherson received any poems, inquire particularly what the poems were which he so received, the manner in which he received them, and how he wrote them down; shew those persons, if you have an opportunity, his translation of such poems, and desire them to say if the translation is exact and literal; or, if it differes, in what it differs from the poems, as they repeated them to Mr Macpherson, and can now recollect them.

v. Be so good to procure every information you conveniently can, with regard to the traditionary belief, in the country in which you live, concerning the history of Fingal and his followers, and that of Ossian and his poems; particularly concerning those stories and poems published by Mr Macpherson, and the heroes mentioned in them. Transmit any such account, and any proverbial or traditionary expression in the original Gaelic, relating to the subject, to the Committee.

vi. In all the above inquiries, or any that may occur to in elucidation of this subject, he is requested by the Committee to make the inquiry, and to take down the answers, with as much impartiality and precision as possible, in the same manner as if it were a legal question, and the proof to be investigated with a legal strictness.

...

SIR,

Kincardine, 4 March 1801

As I have not seen Mr Laing's history, I can form no opinion as to the arguments wherewith he has attempted to discredit Ossian's poems: the attempt could not come more naturally than from Orcadians*. Perhaps the severe checks given by the ancient Caledonians to their predatory Scandinavian predecessors raised prejudices not yet extinct. I conceive how an author can write under the influence of prejudice, and not sensible of being acted upon by it.

I stand persuaded, that Mr Laing's arguments cannot stagger my

---

* Mr Laing is a native of Orkney.

I shall endeavour to recollect what I can of the war song, and to give it you; but I must observe, though I had my memory refreshed by the manuscript, as it is more than 40 years back, that my edition of it cannot be considered as perfectly full and correct.

belief in the authenticity of Ossian's poems. Before Mr Macpherson could know his right hand from his left, I have heard fragments of them repeated, and many of those fragments I recognized in Mr Macpherson's translation.

Fingal's standard was my very early acquaintance: 'Togair Deo Grein e re Crann, Brattach Fhinn'sbu mhor a meas.' The concluding conflict betwixt Fingal and the king of Lochlin engaged my young fancy so much, that the following stanza is still remembered by me.

'Tilgidar dhubh 'n airm dhaithte
Fiachadar spairn 'nda laoich.
Clachan agus talamh trom
Do ghluaisd iad le bonn 'n cos.'

### VERBATIM IN ENGLISH

Their burnished arms are laid aside;
The strength of the heroes is tried;
Stones and solid earth
Are overturned by their feet in the contest.

I know not if this makes any part of what Mr Macpherson detailed of the exploits of Fingal; my memory has failed me even in the very line in which it is most exercised. Had its decline kept off, I could give your honourable Society more specimens, with which I had the honour of being early acquainted. Here I cannot get my memory refreshed. The pride of ancestry, the *fortia facta patrum*, are obsolete themes: the pressure of the times, the change of system, have brought forward other feelings and speculations. Little else is left us of the ancient Caledonians than the refuse of their remains; occupants hold their possessions, who are more able to advance the interest of landlords, and who are more attached to Plutus than to Mars, to Tellus than to the Muses.

What Sir John Dalrymple predicted concerning the Highlanders, at the close of the battle of Killicranky, seems to be coming forward with hasty strides. Let Mr Laing read their character as drawn by that masterly pen, and it will not seem to him incredible, that a former age should, among the Caledonians, furnish such a hero as Fingal, or such a bard as Ossian.

I remember, when I first read Fingal in English, I quarrelled a term in the war song, (prosnacha cath.) I heard it in early life repeated, and *snorting* steeds was the expression, and, if I forget not, it so stood in the Gaelic manuscript; and I did not then, neither do I now think it an improvement to have it translated *generous* steeds.

I must confess, that I heard in early life, among some of the most vulgar Senachies and singers, some parts of Ossian's poems interlarded with what was marvellous in the extreme; and I have heard them repeated by others, then and afterwards, without that disagreeable mixture.

The names of Ossian, Fingal, Cumhal, Trenmor, their fathers and their heroes, are still familiar, and held in the greatest respect. Straths, [valleys] mountains, rocks and rivers, out of compliment to them, are named after them. We have a Strathconan in this same county, and a high and craggy mountain in this same neighbourhood, perpetuates the same of Fingal's favourite dog Bran.

Every great and striking remain of antiquity, whose origin and use cannot be traced, is ascribed to Fingal and his followers; such as the roads in the glens of Lochaber, the circular buildings called Duns, and the subterranean excavations, which are of the greatest magnitude.

If the tender feelings, the chaste and delicate sentiments, the striking appearances of the face and works of nature, under a vast variety of vicissitudes, which abound in Ossian, give offence, and create incredulity concerning him, one need not be at a loss to make a large collection of such from bards in our own days, whose geniuses were not cultivated by education, and who were strangers to the benefits of improved society.

If I had not the benefit of education, were Ossian and Virgil named, I would declare my belief in the one, and would be excused for being silent as to the other.

Had Mr Laing been born and bred in the Highlands 60 years ago, I am persuaded he would think and judge concerning Ossian as I do, and would be most happy at having his early prepossessions immoveably established, by seeing the manuscripts to which I referred in my former correspondence with the Highland Society.

It is partly owing to my infirm state of health, that what I now give you, at the request of the Society, communicated by Dr Kemp, was so long delayed. I use the freedom to write to him, and beg to be excused for using a borrowed hand.

Mr Macpherson could not make his Highland tour earlier than the 60, for the reasons formerly given.

The queries sent me may be elucidated in Badenoch and Lochaber. You may gather from what is above, that this corner can do little in that line.

When summer comes, if my health serves me, I shall make it my buiness to see certain old men, though at a considerable distance from here, who, I am told, do still retain some of Ossian's poems.

The gentleman to whom I referred in my former correspondence, as a familiar acquaintance of Mr Macpherson's and mine, and distinguished for his acquaintance with the Gaelic language, is, alas! no more. His name was Lachlane Macpherson of Strathmashy. He died in the 1767. I have the honour to be, with great respect, Sir, the Highland Society's, and your, most obedient humble servant,

ANDREW GAILLIE

...

On the whole, the Committee beg leave to
REPORT,

That there are two questions to which it has directed its inquiries, on the Subject which the Society was pleased to refer to it, and on which it now submits the best evidence it has been able to procure.

1ST What poetry, of what kind, and of what degree of excellence, existed anciently in the Highlands of Scotland, which was generally known by the denomination of *Ossianic*, a term derived from the universal belief that its father and principal composer was Ossian the son of Fingal?

2ND How far that collection of such poetry, published by Mr James Macpherson, is genuine?

As to the first of those questions, the Committee can with confidence state its opinion, that such poetry did exist, that it was common, general, and in great abundance; that it was of a most impressive and striking sort, in a high degree eloquent, tender, and sublime.

The second question it is much more difficult to answer decisively. The Committee is possessed of no documents, to shew how much of his collection Mr Macpherson obtained in the form in which he has given it to the world. The poems and fragments of poems which the Committee has been able to procure, contain, as will appear from the article in the Appendix, No. 15. already mentioned, often the substance, and sometimes almost the literal expression (the *ipsissima verba*), of passages given by Mr Macpherson, in the poems of which he has published the translations. But the Committee has not been able to obtain any one poem the same in title and tenor with the poems published by him. It is inclined to believe that he was in use to supply chasms, and to give connection, by inserting passages which he did not find, and to add what he conceived to be dignity and delicacy to the original composition, by strinking out passages, by softening incidents, by refining the language, in short by changing what he considered as too simple or too rude for a modern ear, and elevating 'what in his opinion was below the standard of good poetry. To what degree, however, he exercised these liberties, it is impossible for the Committee to determine. The advantages he possessed, which the Committee began its inquiries too late to enjoy, of collecting from the oral recitation of a number of persons now no more, a very great number of the same poems, on the same subjects, and then collating those different copies or editions, if they may be so called, rejecting what was spurious or corrupted in one copy, and adopting from another something more genuine, and excellent in its place, afforded him an opportunity of putting together what might fairly enough be called an original whole, of much more beauty, and with much fewer blemishes, than the Committee believes it *now* possible for any person, or combination of persons, to obtain.

The Committee thinks it discovers some difference between the style both of the original (one book of which is given by Macpherson) and translation of *Temora* and that of the translation of Fingal, and of the small portion of the original of that poem, which it received from his executors. There is more the appearance of simplicity and originality in the latter than in the former. Perhaps when he published Fingal, Mr Macpherson, unknown as an author, and obscure as a man, was more diffident, more cautious, and more attentive, than when at a subsequent period he published Temora, flushed with the applause of the world, and distinguished as a man of talents, and an author of high, and rising reputation. Whoever will examine the original prefixed to some of the editions of the 7th book of Temora, and compare it with the translation, will, in the opinion of the Committee, discover some imperfections, some *modernisms*, (if the expression may be allowed) in the Gaelic, which do not occur in the specimen of Fingal, given in the Appendix to this Report; and, in the English, more of a loose and inflated expression (which however was an error into which Macpherson was apt to fall), than is to be found in his earlier translations. He had then attained a height which, to any man, but particularly to a man of a sanguine and somewhat confident disposition like Macpherson, is apt to give a degree of carelessness and presumption, that would rather command than conciliate the public suffrage, and, in the security of the world's applause, neglects the best means of obtaining it. He thought, it may be, he had only to produce another work like Fingal, to reap the same advantage and the same honour which that had procured him; and was rather solicitous to obtain these quickly, by a hasty publication, than to deserve them by a careful collection of what original materials he had procured, or by a diligent search to supply the defects of those materials.

# BIBLIOGRAPHY

## PRIMARY SOURCES

Joseph Addison, 'From the Spectator, (1712–1714)' in A. Ashfield and P. de Bolla (Eds) The Sublime: A Reader in British Eighteenth-Century Aesthetic Theory (Cambridge: Cambridge University Press, 1996), pp. 62–69

Hugh Blair, 'Preface' in Macpherson, Fragments of Ancient Poetry, Collected in the Highlands of Scotland and Translated from the Galic or Erse Language (Edinburgh: G. Hamilton and J. Balfour, 1760)

—, A Critical Dissertation on Ossian, The Son of Fingal (London: T Becket and P. A. Hondt, 1763)

—, A Critical Dissertation on the Poem Hugh Blair, A Critical Dissertation on the Poems of Ossian, The Son of Fingal, 2nd ed. (London: T. Becket and P.A. De Hondt, 1765)

Thomas Blackwell, 'From An Enquiry into the Life and Writings of Homer (1735)' in A. Ashfield and P. de Bolla (Eds.), The Sublime: A Reader in British Eighteenth-Century Aesthetic Theory (Cambridge: Cambridge University Press, 1996), pp. 163–165

James Boswell, The Life of Samuel Johnson, Vol. 1 (London: Henry Baldwin for Charles Dilly, 1791)

Edmund Burke, A Philosophical Enquiry into the Origin of our Ideas of the Sublime and Beautiful (London, 1757)

Edmund Burt, Burt's Letters from the North of Scotland as related by Edmund Burt, Ed. A. Simmons (Edinburgh: Birlinn, 1998)

Charles Churchill, The Poetical Works of Charles Churchill, Ed. Douglas Grant. (Oxford: Clarendon, 1956)

David Erskine-Baker, The Muse of Ossian a Dramatic Poem, of Three Acts. Selected from the Several Poems of Ossian the Son of Fingal. As it is Performed at the Theatre in Edinburgh (Edinburgh, 1763)

Highland Society of Scotland, Reports of the Committee of the Highland Society of Scotland: appointed to enquire into the nature and authenticity of the poems of Ossian (Edinburgh: Constable, 1805)

Samuel Johnson, A Journey to the Western Islands of Scotland (London: W. Strahan and T. Cadell, 1775)

James Macpherson, The Highlander: A Poem: In Six Cantos (Edinburgh: Wal. Ruddiman jun. and Company, 1758)

—, Fragments of Ancient Poetry, Collected in the Highlands of Scotland and Translated from the Galic or Erse Language (Edinburgh: G. Hamilton and J. Balfour, 1760)

—, Fingal, An Ancient Epic Poem in Six Books: Together with Several Other Poems Composed by Ossian, the Son of Fingal (London: T. Becket and P. A Hondt, 1762)

—, Temora, An Ancient Epic Poem in Eight Books: Together with Several Other Poems Composed by Ossian, the Son of Fingal (London: T. Becket and P. A Hondt, 1763)

—, The Works of Ossian, The Son of Fingal, 3rd ed., Vol. I (London: T. Becket and P. A Hondt, 1765)

—, The Works of Ossian, The Son of Fingal, 3rd ed, Vol. II (London: T. Becket and P. A Hondt, 1765)

—, Original Papers, Containing the Secret History of Great Britain from the

Restoration to the Accession of the House of Hanover, with Memoirs of James II, 2 vols. (London: W. Strahan and T. Cadell, 1775)

—, The Rights of Great Britain Asserted Against the Claims of America (London: Strahan and T. Cadell, 1776)

—, The History and Management of the East India Company from its Origin in 1600 to the Present Times (London: Strahan and T. Cadell, 1779)

—, A Short History of the Opposition during the Last Session (London: T. Cadell, 1779)

Malcolm Laing, The Poems of Ossian,&c, Containing the Poetical Works of James Macpherson, Esq. in Prose and Rhyme: With Notes and Illustrations, 2 vols. (Edinburgh: Archibald Constable, 1805)

Donald McNicol, Remarks on Dr Samuel Johnson's Journey to the Hebrides (London: Cadell, 1779)

Thomas Pennant, A Tour in Scotland and Voyage to the Hebrides, 1772 (Chester: J. Monk, 1774 and 1776)

John Pinkerton, An Enquiry into the History of Scotland preceding the reign of Malcolm III. Or the Year 1056, 2 vols. (London: John Nicols, 1789)

Tobias Smollett, The Expedition of Humphry Clinker, Vol.II (London: J. Wren and W. Hodges, 1795)

—, Poems, Plays and the Briton, Introductions and Notes by Byron Gassman (Athens: University of Georgia Press, 1993)

J. Sinclair, The Correspondence of the Right Honourable Sir John Sinclair, Vol.I, (London: H. Colburn & R. Bentley, 1831).

SECONDARY SOURCES

Malcolm Andrews, In Search of the Picturesque: Landscape Aesthetics and Tourism in Britain, 1760–1800 (Aldershot: Scolar Press, 1989)

Alexander Broadie, The Scottish Enlightenment: The Historical Age of the Historical Nation (Edinburgh: Birlinn, 2001)

Linda Colley, Britons: Forging the Nation 1797–1837 (London: Vintage, 1997)

Leith Davis, Acts of Union: Scotland and the Literary Imagination of the British Nation, 1707–1830 (Stanford: Stanford University Press, 1998)

Paul J. deGategno, James Macpherson. Twayne's English Authors Series No.467. (Boston: Twayne Publishers, 1989)

Ian Duncan, 'The Pathos of Abstraction: Adam Smith, Ossian and Samuel Johnson' Leith Davis, Ian Duncan and Janet Sorensen (Eds.) Scotland and the Borders of Romanticism (Cambridge: Cambridge UP, 2004), pp.38–56

John Dwyer, 'The Melancholy Savage: Text and Context in the Poems of Ossian.' Howard Gaskill (Ed.) Ossian Revisited (Edinburgh: Edinburgh University Press, 1991), pp.164–206

William Ferguson, The Identity of the Scottish Nation: An Historic Quest (Edinburgh: Edinburgh University Press, 1998)

Howard Gaskill (Ed.) Ossian Revisited (Edinburgh: Edinburgh University Press, 1991)

—, 'Introduction' Howard Gaskill (Ed.) Ossian Revisited (Edinburgh: Edinburgh University Press, 1991), pp.1–18

—, The Reception of Ossian in Europe (London: Thoemmes Continuum, 2004)

Luke Gibbons, 'The Sympathetic Bond: Ossian, Celticism and Colonialism.' Terence Brown, Celticism (Amsterdam: Atlanta, 1996), pp.276-77.

T. F. Henderson, 'Laing, Malcolm

(1762–1818)', rev. Paul J. deGategno, *Oxford Dictionary of National Biography*, (Oxford University Press, 2004) Online edition [http://www.oxford-dnb.com/view/article/15890, accessed 25 Jan 2011]

Hugh Honour, *Neo-Classicism*, 2nd ed. (London: Penguin,1991)

Colin Kidd, *Subverting Scotland's Past: Scottish Whig Historians and the Creation of an Anglo-British Identity, 1689–c.1830* (Cambridge: Cambridge University Press, 1993)

Mícheál MacCraith, 'Fingal: Text, Context, Subtext' Fiona Stafford and Howard Gaskill (Eds.) *From Gaelic to Romantic* (Amsterdam: Rodopi, 1998), pp.67–78

Susan Manning, 'Ossian, Scott and Nineteenth-Century Scottish Literary Nationalism' *Studies in Scottish Literature* 17 (1982), pp.19–54

—, 'Why Does It Matter that Ossian Was Thomas Jefferson's Favourite Poet?' *Symbiosis* 1 (Oct. 1997), pp.219–36

Dafydd Moore, *Enlightenment and Romance in James Macpherson's The Poems of Ossian: Myth, Genre and Cultural Change* (Aldershot: Ashgate, 2003)

Murray Pittock, *Inventing and Resisting Britain: Cultural Identities in Britain and Ireland 1685–1789* (London: Palgrave Macmillan, 1997)

George Nobbe, *The North Briton: A Study in Political Propaganda* (New York: Columbia University Press, 1939)

David Punter, 'Ossian, Blake, and the Questionable Source' in Valeria Tinkler-Villani et al (Eds.) *Exhibited by Candlelight: Sources and Developments in the Gothic Tradition* (Amsterdam: Rodopi, pp.25–42

John Robertson, *The Scottish Enlighten-ment and the Militia Issue* (Edinburgh: Donald, 1985)

Bailey Saunders, *Life and Letters of James Macpherson* (London: MacMillan, 1894)

Richard B. Sher, *Church and University in the Scottish Enlightenment: The Moderate Literati of Edinburgh* (Edinburgh: Edinburgh University Press, 1985)

Christopher Smith, 'Ossian in Music' in Howard Gaskill (Ed.) *The Reception of Ossian in Europe* (London: Thoemmes Continuum, 2004), pp.389–91

Fiona Stafford, *The Sublime Savage: James Macpherson and the Poems of Ossian* (Edinburgh: Edinburgh University Press, 1988)

—, 'Introduction: The Ossianic Poems of James Macpherson' in Howard Gaskill (Ed.), *The Poems of Ossian and Related Works* (Edinburgh: Edinburgh University Press, 1996), pp.v–xviii

Derick S. Thomson, 'Macpherson, James (1736–1796)', *Oxford Dictionary of National Biography*, Oxford University Press, 2004; online edn, May 2006 [http://www.oxforddnb.com/view/article/17728, accessed 25 Jan 2011]

Katie Trumpener, *Bardic Nationalism: The Romantic Novel and the British Empire*, (Princeton: Princeton UP, 1992)

Howard D. Weinbrot, *Britannia's Issue: The Rise of British Literature from Dryden to Ossian* (Cambridge: Cambridge University Press, 1993)

Lois Whitney, *Primitivism and the Idea of Progress: In English Popular Literature of the Eighteenth Century*, 2nd. Ed. (New York: Octagon Books, 1973)

Peter Womack, *Improvement and Romance: Constructing the Myth of the Highlands* (Macmillan, 1989)

## **Luath** Press Limited
*committed to publishing well written books worth reading*

LUATH PRESS takes its name from Robert Burns, whose little collie Luath (*Gael.*, swift or nimble) tripped up Jean Armour at a wedding and gave him the chance to speak to the woman who was to be his wife and the abiding love of his life. Burns called one of 'The Twa Dogs' Luath after Cuchullin's hunting dog in Ossian's *Fingal*. Luath Press was established in 1981 in the heart of Burns country, and now resides a few steps up the road from Burns' first lodgings on Edinburgh's Royal Mile.
Luath offers you distinctive writing with a hint of unexpected pleasures.

Most bookshops in the UK, the US, Canada, Australia, New Zealand and parts of Europe either carry our books in stock or can order them for you. To order direct from us, please send a £sterling cheque, postal order, international money order or your credit card details (number, address of cardholder and expiry date) to us at the address below. Please add post and packing as follows: UK – £1.00 per delivery address; overseas surface mail – £2.50 per delivery address; overseas airmail – £3.50 for the first book to each delivery address, plus £1.00 for each additional book by airmail to the same address. If your order is a gift, we will happily enclose your card or message at no extra charge.

**Luath** Press Limited
543/2 Castlehill
The Royal Mile
Edinburgh EH1 2ND
Scotland

Telephone: 0131 225 4326 (24 hours)
Fax: 0131 225 4324
email: sales@luath.co.uk
Website: www.luath.co.uk